Practice Theory and Research

There has been an upsurge in scholarship concerned with theories of social practices in various fields including sociology, geography and management studies. This book provides a systematic introduction and overview of recent formulations of practice theory organised around important themes such as: the importance of analysing the role of the non-human alongside the human; the reflexive nature of social science research; the conceptualisation of human agency and macrophenomena; and the dynamics of social change. Combining a rich variety of detailed empirical research examples with discussion of the relevance of practice theories for policy and social change, this book represents an excellent sourcebook for all academic and professional researchers interested in working with practice theory.

Gert Spaargaren is Professor and Chair of the Environmental Policy Group at Wageningen University, the Netherlands.

Don Weenink is an Associate Professor at the Department of Sociology at the University of Amsterdam, the Netherlands.

Machiel Lamers is Assistant Professor at the Environmental Policy Group at Wageningen University, the Netherlands.

Practice Theory and Research

Exploring the dynamics of social life

Edited by Gert Spaargaren, Don Weenink and Machiel Lamers

Routledge
Taylor & Francis Group

LONDON AND NEW YORK

First published 2016
by Routledge
2 Park Square, Milton Park, Abingdon, Oxon OX14 4RN

and by Routledge
711 Third Avenue, New York, NY 10017

Routledge is an imprint of the Taylor & Francis Group, an informa business

British Library Cataloguing-in-Publication Data
A catalogue record for this book is available from the British Library

Library of Congress Cataloging in Publication Data
Names: Spaargaren, Gert, editor. | Weenink, Don, editor. |
Lamers, Machiel, editor.
Title: Practice theory and research : exploring the dynamics of
social life / edited by Gert Spaargaren, Don Weenink and Machiel
Lamers.
Description: Abingdon, Oxon ; New York, NY : Routledge, 2016.
Identifiers: LCCN 2016002704 | ISBN 9781138101517 (hardback)
| ISBN 9781315656908 (ebook)
Subjects: LCSH: Social sciences–Research. | Social sciences–
Methodology.
Classification: LCC H61 .P6337 2016 | DDC 300.72–dc23
LC record available at http://lccn.loc.gov/2016002704

ISBN: 978-1-138-10151-7 (hbk)
ISBN: 978-1-315-65690-8 (ebk)

Typeset in Times New Roman
by Wearset Ltd, Boldon, Tyne and Wear

Contents

Figures

Tables

Contributors

Bas Arts (Prof. Dr) is Chair of the Forest and Nature Conservation Policy group at Wageningen University, the Netherlands. His main research interests and publications are in the fields of international environmental governance, natural resource management and their connections ('global-local nexus'). His latest books are: *The Disoriented State: Shifts in Governmentality, Territorialization and Governance* (edited with Arnoud Lagendijk and Henk van Houtum, Springer 2009) and *Forest and Nature Governance: A Practice-Based Approach* (edited with Jelle Behagel, Severine van Bommel, Jessica de Koning and Esther Turnhout, Springer 2013).

Sven Bakker (MSc) is a researcher at the Mulier Institute, a social scientific research centre for sports in the Netherlands. His research focuses on sport facility planning, sport management, sport events and tennis. With Hugo van der Poel he co-edited a book on tennis in the Netherlands (Arko Sports Media 2015). Sven plays tennis at a quite high level.

Jan den Bakker (MSc) is the owner of a consultancy business in the Netherlands and former healthcare manager. He applies a care ethical perspective on change and management in healthcare and welfare organisations. His ambition as chairman of the foundation, Critical Ethics of Care, is to gain knowledge by studying the burning issues in care and welfare practices from a care ethical perspective.

Karin Dobernig (Dr) has recently completed her doctorate at the Institute for Ecological Economics of the Vienna University of Economics and Business in Austria with a dissertation on urban agriculture in New York City. During her studies, she also was a Visiting Scholar at the Center for European and Mediterranean Studies (CEMS) and the Department of Nutrition, Food Studies and Public Health at New York University in the United States. Her main research interests lie in the areas of sustainable consumption and pro-environmental behaviour.

René van der Duim (Prof. Dr) is Personal Professor at the Cultural Geography Group at Wageningen University. His main research interest is the relation between tourism, conservation and development, particularly focusing on Eastern Africa. His latest books are *Tourism Encounters and Controversies. Ontological Politics of Tourism Development* (edited with Gunnar Thór Jóhannesson and Carina Ren, 2015 Ashgate) and *Institutional Arrangements for Conservation, Development and Tourism in Eastern and Southern Africa* (edited with Machiel Lamers and Jakomijn van Wijk, 2015 Springer).

Andrew Glover (Dr) is a Postdoctoral Research Fellow in the School of Media & Communications at RMIT. He currently works in the Sustainable Urban Precincts Project (SUPP), researching academic air travel, mobility and remote presence as part of contemporary academic work life ecology. More broadly, his research interests lie in sustainability, theories of practice, consumption, reuse and waste. Prior to his current research at RMIT, Andrew completed his PhD at the UTS Institute for Sustainable Futures on the topic of household material divestment. He is a member of the Australian Sociological Association.

Daniela Kleinschmit (Prof. Dr) is head of the chair group of Forest and Environmental Policy at the University of Freiburg, Germany. Her main interest is on land use governance at multiple levels and across different sectors. Her research and publications particularly deal with questions of policy integration, communication and discourses as well as legitimacy and democracy. Her policy research is taken up in diverse international political fora.

Machiel Lamers (Dr) is Assistant Professor at the Environmental Policy Group at Wageningen University, the Netherlands. His main research interests are in new modes of governance in sustainable tourism and conservation tourism across the world. His latest books are *Antarctic Futures: Human Engagement with the Antarctic Environment* (edited with Tina Tin, Daniela Liggett and Pat Maher, Springer, 2014) and *Institutional Arrangements for Conservation, Development and Tourism in Eastern and Southern Africa: A Dynamic Perspective* (edited with Rene van der Duim and Jakomijn van Wijk, Springer, 2015).

Peter Oosterveer (Dr Ir.) is Personal Professor at the Environmental Policy Group at Wageningen University, the Netherlands. His main research interests are in the sustainability of food in globalizing food networks, and equity in access to sufficient, safe and sustainable food. Among his recent books are *Food, Globalisation and Sustainability* (with David A. Sonnenfeld, Routledge, 2012) and *Food in a Sustainable World; Transitions in the Consumption, Retail and Production of Food* (edited with Gert Spaargaren and Anne Loeber, Routledge, 2012).

Hugo van der Poel (Dr Ir.) is Director of the Mulier Institute, a social scientific research centre for sports in the Netherlands. His research interests are in theory, policy, space and facilities in the field of sports. He is project leader of the NWO Research Programme Sport Facilities and Sport Participation. With Sven Bakker he co-edited a book on tennis in the Netherlands (Arko Sports Media 2015). His tennis skills remain poor, but until spring 2015 he was Chairman of a tennis club for eight years.

Helga Pülzl (Dr) is a senior researcher at the European Forest Institute's Central Eastern European Regional Office, EFICEEC, and the Institute of Forest, Environmental, and Natural Resource Policy at the University of Natural Resources and Life Sciences, Austria. She graduated with a PhD thesis focusing on global forest governance from a discourse theoretical perspective. Her main research interests and publications are in the field of international and European forest governance, implementation of forest policy related decisions, sustainability indicator development and policy change.

Theodore Schatzki (Prof. Dr) is Senior Associate Dean and Professor of Philosophy and Geography in the College of Arts and Sciences at the University of Kentucky, United States. His research interests primarily lie in social ontology, theory of action and the philosophy of social science. He is the author of *Social Practices* (Cambridge University Press, 1996), *The Site of the Social* (Pennsylvania State University Press, 2002), *Martin Heidegger: Theorist of Space* (Steiner, 2007) and *The Timespace of Human Activity* (Lexington, 2010).

Robert Schmidt (Prof. Dr) is Professor for Process-Oriented Sociology at the History and Social Science Faculty of the Catholic University Eichstätt-Ingolstadt, Germany. His research focuses on the sociology of social practices, the ethnography of organization, intellectual teamwork and process-oriented methodology. His recent publications include *Soziologie der Praktiken. Konzeptionelle Studien und Empirische Analysen* (Suhrkamp 2012) and *Siting Praxeology. The Methodological Significance of 'Public' in Theories of Social Practices* (with Jörg Volbers in the *Journal for the Theory of Social Behaviour*, 41, 2011).

Gert Spaargaren (Prof. Dr Ir.) is Professor and Chair of the Environmental Policy Group of Wageningen University, the Netherlands. His main research interests and publications are in the field of environmental sociology, sustainable consumption and behaviour, and the globalisation of environmental reform. His latest books are *The Ecological Modernisation Reader* (edited with Arthur Mol and David Sonnenfeld, 2009 Routledge) and *Food in a Sustainable World; Transitions in the Consumption, Retail and Production of Food* (edited with Peter Oosterveer and Anne Loeber, Routledge, 2012).

Esther Veen (Dr) recently started as a lecturer for the Rural Sociology Group of Wageningen University, the Netherlands, where she gives courses on the sociology of food and health. Before this she worked as a researcher for Applied Plant Research (part of Wageningen University and Research Centre), where she participated in research projects on urban agriculture and multifunctional agriculture. In June 2015 she graduated for her PhD at the Rural Sociology Group of Wageningen university, with a study on community gardening in the Netherlands.

Frans Vosman (Prof. Dr) is Professor of Care Ethics at the University of Humanistics in the Netherlands. He is a member of the Dutch-Flemish research group on Care and Contested Coherence.

Don Weenink (Dr) is a member of the Sociology Department at the University of Amsterdam. His main area of research is the micro-sociology of violence. Recently, he published on this topic in *Sociological Forum* (2015), the *British Journal of Sociology* (2014) and *Human Figurations* (2013). Currently, he is conducting research projects on the video analysis of robberies and street violence in which he combines praxeological and micro-sociological approaches. More generally, he takes an interest in specifying and further developing social theories by applying them in empirical research. In a new publication (together with Christian Bröer) which appeared in the *Journal of Health, Risk, and Society* (2015), he combined micro-sociology with material semiotics to understand how health risk prevention technology can become a symbol of collective identity.

Preface

Practice theory is gaining popularity in the social sciences. Recently, there has been an upsurge of scholars who have revisited theories of (social) practices in a variety of fields. Within sociology and social philosophy, Theodore Schatzki, Elizabeth Shove, Theodore Reckwitz, David Nicolini and Robert Schmidt, amongst others, have elaborated, complemented and also reformulated the practice ontologies as they were developed in sociology in the 1970s and 1980s by Pierre Bourdieu and Anthony Giddens in particular. Broadly speaking, all formulations of practice theory depart from the idea that social life consists of social interactions through which people make and transform their world and themselves. Despite this growing popularity practice theory has not yet acquired the status of a permanent section or category in social theory introductions and handbooks that appear regularly. Practice theories and their authors form a lively field of debate, conceptual innovation and research. Practice theory represents a contemporary social theory that inspires and appeals to many new (PhD) students because of the practical guidelines it provides for academic social science researchers. This book has been developed for this purpose as it is focused on practice theories and their authors, the interaction they have with their critics, and the various applications in widely different societal themes and contexts.

The book provides a systematic introduction and overview of these recent formulations of practice theory as suggested by key authors in this tradition while at the same time showing how practice theories can be applied in empirical research on social change. More explicitly the book aims to contribute to a recent shift in the practice theory literature to not only explain small but also large social phenomena, including processes of societal change and governance. The diversity and depth of the empirical research examples and the discussion on the relevance of practice theories for (the management of) social change make this book an excellent starter for all academic and professional researchers who plan to 'do something with' practice theory.

This book is timely as it holds a message that could only emerge here and now. Without the methodological reflections of Schmidt, the publications of Schatzki and Shove and their Giddens' inherited struggle with the agency-structure theme, without their lively debate with ANT and the recent school of transition theories, this book would not be here or would have at least had a substantially different content.

This multi-author edited volume is the result of extensive debates among the editors and the team of authors. This process shows that writing a book like this should not be seen primarily as the result of writing and thinking individuals, but instead as emerging from the practices of reading, writing, sharing, meeting, debating and rewriting that are the key source of new ideas and theories. The book is a follow-up of an international symposium organised by the editors in June 2013 at Wageningen University in the Netherlands in which a number of internationally renowned practice theorists (i.e. Theodore Schatzki, Elizabeth Shove), as well as researchers applying practice theory to various domains, participated to present and discuss the innovations, challenges and relevance of practice theory. A selection of the presenters at the symposium was invited to write full-fledged chapters for this book project. In addition, a selection of internationally recognised scholars were asked to participate in this book project, to increase its international character and expand the thematic scope of the topics covered. The international symposium was followed by two author workshops organised at Wageningen University, in November 2013 and November 2014 respectively, during which the overall theme of the book and drafts of the contributing chapters were discussed and aligned. Some of the international contributing authors participated in the workshops through Skype. We are very grateful for the fruitful interactions with the author team, and we hope it has brought as much to them as it has to us. In addition, we look back with great pleasure to the numerous editorial meetings at Gert Spaargaren's kitchen table. The informal setting has been indispensable for discussing practice theories, the progress of the project, the thematic scope of this volume and the contents of our joint chapters.

We are grateful for the financial support from the Wageningen School of Social Sciences (WASS), the Environmental Policy Group and the Rural Sociology Group, for organising the symposium and the author workshops. We are very thankful for the practical support received from Corry Rothuizen, secretary of the Environmental Policy Group at Wageningen University. Thanks also to Alyson Claffey of Routledge for the regular and constructive communication regarding this book project. Finally, we would like to thank the contributing authors, without whom we would not have been able to produce this volume.

Gert Spaargaren, Don Weenink and Machiel Lamers
January 2016

Abbreviations

AGM	Annual General Meeting
AM	Ante Meridiem
ANT	Actor-Network Theory
AWF	African Wildlife Foundation
C&I	Criteria and Indicators for Sustainable Forest Management
CBD	Convention on Biological Diversity
CEO	Chief Executive Officer
CITES	Convention on International Trade of Endangered Species
CPF	Collaborative Partnership on Forests
CTP	Conservation Tourism Partnership
EU	European Union
FAO	Food and Agriculture Organization of the United Nations
FLEGT	Forest Law Enforcement, Governance and Trade
FSC	Forest Stewardship Council
ICT	Information and Communication Technology
IFF	International Forum on Forests
INC	International Negotiation Committee
IPCC	Intergovernmental Panel on Climate Change
IPF	International Panel on Forests
ITTA	International Tropical Timber Agreement
ITTO	International Tropical Timber Organization
KNLTB	Royal Dutch Lawn Tennis Association (*Koninklijke Nederlandse Lawn Tennis Bond*)
MCPFE	Ministerial Conference on the Protection of Forests in Europe (renamed 'Forest Europe')
MLG	Multi-Level Governance
MLP	Multi-Level Perspective
NFP	National Forest Programmes
NGO	Non-Governmental Organization
OECD	Organisation for Economic Co-operation and Development
PEFC	Program for the Endorsement of Forest Certification
PFM	Participatory Forest Management

PROFOR	Program on Forests (at World Bank)
RSPO	Round Table of Sustainable Palm Oil
SFM	Sustainable Forest Management
SIR	Study of International Relations
UN	United Nations
UNCCD	United Nations Convention to Combat Desertification
UNCSD	United Nations Commission for Sustainable Development
UNDP	United Nations Development Program
UNFCCC	United Nations Framework Convention on Climate Change
UNFF	United Nations Forum on Forests
US$	United States dollar

Part I

Theoretical and methodological contributions to practice theories

Chapter 1

Introduction

Using practice theory to research social life

*Gert Spaargaren, Machiel Lamers
and Don Weenink*

> Not, then, men and their moments. Rather moments and their men
>
> Erving Goffman, 1967, p. 3

Introduction

Why and how are you reading this book? Maybe you read a review of it in a social science journal. Perhaps you were advised to do so by your lecturer to prepare that paper on practice-based research. Maybe you noticed a new cover and interesting title during your monthly stroll through the local library and read for another two minutes before deciding to take it on loan. Or perhaps you are sitting behind your office-desk and just received the book that you ordered online after a 'content alert' from the publisher.

Whatever made you reading this text as part of your daily activities, it is you as a unique individual who knows what you are up to do next. You are familiar with the situation and you know how to go on in daily life, how to take the next step. But suppose you were asked to study the behaviours and motivations of people going through similar moments like you now. People who are about to read and study a book on practices. How would you, in this particular case, frame and organize your research, both theoretically and methodologically? Theoretically, by asking yourself what kind of 'decisions' are at stake, and which factors are assumed to influence the process. Do emotions play a role in this? Do you happen to know the authors? Did the title of the book seduce you? The theoretical lens you decide to use will influence what you see and how much emphasis you will give to particular items and factors. Methodologically, you might wonder what qualitative and quantitative methods are available for getting to the situation in such a way that you gain the knowledge needed to understand similar situations elsewhere.

The methodological approach which is often suggested in situations like this is that you develop a survey or interview topic list to ask people about their motivations, meanings, experiences and interests for reading books in the first place and for selecting this book on practices in particular. Your research-focus in that case could be on a set of more or less well-known background variables (education, income, job, discipline, gender) combined with some stated preferences and values of the individuals. They are combined methodologically in order to predict future behaviours or to understand their meanings. Maybe you will be able to show that for students income turns out to be a more decisive factor when compared with tenured staff.

There is however an alternative approach possible. One that is challenging the assumptions behind the conventional approaches to study human behaviour and social change. This alternative approach is the central theme of the present volume. Theoretically, it suggests shifting the research focus away from studying individuals, their motives and background features primarily, towards a more in-depth investigation of 'context', or the activities, the social practices, they engage in. For our example of reading this book, the classroom, the library and the office are now included in the enquiries, as are the time-slots and the reading time being available (or not) for actually reading the book. The projected activities of the reading – glancing through, reading-with-highlighting, studying-while-abstracting – are not just contextualized but also investigated for their functionality in relation to the wider projects or programmes in which the reading activities of individuals are embedded. For example, perhaps you aimed to share your findings with a group of fellow students in next week's class or you intend to write a book review for the journal of which you are an associate editor. Methodologically, the alternative approach suggests to employ methods of data collection and techniques of data analysis that allow you to gain a rich and detailed understanding of the situation. This implies that you consider using a range of techniques that are particularly relevant for 'praxeologizing' the would-be readers and their contexts. Both the theoretical and the methodological aspects of the alternative approach will be introduced and enhanced in this volume, by presenting key characteristics of contemporary practice theories and by showing how they can be put to use in empirical research.

The idea of shifting the analytical emphasis from the individual to the situation however is not new at all. When the sociologist Erving Goffman developed his micro-sociological or interactionist approach in the early 1960s, he emphasized the impact of contextual factors on even our 'smallest behaviors'. To understand how people 'behave in public places' (Goffman, 1963) and 'present themselves in everyday life' (Goffman, 1959), sociologists must investigate the particular situations or moments as contexts which co-constitute behaviour. Goffman showed that analysing situations is an indispensable tool for understanding why and how people act and talk the way they do. Together with their fellow actors, individuals create a social unit which cannot be reduced to the motives, intentions and meanings of single individuals. The situation represents more than the sum of its constituting elements. Therefore Goffman (1963: 3) suggests that social scientists better focus their attention to 'moments and their men', or – as in the case of this volume – on 'practices and their participants' instead of using isolated individuals as the privileged starting point for theorizing and doing empirical research on the social.

The Goffman-motto of starting from situations while bracketing the individual is one of the key assumptions which are broadly shared among theorists of practices. We will discuss key assumptions and characteristics of theories of social practices in the sections to follow. The core assumptions refer to the nature of social practices and how they should be defined (or not), to the role of material, both human-made and naturally occurring objects and human agents within social practices, and to the more general assumption that society, social life that is, should be conceived in terms of interconnected practices (and nothing else). These assumptions of course influence the research design and the use of concepts and methodologies for analysing the dynamics of society. Because practice theories are rather young and not yet mainstream in social science, their application in empirical research tends to raise a number of questions that need to be confronted in some detail. With this book, we aimed to select a set of relevant questions and to elaborate them in both theoretical and empirical contexts.

Aims of the book

The family of practice theories, the key ontological assumptions they represent, the methodological and epistemological issues involved in the application of practice theories in empirical research, and the relevance of practice-based research for understanding social change in contemporary societies, are the central topics discussed throughout this volume. This seems like a rather broad agenda, but we will show that it is one with a clear focus. The aims of the book are twofold:

1   to demonstrate how practice theories can be used for empirical analyses that aim to understand social reproduction and social change;
2   to outline the conceptual and methodological challenges related to the use of practice theories when applied to both small and large social phenomena.

To meet these objectives the book includes a number of theoretical chapters that discuss the foundations of practice theory, that propose ways to conceptualize agency and power and their role in social change, and that clarify some of the methodological principles and discussions. Together with this introductory chapter, these theoretical and methodological chapters form Part I of the volume. Next to these theoretical chapters, the book offers empirical chapters that show how practice theories can be put to use in a wide variety of social contexts, while also taking up and discussing the conceptual and methodological challenges of practice approaches along the way. The empirical chapters focus on the analysis and assessment of social change in the situated here and now of single practices or small phenomena, such as being violent, playing tennis and undergoing medical treatment (Part II), as well as on changes in large phenomena, e.g. in bundles of practices extending in a wider scope of time-space, such as conservation tourism partnerships and the sustainable management of forests (Part III).

In order to prepare the reader for what comes next, this introductory chapter aims to provide a brief discussion of central concepts and key assumptions in practice theories, the debate between practice approaches and transition theory approaches with regard to the analysis of social change, and some of the methodological and policy aspects of practice-based empirical research. We conclude this introductory chapter by outlining the subsequent chapters in this volume.

Practice theories: key concepts and assumptions

Since *The Practice Turn in Contemporary Theory* (Schatzki *et al.*, 2001) practice theories seem to be steadily on the rise within the social sciences. Despite their popularity however, practice theories have not yet been assigned the status of a distinct family or category of social thinking, such as post-structuralism or interpretive sociology. So far, they do not appear as separate sections in the social theory handbooks and introductions, which appear so regularly nowadays (Calhoun *et al.*, 2012; Wallace and Wolf, 2006). Of course the authors associated with the emergence of the field of practice theory are discussed in these volumes, most notably Anthony Giddens and Pierre Bourdieu. They are considered the founders of a movement or approach that laid out the conceptualization of the agency-structure relation as one of the key themes in social theory (King, 2004). Giddens and Bourdieu are – together with Bruno Latour – also a source of inspiration for contemporary practice theorists, such as Davide Nicolini, Annemarie Mol, Andreas Reckwitz, Theodore Schatzki, Elizabeth Shove, Alan Warde, Robert Schmidt and many others. These contemporary scholars carry out their practice theory inspired research in a variety of fields, such as food and health, sustainable consumption, sports, work and organization, and urban provisioning of energy, water and food.

Practice theories form a lively field of debates, conceptual innovation and research. They represent a contemporary social theory that inspires and appeals to many (PhD) students, since they expect the theory to offer them guidance on how to organize social science research. When using the lens of practice theories, researchers show particular sensitivities and preferences, while being keen on avoiding well-known pitfalls. The preferences often mentioned are to approach the social world as open, contingent, transitory and horizontal. Practice theories appeal to researchers' intuitions as they seem to match well with the dynamics of the current horizontal, fluid and global network society (Castells, 1996, 2009; Urry, 2000). The pitfalls that practice-based researchers are keen to avoid refer to two forms of reductionism. The first are individualistic accounts of the social and the second are system perspectives of all kinds that emphasize order, systemic principles, structures and hierarchies. Research based on practice theories seeks to find the middle ground between voluntarist or subjectivist (society as the result of actions, values and preferences of sovereign individuals) and structural or objectivist (society as made up by structures which 'govern' the grand totality behind the backs of human actors) accounts of the social.

This book has been developed to comment on the present state of affairs in the field of practice theories and to make visible the kind of contributions practice theories can make to empirical research on social change. It draws upon different streams of practice theories and their authors, and shows the application of their concepts and ideas to a wide variety of social themes and contexts. With the book we do not claim to represent 'the' practice approach. We contend that practice theory should be seen as a family of theories, consisting, among others, of the above mentioned authors and their critics. Their ideas and contributions inspire us and are discussed in different chapters of the book. In this section, we share with the reader some of the conceptual issues and debates that are prominent among practice theorists. For each topic we indicate how we intend to deal with them in the context of the present volume.

Defining social practices?

All practice theorists claim that the study of social life should start with social practices. But what exactly is a 'social practice'? A quick scan of the literature will tell you that there is not a single best definition of social practices around. Some authors even suggest not trying to provide one, since such a definition would run counter to the style of thinking and working represented by the open-ended practices ontology (Nicolini, 2012). We nevertheless selected a few definitions to develop a feel for the game.

Andreas Reckwitz regards practices as 'routines of moving the body, of understanding and wanting, of using things, interconnected in a practice' (Reckwitz, 2002a: 255). So there are elements which interconnect or organize social practices. Taking practices as the unit of analysis implies looking into the properties or elements that go together in human activity and that do not appear when studying human individuals or institutions at large. But what exactly are the components or elements? Practice theorists seem to agree on what they are, but they use different concepts to refer to them and provide different explanations for how they contribute to the organizing of practices. For example, with Shove et al. (2012) practices are constituted by combining (only) three main components: materials (e.g. bodies, things, technologies and tangible physical entities), competences (e.g. skills, know-how, techniques) and meanings (e.g. symbolic meanings, ideas and aspirations). It is through recurrent enactments (i.e. practices-as-performances) that a distinct and recognizable conjunction of these elements is established over time, with social practices then becoming visible as entities (practices-as-entities) which are embedded in broader nexuses or bundles of practices. As Shove et al. indicate themselves, although working with only three components or elements might be helpful when organizing empirical research on social change, it is at the expense of simplifying what social practices are about (Shove et al., 2012: 15).

A more elaborate description of elements of social practices is provided by Schatzki (2002, 2010) who argues that they consist of doings and sayings and material arrangements that hang together, organized by practical understanding, general understanding, rules and teleo-affective structures. A similar, even more elaborate definition of a practice is provided by (again) Reckwitz:

> a routinized type of behaviour which consist of several elements, intercon-
> nected to one other: forms of bodily activities, forms of mental activities,
> 'things' and their use, a background knowledge in the form of understand-
> ing, know-how, states of emotion and motivational knowledge.
>
> (Reckwitz, 2002a: 249)

This definition is among the most cited and used ones. Both his and Schatzki's definitions are very helpful with regard to theoretical clarification and debate, but rather difficult to operationalize into designs for empirical research on social change.

Instead of going for the most adequate definition, we would argue with Nicolini (2012) that practice researchers profit from taking into account the different formulations of the concept of social practices currently in use, using them to shape the research design in a way that fits best the theoretical or empirical tasks at hand. When quickly mapping practices for their key components, elements or dimensions, researchers can create room for more in-depth analyses of specific elements, their hanging together in practices and their dynamics of change. As we will show in the empirical chapters of the book, just mapping designated practices for their (for example three, with Shove *et al.*, 2012) components, will not do when the aim is to arrive at a convincing analysis of the dynamics of change in society. For a more in-depth understanding of social change, the rules and teleo-affective structures that organize practices, the emotions at stake and the ways in which social practices are part of wider bundles of practices, all need to be taken into account.

In our view, going through the set of definitions on offer in the practice literature is a useful and necessary exercise for researchers who engage in practice-based research. When the authors of this book gathered to discuss their particular take on how to define and approach social practices, the editors suggested to combine elements of Giddens, Schatzki and Shove into the following working-definition: social practices are shared, routinized, ordinary ways of doings and sayings, enacted by knowledgeable and capable human agents who – while interacting with the material elements that co-constitute the practice – know what to do next in a non-discursive, practical manner.

The material dimension of social practices

All practice theories acknowledge the important, co-constituting role of material objects in social life. One cannot claim to use a practice-based approach when neglecting the role of material objects, symbols, things, technologies and infrastructures as the crucial hardware of the social. Beyond this broad consensus however, there exist significant differences among practice theorists when it comes to conceptualizing the material in relation to the social. For example both Reckwitz (2002a, 2002b) and Shove (2003) go a long way in arguing for a formulation of practice theory that resembles the strong emphasis of material semiotics, also known as actor network theory, on the independent role of objects vis à vis human agents. Also Rick Wilk (2009) argues for a concept of 'distributed agency' in which objects have their fair share.

Schatzki on the other hand makes an effort to specify the crucial differences between human and non-human activity chains. In his recent work in particular, Schatzki contrasted his formulation of practice theory versus Latour's material semiotics perspective (see Chapter 2 of this volume). Although the plenum of the social is populated by practice-arrangement-bundles that always and inherently so represent the going together of social practices and material arrangements, for Schatzki it is human agency that makes the difference, e.g. that what makes practice theories theories of social practices. With respect to analysing the role and status of material objects in social practices, the approaches of Schatzki and Shove seem to be different as well, for example when it comes to the conceptual position of Shove's material element (Shove *et al.*, 2012) in comparison with Schatzki's material arrangement (Schatzki, 2002). While Shove *et al.* put materials on a par with meanings and competences, Schatzki sees material arrangement as being employed, manipulated and constructed by the participants in their doings and sayings. The theoretical and epistemological debates on what objects 'do' in practices will be one of the recurrent themes in this book. It is to just inform the reader that when discussing the material dimension of practices, the editors are more close to the position of Schatzki (1996, 2002, 2010). Notably, in his conceptualization of the material versus the social, the role of human agency is recognized and defended in a much more explicit way as compared to practice theories that are closer to material semiotics (Latour, 2005; Reckwitz, 2002a, 2002b; Shove *et al.*, 2012). We think that the concept of agency and its relation to social reproduction and change is crucial and hence deserves further discussion and exploration.

Agency and practice theory: social reproduction as a practical, 'taken-for-granted' affair?

Practice theories foreground what people actually do in ordinary life. They emphasize the fact that the social is more than language, discourse or communication. As Warde has argued, practice theorists 'give precedence to practical activity as the means by which people secure their passage through the world, thereby emphasizing doing over thinking, practical competence over strategic reasoning, mutual intelligibility over personal motivation and body over mind' (Warde, 2013: 18). At the same time, practice theories emphasize the fact that the doings and sayings of social life are not only practical in nature but also taken for granted, habitual, and routinized (Evans *et al.*, 2012). This implies that agency and power are exerted most of the times in a non-discursive, non-cognitive and routinized way. Within the family of practice theories, the routi-nized and habitual nature of the social is being discussed at some length, relating the topic of the taken-for-granted nature of doings and sayings with standing debates in the social sciences on the exact meaning of agency, and its relation-ship to power and social change (Wilk, 2009; Welch and Warde, 2015). When summarized in a negative way, the practice stance on agency could be depicted as the homo practicus who, submerged in practices, just follows the existing rou-tines in an intuitive and taken for granted way. This formulation of course does not do justice to all the nuances being made by different authors in this field. It does however indicate in a strong way the difference between practice theories on the one hand and competing approaches in economics and psychology on the other hand, where human agency is connected primarily with the conscious, rational decision making of individuals who follow orders from inside. So how is the 'practical nature' of the reproduction of social practices conceptualized?

Schatzki (2010) introduces the concept of practical intelligibility to discuss the intuitive, practical, embodied ways in which human actors know what to do next in a given situation. Practical intelligibility tells individuals what makes sense for them to do next 'given that such and such is the case' Schatzki (2010: 114). The such and such refers to many things at the same time: the set of goals (telos) that are involved in the practice, the emotions at stake, the ways in which objects invite or trigger certain behaviours, and the relationships of relative auto-nomy and interdependence with other participants of the practice. Although Schatzki claims that his concept of 'practical intelligibility' is more convincing – since more specific and contextual – when compared to Bourdieu's 'sens pra-tique' (Bourdieu, 1977, 1979) and Giddens' 'practical consciousness' (Giddens, 1984), we think these differences are less important than the shared assumption that most of the times most things are being dealt with by human agents in a non-discursive manner. Non-discursivity however does not imply that people are stupid, ignorant of what is going on, or cultural dopes. When things move smoothly, when practices can be enacted on the automatic pilot, and when per-formances are successful the way they have been done in the recent past, there is no need to shift to the 'cognitive driving modality'. Only when special occasions occur, for example when new objects or ideas are brought into the practice, or when practices collapse, are disturbed or de-routinized in ways that courses of future action are no longer innate to the practice and no longer 'obvious' for the practitioners, only then a temporary switch is being made to the discursive, reflexive, cognitive, conflict or consensus generating mode of doing and saying. The fact that social life is taken for granted most of the times, does not preclude creativity, reflexivity and social innovation to play an important role in the process of social (re)production.

When discussing human agency in relation to practice theories, we think that the works of Giddens, Schatzki and Bourdieu represent a perspective on agency and subjectivity that distances itself from more individualist, cognitive and voluntarist accounts of agency. At the same time, however, these authors tried to avoid the portrayal of human agents as 'cultural dopes' or as passive recipients of the dynamics of social structures. Human agents are intelligible, knowledge-able and capable agents who know what to do next most of the time, and how to move around in the world. The 'third way' approach of Giddens and Bourdieu to the issue of subjectivism versus objectivism has gained broad recognition in the social sciences. For the original agency – structure problem there are by now about fifty shades of structuration available in the practice literature. Against this background, we would like to emphasize two items which we consider important for the central theme of this book.

First, we suggest that agency should be discussed and accounted for both in relation to social practices and in relation to how embodied human actors parti-cipate in these practices. The added value of practice theories is their claim that both accounts of agency cannot be developed independently. In some variants of practice theory, the individual seems to almost disappear from view (Shove *et al.*, 2012; Welch and Warde, 2015). We think that being silent about the role of individual human actors in the reproduction of practices is not the most promis-ing strategy. Instead, the role of individual actors as 'practitioners' should be conceptualized in more convincing ways. So yes, individual human actors or agents exert agency, have a lifestyle, and possess transformative capacities. The skills, capacities, competences, values and emotions at stake can be observed, measured and monitored in social science research. However, they cannot be analysed and properly understood when they are treated in isolation, without taking into account the practices they are connected with and originate from. Practice theories argue that the very capacity of individual human actors to act upon and to intervene in the world, is produced in and through existing constel-lations of social practices. Practices produce human agents as much as human agents produce practices. In more historical terms: situated groups of people in a particular society derive their existence as social actors from the very same his-torically evolving patchwork of social practices they are part of and help repro-duce. Those quilts tell their participants who they are, what they should do in different situations and how they can act upon the situation given the opportun-ities and constraints inherent in the practices they engage in. Human agents have no choice other than to accept their destiny to act as the co-creators of society under given, ever changing circumstances which they are never fully aware of and which they can never fully control. Hence the practice theoretical adage of 'bounded agency' can exist side by side to the practice theoretical adage of social life being 'open-ended and dynamic' in nature.

Second, we argue that practice theories can benefit from a new round of dis-cussion and theorizing of the nature and role of human agency in the reproduc-tion and transformation of social practices. Social practices are not just moments of instantiation or the reproduction of a set of programs, or hybrids of the social and the material etcetera. They are as well 'Erlebnissen', fun to do, suffering, exciting, boring, risky, tasteful, abhorrent, etcetera. In Chapter 4 of this volume,

Weenink and Spaargaren make a case for conceptualizing the role of emotions in practices, which has been an almost neglected element of social practices so far. Making use of the sociology of emotions as a prospering branch of sociology, they argue that emotions navigate practices. This may sound like a rather revolutionary approach to the reproduction of social practices. In the work of Schatzki however there are several clues on how to elaborate a theory of emotions in the context of practice theory. When combined with Randal Collins' work on Interaction Ritual chains (1993; 2004), emotions can be shown to be important drivers of change, whether analysed in terms of embodied responses or in terms of emotional energies produced in and through social practices of interaction.

The plenum of the social: populated by practices that are clustered and related in different ways

The fourth and final key element to be discussed here refers to the notion that practice theories represent a flat ontology. This assumption is at the core of the chapter that Schatzki contributes to this volume. Embracing a flat ontology implies that the social is approached as being one of a kind. There is no distinction made into different social realms with distinct characteristics, as for example suggested by micro- versus macro-analyses, by the agency – structure dualism, and by the distinction between landscape, regime and niche actors and dynamics in transition theory (see below). Also Manuel Castells' distinction between the different time-space dynamics of what he labels as 'space of flows' versus 'space of places' would not be a conceptual candidate to be used in the context of a flat ontology. In practice theories, there are no levels of the social which represent different dynamics of social change. A flat ontology entails that practice theories accept no stratification of social reality when it comes to the workings and mechanisms of the social. The constitution of society evolves through, and takes the form of, a myriad of interconnected social practices being (re)produced in time and space. The dynamics of society are one of a kind, even though the reproduction of the web of social practices is generating different kinds of inequalities. Unequal relations of power and the unequal distribution of emotional energies, values, knowledge and skills among groups of social actors do not go against the flat ontology of practice theories.

When reviewing the empirical examples used by practice theorists and the kind of empirical studies conducted with the help of practice approaches so far, there seems to exist a preference for studying everyday life, ordinary, rather 'small' social phenomena. The typical examples in Shoves' work for example are about doing the laundry, taking a shower and going for a Nordic walk. With such an emphasis on small phenomena, it is difficult to provide inputs to actors and organizations involved in the governance of social change at the national and international levels. In this volume, we are keen to elaborate the consequences of working with a flat ontology in empirical research when the focus is on 'larger' social phenomena as well. Largeness here refers to extension of bundles of practices in time and space. Since it is ontologically inadequate to distinguish between different levels or layers within the social, we have to find or invent other concepts that specify what is 'large' and what is 'small' within the framework of practice theory. Shove *et al.* (2012), Schatzki (2015; forthcoming) and Nicolini (2012) have set themselves to the task of further elaborating practice theories so that they allow for the analysis and investigation of larger social phenomena.

Social practices can be more or less frequent, prominent and visible in the plenum. They can show different patterns of distribution through time-space, they can be more or less firmly clustered and embedded in wider networks of practices and they can be related to and (made) dependent from other practices in more or less stringent and enduring ways. In the past few years, a number of concepts has been suggested by practice theorists to specify the distribution of practices over time-space and to characterize their modalities of being interconnected and clustered. Schatzki uses the concept of bundles – or more correctly practice-arrangement-bundles –, to organize the discussion on small versus larger social phenomena (Schatzki, forthcoming). Practice-arrangement bundles refer to sets of social practices and material arrangements that hang together and are interconnected in more or less strong and enduring ways. When studying larger practice-arrangement bundles in particular, it seems attractive from a methodological point of view to approach the plenum of practices in what Nicolini (2012) refers to as the zoomed-out modus. Taking a helicopter view of the plenum is instrumental for identifying smaller and larger bundles of practices and the patterns they weave through time-space.

When practice-arrangement bundles are anchored at specific places – as in the case of airports, hospitals or industrial parks – Shove refers to them as complexes. In the case that well-defined strings of interconnected practices are lightened up by the practice lens, they can be called chains or nexuses, for example in the empirical study of international food chains (Oosterveer and Sonnenfeld, 2012). When particular kinds of practices are shown to appear together with two other kinds of social practices often, they could be referred to in terms of connecting or mediating practices (see Chapter 10 of this volume). Shove *et al.* (2012) also discuss recurring patterns of practices in time-space using the concepts of dominant pathways and circuits of reproduction. Again, for these dominant pathways to become visible for the researcher, one has to zoom-out and consider a larger slice of the plenum through the lens of practice theory. Without going into more detail here, the reader will grasp the basic idea of what it is like to research aspects of the plenum of practices with the analytical lens on a wider scope. Such a modality of looking at social practices was referred to by Giddens (1984) in terms of 'institutional analyses' of social practices. In such a mode of doing research, practices as embedded entities and practice-arrangement bundles are being investigated while bracketing the performances of the practices through the interplay of agents and objects.

Throughout the book, we will provide further discussion and empirical examples to substantiate the claim that practice theories are not just valuable when the analysis focuses on the enactment of situated practices with the analytical lens zoomed-in, but that they also have promising potential when larger social phenomena are considered, analysed with a zoomed-out practice lens to grasp recurring patterns within the plenum. Before we introduce some methodological considerations that are specifically related to doing practice-based research, we have one more set of theoretical issues to deal with: the ways in which practice theories approach and conceptualize social change.

Practice theories and research on social change

In Chapter 2 of this volume, Schatzki argues in some detail why there is nothing beyond 'the level of social practices' and why, for that reason, the multi-level perspective as implied in transition theory (Grin *et al.*, 2012; Geels *et al.*, 2015) is difficult to reconcile with a practice ontology. According to some authors, however, the 'flat ontology assumption' of theories of social practices can be shown to seriously hamper the potential of practice theories to analyse and understand the bigger picture of 'episodic transformations' (Giddens, 1984) or 'transitions (Geels, 2002; De Haan and Rotmans, 2011).[1] The flat ontology thereby seems to stand in the way of practice theories' potential to gain direct relevance for the understanding and governance of social change of large phenomena in particular. How can social scientists be so naive to think that the worlds of multinationals and the unemployed, of global superpowers and small-island states, of Nobel prize winners and the illiterate or of dictators and prisoners, can be regarded as made from the same ground materials and as essentially the same? Are there no institutions (e.g. the Roman Catholic Church, Museums, Capitalism, the Olympics Games) of hundreds of years old that play a dominant role in the development of society as a whole? The flat ontology assumption in general seems to generate fierce discussions among a broader range of authors who raise different kinds of criticisms in this respect (Shove *et al.*, 2007; Thornton *et al.*, 2012; Shove *et al.*, 2012; Nicolini, 2012; Elder-Vass, 2010; Sayer, 2013; Geels *et al.*, 2015).

In this volume, the supposed incommensurability of transition theory and practice theories is foregrounded and discussed both in theoretical chapters and in chapters reporting on empirical analyses. We think this debate is much needed and to be welcomed, especially since it is the ambition of practice research to move beyond analysing and researching 'small' social phenomena only. We shortly comment on one chapter of the book in some more detail here, since it offers a nice illustration of the way in which practice theory can be used to confront social change in relation to both smaller and larger social phenomena. Van der Poel and Bakker (Chapter 8) take playing tennis as their starting point, a social practice which has been analysed before in relation to the works of Elias and Bourdieu (Bowen *et al.*, 2013). Having their lens zoomed in on the performances of the

practice, van der Poel and Bakker show how in time-space specific performances, bodies and both smaller and larger material objects play a crucial role.
They argue that small material objects like tennis-balls, tennis-shoes and rackets
are material elements of a different kind as compared to the larger material
objects and infrastructures that form the surfaces on which the tennis-play is performed. With their lens in the zoomed out position, they then go on to show how
playgrounds are involved not just in the situated performances of tennis players,
but also in the organization and management of tennis as a field of sports, with
particular standards, and designated roles and responsibilities of governing
bodies. Using the concept of 'affordances', they elaborate on Shove's analyses
with respect to the role of material objects and they show how both small and
large objects co-determine future performances, albeit in ways that are different
for smaller and larger objects. We offer this as an example of how we think practice theories could and should be developed both conceptually and methodologically in order to cover not just small but larger phenomena as well.

With respect to analysing the dynamics of larger scale social phenomena,
authors who work in the tradition of transition theory have made significant contributions to the social sciences over the past decades. Transition studies have
become famous for their sensitivity to history and their relevance for policy processes, the governance of sustainability transitions in particular. Historical
studies and integrated assessments have appeared on transitions in systems of
(auto)mobility (Geels *et al.*, 2012), food consumption, -retail and -production
(Spaargaren *et al.*, 2012), the uses of energy (Verbong *et al.*, 2013) and of health
care (Broerse *et al.*, 2012). The concepts and ideas developed by Johan Schot,
Rene Kemp, Frank Geels, Jan Rotmans, Derk Loorbach, John Grin, Tom Hargreaves, Ken Green, Frans Berkhout and many others explicitly aim to illustrate
specific dynamics of social change based on models that are built on historical
cases. Firmly anchored in the Science and Technology Studies school of thought,
concepts such as lock-in, strategic niche management, acceleration, momentum,
and dominant and alternative regimes, were added to the jargon of the social sciences. A multi-level perspective is used to show that social changes take distinct
shapes at different levels (i.e. niches, regimes and landscapes, in the terminology
of transition theory) of the social. Niche developments that occur in socio-
technical innovations are of a different kind and thereby require different governance and management approaches as compared to the higher level of
well-established regimes which appear in the reproduction of large socio-
technical systems. Also, so called landscape factors which are conceptualized as
being 'external' to even the largest socio-technical systems, represent their own
specific dynamics of social change.

Practice theories and their flat ontology collide with transition theoretical
studies not so much – so we would argue – on the relevant units of analysis. It
can be argued that the concept of practice-arrangement bundles as recently suggested by Schatzki, is of a similar theoretical kind as the notions of socio-
technical or socio-material systems used in transition studies (McMeekin and

Southerton, 2012). When Shove *et al.* (2012) discuss how novel practices emerge and go through early phases of development and stabilization, one could easily recognize the similarities with the niche-innovation concept. Also, their 'dominant circuits' and 'pathways of reproduction' are not that far removed from what is called 'dominant regimes' in transition theory. However, both approaches seem less reconcilable with respect to their basic assumptions about the nature and dynamics of social change, and in particular the multi-level perspective assumption in transition theory that the social is made up of three different kinds of dynamics of social change. In a flat ontology it is not possible to speak of a 'landscape' level (i.e. macro level) that represents fundamentally different dynamics of change in relation to processes of social change at the levels of regimes (i.e. meso) or niches (i.e. micro) level. In practice-theoretical terms, there is no area or region within the plenum where human agency does not appear or where it plays a different role in the reproduction of socio-technical systems and their regimes.

In the concluding chapter of the book, we argue for a continued debate and exchange of ideas between practice theorists and authors from the school of transition studies. Both streams of social scientific research have specific contributions to make to the analysis of social change, and there is an increasing number of authors combining both approaches or at least showing an open attitude towards finding syntheses and building bridges (Hargreaves *et al.*, 2013; Geels *et al.*, 2015; Rauschmayer *et al.*, 2015). As the work of Shove *et al.* (2012) and Schatzki (forthcoming) demonstrate, efforts are now being made to develop more elaborate and concrete ideas on 'pathways of change' within configurations of social practices. We consider the shared interest in looking for historical patterns or pathways of change with respect to large social phenomena to be an important meeting ground of practice theories and transition theories.

Finally, with respect to the analyses of social change in contemporary societies, we think practice theorists could benefit from a suggestion made by Anthony King (2010) to take a critical and more distant look at the kind of conceptual issues – agency, structure, objectivism, subjectivism – that kept social theorists busy over the last decades. The question is how relevant agency-structure debates still are, when they are reviewed from the perspective of sociological theories of the network-society as formulated by Manuel Castells (1996, 2009), John Urry (2000), Saskia Sassen (2006) and others. Network theories seem to offer a range of concepts that are particularly useful when researching the plenum of the social with the practice-lens in the zoomed-out modality. Agency and power in the global network society gain particular characteristics which deserve the analytical attention of practice theorists as well. The role of network codes and standards as well as the idea of groups of actors being actively involved in the making and breaking of linkages between different networks are two examples that are in need of further elaboration from a practice theoretical point of views We will follow-up on King's suggestion in different chapters of the book, and in the concluding chapter in particular.

Methodological issues in practices-oriented research

According to Davide Nicolini (2012), practice-based research approaches are not just build upon a flat ontology, they also use a specific methodology and a particular 'style of writing'. The latter points refer to a particular reflexive style of engagement in social science research that is further elaborated by Robert Schmidt in Chapter 3 of this volume. Since one of our aims of this book is to demonstrate that practice theories can be used for empirical analyses, some further reflection on epistemological and methodological issues seems inevitable and useful. What can be said about the position of practice theory researchers vis-à-vis their objects of research? How do researchers themselves connect to the practices they study? We shortly discuss two modalities of looking at and investigating practices: analysing them with the lens zoomed-in, and taking a helicopter view on the plenum with the lens zoomed-out.

Practice research with the lens zoomed-in: focusing on situated practices and their (historical) development

According to Robert Schmidt (Chapter 3), participation of researchers in the social practices they investigate is necessary and a prerequisite. His praxeology shows a clear and substantively justified preference for ethnographic methods, such as participant observation, manipulative observation, shadowing and first and second person observation. Such methods bring along different forms of participation from the part of researchers. Only by actively participating in the practices under study, researchers gain practical understanding and are able to acquire inside knowledge and skills in relation to the nature of the practices, their rules and teleo-affectivities. However, forms of participation from the side of researchers are not unproblematic and can generate both intended and unintended results and have effects on the practice which themselves can be turned into further objects of empirical research. Schmidt's contribution is not intended as the final word on the relationship between practice theories and research methodology. Nevertheless, a consensus seems to exist on the primacy of qualitative methods. Some authors argue on theoretical grounds against the use of quantitative survey methods (Arts et al., 2012; Nicolini, 2012). Others however argue that practice theories are tolerant to all types of research methodology, including forms of (practice-based) modelling (Holtz, 2014) and quantitative representations and investigations on the rhythms of practices (Pantzar, 2013).

Although we tend to take a pragmatic approach with regard to the use of more or less standardized or more or less qualitative or quantitative research methods, we do think that more open, qualitative methodological approaches are indispensable to conduct research on practices. This is because such approaches reveal the rich detail of practices and the ways they unfold. The *in situ* reproduction of practices (Stones, 2005) can be researched by using ethnographic methods for deciphering the codes of situated practices, for carefully describing the objects involved and their particular uses. Qualitative methods are indispensable when seeking to describe the emotions at stake, the shifting of performances from front-stage to back-stage and vice versa, and for investigating the things being taken for granted or made into objects of reflection and discussion.

To refer to all the detailed, close-up, engaged ways of looking at and diving in to situated performances, Nicolini (2012) has suggested the metaphor of 'zooming in' on social practices. Zooming in is about taking a closer look, and taking a closer look means first of all getting engaged, becoming submerged in the practices and experiencing first-hand what it is like to be a participant to the practice. The best way to dive into kitchen practices is to participate in doing the cooking or dish-washing (Martens, 2012). By using different forms of participating and participatory observation, the researcher develops a feel for the game, a first-hand experience of the doings and sayings at stake. He or she is able to record in detail the physical aspects of local context, the objects and material elements involved and the codes of the practices as enacted by the participants of the practice. Methods developed by ethno-methodologists can be used to crack the code, for example by creating circumstances that go against the rules of the practices.

A well-known method for getting to know the rules and teleo-affective structures of the practices is to enter into the practice as a novice. Recognized newcomers to the practice are often granted the right to experiment, to ask basic or stupid questions, to find out about the expected doings and sayings, to learn how activities and projects are being carried out, and what kind of power relations are at stake. Their position of 'legitimate peripheral participators' (Nicolini, 2012; Lave and Wenger, 1991) makes things possible that otherwise would be regarded as being out of order.

Another method or circumstance would be to observe and participate in the temporary breakdown of routines and the ensuing attempts of normalization or re-routinization. Goffman's discussion of the many ways in which the interaction order can be endangered by the behaviour of its participants, is required reading for all practice-oriented researchers (Goffman, 1967). When routines are disrupted, doings and sayings which are normally taken for granted can become an object of reflection from the side of participants, which may result in a discussion of the key characteristics of the practice among the participants (Spaargaren *et al.*, 2013). De-routinization does not have to be triggered by human agents but can result from breakdowns in technologies and infrastructures involved in the reproduction of practices as well: the energy system going down and the city being flooded as the result of extreme rainfall are examples here.

Finally, an important form of practice research with the lens zoomed-in is to closely follow the trajectory or the life of a specific social practice. By studying the 'life of practices' (Shove *et al.*, 2012), researchers try to find out how and when a practice emerged, how it developed, matured, aged and perhaps disappeared or dissolved into other practices. It can be investigated how specific practices 'travel' through time-space and with what other kind of practices they tend to team up, or not. Historicizing social practices provides knowledge about the robustness or resilience of the practice, about the contextual conditions under which it prospers and about the ways in which particular emotions can become attached or detached from the practice (Wertheim-Heck and Spaargaren, 2015).

It is difficult to image practice-based research in which the lens is not at any one time being brought into the zoomed-in position. This is because of the assumption of practice theories that performances, bodily presence, emotions, practical intelligibilities and more in general forms of 'social integration' are the heart of the matter. Without 'thick' analyses of the life of situated practices, no valid sociological knowledge on the constitution of social practices is possible. In the process of reproduction, social practices create meanings, symbols, ways of using things, emotions, projects and programmes to be further developed. Social practices are at the origin of the social and studying them in detail informs researchers about the ways things are.

Practice research with the lens in the zoomed-out position: connectivity and dynamic patterning

While most practice theorists still would agree upon the primacy of zoomed-in methodologies and the kind of knowledge they generate, there has recently emerged a debate on the limitations and potential weaknesses of just doing analyses of situated practices. Especially when the interest is about understanding and explaining wider processes of social change, is it recognized that the zoomed-in methods, data and interpretations need to be complemented with questions, data and methodologies that require the practice-lens being put in the zoomed-out modality. Or more correctly formulated, when researching social change, researchers inspired by practice theories are advised to use their analytical lens alternately in a zoomed-in and zoomed-out position. What kind of questions guide practice inspired research that looks at the plenum in the zoomed-out modality? What kind of methods are being used and what kind of knowledge is expected to result from this? When searching for answers to these questions, there are at least three topics we think need to be considered: connectivity between social practices, dynamic patterning within the plenum and identifying promising entry points for ensuing research in the zoomed-in modality.

Connectivity has been discussed already in terms of social practices hanging together in practice-arrangement bundles of smaller or larger size. The bindings between practices can be shown to be of different kinds, more or less enduring, in some cases place-specific and organized via one or more elements of the practices. At the moment, a number of authors in the field of practice theories are busy elaborating the theme of connectivity between practices, thereby suggesting new concepts to be added to the vocabulary of practice theories (Shove *et al.*, 2012; Warde, 2013; Kuijer, 2013; Lamers and Pashkevich, 2015). Next to the hanging together via shared rules, values, emotions, material objects, competences or teleo-affective structures, practices can also be connected via groups of human agents with similar lifestyles (Giddens, 1991) or a corresponding habitus (Bourdieu, 1977, 1979). When discussing the role of human actors as 'bodily intersections' of social practices, it would be interesting to investigate how people reflect upon the status of the practices they are involved in. As Elder-Vass (2012) has suggested in relation to norm circles, it could perhaps be interesting to investigate the (causal) power of practices and practice-arrangement bundles as perceived by and acted upon from the side of the practitioners. How widely dispersed in time-space do practitioners think the practice-arrangement bundles to be? Is 'it' being done in China and Brazil as well, and has it been around for a long time already? Think about Nordic walking, or playing soccer or growing food at your rooftop in the city. The size of the 'imagined practice-arrangement bundle' influences the enactment of the practitioners, their assessment of the competences and the emotional energy they might derive from doing it. When entering into this kind of research, we discuss connectivity not just in terms of practices being interconnected but as well in terms of being enacted as power relation (see Chapter 10).

Dynamic patterning is about the ways in which practice-arrangement bundles develop over time. Without going into detail on the kind of patterns to be discerned and the kind of dynamics at play, we think there is a common ground for research on social change between practice theories on the one hand and transition theories on the other. Transition studies have identified pathways of change based on historical research. Next to transitions being successful or failing, a number of patterns have been identified that vary with respect to their pace of change and overall impact on the plenum. Thus, in terms of transition theory, 'substitution' and 'transformation' indicate changes in the overall configuration of practices that are less profound, spectacular and visible as compared with 'reconfiguration' and 'de- and re-alignment' (Grin *et al.*, 2010). Departing from a practice theory perspective, Schatzki has recently suggested a number of concepts that very much resemble these forms of dynamic patterning. Practice-arrangement bundles can diffuse, collide, collapse, co-evolve, be transformed or de-aligned, etcetera. (Schatzki, forthcoming). In the concluding chapter we will return to this issue of how to conceptualize social change within the flat ontology of practice theories. There, we are going to make a case for thinking about and analysing dynamic patterning without losing sight of human agency and subjectivity. Patterns are not just the result of technological innovations diffusing through the plenum. Patterns are made, constructed, attempted and achieved by groups of actors using their powers to achieve certain ends.

The helicopter-view that comes along with the zoomed-out modality allows for the identification of promising spots to be investigated in the next round of research with the lens zooming in on particular practices or practice-arrangement bundles. When particular connections between practices are rare or abundant, they might deserve a next round of investigation. When bundles of practices seem to break down into smaller bundles at particular sites or moments, this asks for zooming in and finding out what causes the breakdown or split. Only when alternating the lens between the zoomed-in and the zoomed-out modality, a rich account of social change in the plenum of practices can be realized. And this is what explains the structure of the book as discussed in the next section.

Outline of the book

The book is organized in three Parts and 12 Chapters. The first part discusses theoretical and methodological issues, and includes three chapters in addition to the present introductory chapter. Parts II and III present empirical research conducted with the practice lens alternating between zoomed-in and zoomed-out modalities. The chapters in Part II primarily use the zoomed-in modality while those in Part III represent studies with the lens zoomed-out.

In Chapter 2, Schatzki presents the claim that practice theory as social ontology holds that the realm of the social is entirely laid out on a single level. The chapter discusses the kind of social ontology that is promulgated in practice theories and emphasizes one particular feature of this ontology, namely, its 'flat' character. The chapter discusses his claim in relation to other social theories that advance flat social ontologies, as well as theories that proclaim a multi-level perspective (transition theory). Schatzki concludes that practice theory presents a unique flat ontology that has significant implications for investigation and explanation.

In Chapter 3, Schmidt addresses the praxeological implications of conducting research based on practice theory, or the methodology and methods of the practice of doing research on practices. Using the empirical example of academic writing, the chapter proposes a procedure of praxeologizing the objects of inquiry. The focus is on the methodological tasks and empirical challenges, the epistemological aspects, and the conceptual tool kit for the task of praxeologizing. Schmidt argues for a double hermeneutic of understanding social phenomenon as being members' work, that is, as being naturally organized and accomplished by the participants (including the researcher).

In Chapter 4, Weenink and Spaargaren review the role of human agency and power in practice theory and argue for the relevance of emotion in the analysis of social change in (networks of) practices. Their exploration of the concepts of emotions, emotional agency and emotional energy is framed in relation to the practice theory family while using insights from the sociology of emotions and Randall Collins' (2004) theory of Interaction Rituals. The chapter concludes with a discussion of the role of power, agency and social change, informed by Manuel Castells' concept of power in network society.

Part II: Zooming in on practices as performances

The second part contains five empirical chapters which have the lens 'zoomed in', focusing on understanding situated practices of such diverse nature as youth violence, home divestment, playing tennis and the role of good care in complex hospital practices. Here the concepts of shared understandings, portfolios of skills, experiences and competences, distributed agency, transformative capacity, lifestyles, power in interaction, teleo-affective structures, learning and being participants in practices are all shown to contribute in a particular way to understanding practice as performance, e.g. to the reproduction and change of situated, individual practices by knowledgeable and capable human agents.

In Chapter 5 Glover outlines and analyses practices of material divestment for household durable objects. Based on a series of interviews with households in Australia and the Netherlands, participant observation, and a review of documentation, the chapter yields three identifiable sets of practices for material divestment, i.e. making do, passing on and selling. Glover shows that a practice approach captures the emotional and procedural rationales of digitally mediated forms of divestment as much as analogue, and that innovations in divestment practice are not occurring in isolation, since they reflect more widespread innovations in practices, such as the proliferation of internet connectivity, e-commerce, and digital photography.

In Chapter 6, Weenink analyses actual interactions in youth street violence, as interactions are generally overlooked in the violence literature that focuses on features of perpetrators, victims or neighbourhoods to assess the likelihood for violence to occur. Based on an analysis of judicial files, this chapter discusses how and why violence can be regarded as a practice in which people mutually attune their actions toward a shared goal, how these teleological actions are related to material arrangements, and what can be learnt from approaching violence in this way. The chapter also attempts to evaluate how a practice approach may contribute to the study of violence compared with other perspectives that give analytical priority to the situation rather than to individuals or institutions, such as interactionist and micro-sociological approaches.

In Chapter 7, Vosman, Den Bakker and Weenink argue that possibility (Ricoeur's possibilité) is crucial to understand the role of patients in care practices: to be subjected to what comes and what that brings about in the form of inner movements, experiences and emotions. While possibility is often not manifestly open to the immediate gaze, its latency can be turned into a focus of attention. The authors identify two leads in this respect. The first is by position-taking, an awareness of stepping to another position, to the patients as co-actors and to get in touch with possibility as it acts. The second is to acknowledge that suffering, undergoing, is a crucial part of the practice of care.

In Chapter 8, van der Poel and Bakker address the role of material elements in the constitution of practices, using tennis as a case study. Based on a large-scale survey among Dutch tennis players, the authors analyse how various surface types make a difference in the performance of tennis as a practice. The authors claim that a conceptual distinction between various kinds of material arrangements has to be made, as changing court surfaces or tennis rackets require a different kind of agency. The chapter therefore also discusses the practice of managing tennis facilities and how outcomes of this practice have an affect in the practice of playing tennis.

Part III: Zooming out on practices as embedded entities

In the third part of the book the emphasis shifts by presenting three chapters written while using the zoomed-in and zoomed-out modus more interchangeably. The social practices of urban gardening, conservation tourism and sustainable forestry are discussed both for their contents and performances as well as for being embedded in wider nexuses, networks or chains of practices. These chapters focus on understanding the dynamics of change in practices that originate from the fact that practices are part of complexes or bundles of practices. Understanding the kind of relationships or 'bindings' that exist in time and space between practices as entities is shown to be of particular relevance for understanding institutional changes in contemporary societies. Here it is argued that, especially for the practice bundles or complexes that are more extended in time and space, the combination of qualitative and quantitative methods is of special relevance.

In Chapter 9, Dobernig, Veen and Oosterveer demonstrate that the comparative study of the emergence, persistence and disappearance of practices is a way to understand social change from the perspective of practice theory. By comparing two urban food production projects in Amsterdam, the Netherlands, and New York, the United States, the chapter asks what we mean by urban food growing as a practice, and how this practice relates to other relevant social practices already in existence and unfolding in urban spatial contexts. By developing a three-step analysis of synchronic comparison, diachronic comparison and tracing the embedding of the practice in wider networks of practices, the chapter argues that particularly the New York case represents a really new, distinct social practice of urban food growing with new combinations of elements or components, a specific historical trajectory and a unique set of relationships with other sustainability practices in urban space.

In Chapter 10, Lamers and Van der Duim conceptualize conservation tourism partnerships as deliberate attempts to create connections between existing practices and material arrangements to tackle societal challenges. The empirical setting of this study are the tourism conservation enterprises developed and implemented by the African Wildlife Foundation in various Eastern African countries. Based on a comparison of two cases in Kenya, the authors argue that, and examine how, tourism conservation enterprises emerge out of connections between three existing practices: conservation practices of NGOs, livelihood practices (pastoralism) of local communities and business venturing practices of tourism entrepreneurs. These three constituting practices hang together through a new hybrid nexus of practices, so called connecting practices, such as the brokering of the partnership, the funding and building of a lodge, the zoning of land, the communication at trust meetings and the sharing of benefits.

In Chapter 11, Arts, Kleinschmit and Pülzl argue that the way forests are being governed and managed in many countries and sites around the world has been influenced by discourses and practices of sustainable forest management, decentralized forest management and participatory forest management. Contrary to dominant hierarchical perspectives (regime theory or international political economy), this chapter advocates a 'flat ontology' by analysing how ideas, norms and rules travel through 'glocal' networks that bind practices at a world-wide scale. The authors show that global discourses on National Forest Pro-grammes and Participatory Forestry Management have diffused in tailor-made ways to various sites around the world.

In the final chapter, we make up the balance of the book and present a number of key findings that are relevant in the light of the two main aims of the book as identified above. Also, we consider the future research agenda of practice theories and the kind of theoretical and methodological challenges which have to be confronted in order for practice-based research to further develop into a recognized and valued strand of social science.

Note

1 Both the concept of 'episodic transformation' and 'transitions' are used to discuss longer-term and wider processes of change in societies, taking place in specific time-spaces, and characterized by a certain direction or telos. Think about the industrial revolution or the emergence of automobility.

References

Arts, B., Behagel, J., van Bommel, S., de Koning, J. and Turnhout, E., eds, 2013. *Forest and Nature Governance. A Practice-Based Approach.* Dordrecht: Springer.

Beck, U., 2005. *Power in the Global Age. A New Global Political Economy.* Cambridge: Polity Press.

Bourdieu, P., 1977. *Outline of a Theory of Practice.* Cambridge: Cambridge University Press.

Bourdieu, P., 1979. *Distinction: A Social Critique of the Judgement of Taste.* London: Routledge and Kegan Paul.

Bowen, P., Van Heerikhuizen, B. and Emirbayer, M., 2013. 'Elias and Bourdieu'. In: S. Susan and B.S. Turner, eds. *The Legacy of Pierre Bourdieu.* London: Anthem Press, 145–172.

Calhoun, C., Gerteis, J., Moody, J., Pfaff, S. and Virk, I., 2012. *Contemporary Sociological Theory.* Malden: Wiley-Blackwell.

Castells, M., 1996. *The Rise of the Network Society. Volume I of The Information Age: Economy, Society and Culture.* Malden, MA/Oxford: Blackwell.

Castells, M., 2009, *Communication Power.* Oxford: Oxford University Press.

Collins, R., 1993. 'Emotional Energy as the Common Denominator of Rational Choice'. *Rationality and Society*, 5 (2), 203–230.

Collins, R., 2004. *Interaction Ritual Chains.* Princeton: Princeton University Press.

Elder-Vass, D., 2010. *The Causal Power of Social Structures; Emergence, Structure, Agency.* Cambridge: Cambridge University Press.

Elder-Vass, D., 2012. *The Reality of Social Construction.* Cambridge: Cambridge University Press.

Evans, D., McMeekin, A. and Southerton, D., 2012. 'Sustainable Consumption, Behaviour Change Policies and Theories of Practice'. In: A. Warde and D. Southerton, eds. *The Habits of Consumption*. Helsinki: Open Access Book Series of the Helsinki Collegium of Advanced Studies, 113–129.

Geels, F.W., 2002. 'Technological Transitions as Evolutionary Reconfiguration Processes: A Multi-Level Perspective and a Case-Study'. *Research Policy*, 31 (8/9), 1257–1274.

Geels, F.W., Kemp, R., Dudley, G. and Lyons, G., eds, 2012. *Automobility in Transition?; A Socio-Technical Analysis of Sustainable Transport.* New York: Routledge.

Geels, F.W., McMeekin, A., Mylan, J. and Southerton, D., 2015. 'A Critical Appraisal of Sustainable Consumption and Production Research: The Reformist, Revolutionary and Reconfiguration Positions'. *Global Environmental Change*, 34, 1–12.

Giddens, A., 1984. *The Constitution of Society*. Cambridge: Cambridge University Press.

Giddens, A., 1991. Modernity and Self-Identity. Cambridge: Polity Press.

Goffman, E., 1959. *The Presentation of Self in Everyday Life*. London: Penguin Books. Harmondsworth.

Goffman, E., 1967. *Interaction Ritual; Essays on Face-to-Face Behavior*. New York: Pantheon Books.

Goffman, E., 1963. *Behavior in Public Places*. New York: The Free Press.

Grin J., Rotmans, J., Schot, J., with Loorbach, D. and Geels, F.W., 2010. *Transitions to Sustainable Development; New Directions in the Study of Long Term Transformative Change*. New York: Routledge.

Haan, J. de and Rotmans, J., 2011. 'Patterns in Transitions: Understanding Complex Chains of Change'. *Technological Forecasting & Social Change*, 78 (1), 90–102.

Hargreaves, T., Longhurst, N. and Seyfang, G., 2013. 'Up, Down, Round and Round: Connecting Regimes and Practices in Innovation for Sustainability'. *Environment and Planning A*, 45 (2), 402–420.

Holtz, G., 2014. 'Generating Social Practices'. *Journal of Artificial Societies and Social Simulation*, 17 (1), 17.

King, A., 2010. 'The Odd Couple: Margaret Archer, Anthony Giddens and British Social Theory'. *The British Journal of Sociology*, 61 (1), 253–260.

Kuijer, S.C., 2014. *Implications of Social Practice Theory for Sustainable Design*. PhD Dissertation at Delft University of Technology. Pijnacker: Impressed.

Lamers and Pashkevich (2015). 'Short-Circuiting Cruise Tourism Practices along the Russian Barents Sea Coast? The Case of Arkhangelsk'. *Current Issues in Tourism*. OnlineFirst.

Latour, B., 2005. *Reassembling the Social–An Introduction to Actor-Network Theory*. Oxford: Oxford University Press.

Lave, J. and Wenger, E., 1991. *Situated Learning: Legitimate Peripheral Participation.* Cambridge: Cambridge University Press.

Martens, L., 2012. 'Practice "in Talk" and Talk "as Practice": Dish-Washing and the Reach of Language'. *Sociological Research on line*, 17 (3), 22.

McMeekin, A. and Southerton, D., 2012. 'Sustainability Transitions and Final Consumption: Practices and Socio-Technical Systems'. *Technology Analysis and Strategic Management*, 24 (4), 345–361.

Nicolini, D., 2012. *Practice Theory, Work & Organization. An Introduction.* Oxford: Oxford University Press.

Oosterveer, P. and Sonnenfeld, D., 2012. *Food, Globalisation and Sustainability*. London: Earthscan.

Pantzar, M., 2013. *Towards Rhythm-Based Service Economy: Preliminary Outlines.* Keynote paper presented at the 2nd Nordic Conference on Consumer Research, Göteborg, May 2013.

Rauschmayer, F., Bauler, T. and Schäpke, N., 2015. 'Towards a Thick Understanding of Sustainability Transitions – Linking Transition Management, Capabilities and Social Practices'. *Ecological Economics*, 109, 211–221.

Reckwitz, A., 2002a. 'Toward a Theory of Social Practices; a Development in Culturalist Theorizing'. *European Journal of Social Theory*, 5 (2), 243–263.

Reckwitz, A., 2002b. 'The Status of the "Material" in Theories of Culture. From "Social Structure" to "Artefacts"'. *Journal for the Theory of Social Behaviour*, 32 (2), 195–217.

Sayer, A., 2013. 'Power, Sustainability and Well Being'. In: E. Shove and N. Spurling, eds. *Sustainable Practices: Social Theory and Climate Change*. London: Routledge, 167–180.

Sassen, S., 2006. *Territory-Authority-Rights. From Medieval to Global Assemblages.* Princeton: Princeton University Press.

Schatzki, T., 1996. *Social Practices. A Wittgensteinian Approach to Human Activity and the Social.* Cambridge: Cambridge University Press.

Schatzki, T., 2002. *The Site of the Social. A Philosophical Account of the Constitution of Social Life and Change.* Philadelphia: Penn State University Press.

Schatzki, T., 2010. *The Timespace of Human Activity. On Performance, Society, and History as Indeterminate Teleological Events.* Plymouth: Lexington Books.

Schatzki, T. Forthcoming. 'Keeping Track of Large Phenomena'. *Geographische Zeitschrift*, 2.

Schatzki, T.R., Knorr Cetina, K. and Von Savigny, E., eds. 2001. *The Practice Turn in Contemporary Theory*. London and New York: Routledge.

Schmidt, R., 2012. *Soziologie der Praktiken. Konzeptionelle Studien und empirische Analysen*. Berlin: Suhrkamp Verlag.

Shove, E., 2003. *Comfort, Cleanliness + Convenience; The Social Organization of Normality*. Oxford: Berg.

Shove, E. and Walker, G., 2007. 'CAUTION! Transitions Ahead: Politics, Practice and Sustainable Transition Management'. *Environmental Planning A*, 39, 763–770.

Shove, E., Pantzar, M. and Watson, M., 2012. *The Dynamics of Social Practice; Everyday Life and How It Changes.* London: Sage.

Spaargaren, G., Oosterveer, P. and Loeber, A., eds. 2012. *Food Practices in Transition; Changing Food Consumption, Retail and Production in the Age of Reflexive Modernity.* New York: Routledge.

Spaargaren, G., Van Koppen, C.S.A. (Kris), Janssen, A.M., Hendriksen, A. and Kolfschoten, C.J., 2013. 'Consumer Responses to the Carbon Labelling of Food: a Real Life Experiment in a Canteen Practice'. *Sociologia Ruralis*, 53 (4), 432–453.

Stones, R., 2005. *Structuration Theory*. New York: Palgrave MacMillan.

Thornton, P.H., Ocasio, W. and Lounsbury, M., 2012. *The Institutional Logics Perspective; a New Approach to Culture, Structure, and Process*. Oxford: Oxford University Press.

Urry, J., 2000. *Sociology Beyond Society*. London: Routledge.

Verbong, G. and Loorbach, D., eds. 2012. *Governing the Energy Transition; Reality, Illusion or Necessity?* New York: Routledge.

Wilk, R., 2009. 'The Edge of Agency: Routines, Habits and Volition'. In: E. Shove, F. Trentmann and R. Wilk, eds. *Time, Consumption and Everyday Life: Practice, Materiality and Culture*. Oxford: Berg.

Wallace, R.A. and Wolf, A., 2006. *Contemporary Sociological Theory* (sixth edition). New Jersey: Pearson, Prentice Hall.

Warde, A., 2004. *Practice and Field: Revising Bourdieusian Concepts*; CRIC Discussion Paper No 65. Manchester: CRIC (35 pp.).

Warde, A., 2013. 'What Sort of a Practice Is Eating'. In: E. Shove and N. Spurling, eds. *Sustainable Practices; Social Theory and Climate Change.* New York: Routledge, 17–30.

Warde, A. and Southerton, D., eds. 2012. 'The Habits of Consumption'. COLLeGIUM, Volume 12. Helsinki: Helsinki Collegium for Advanced Studies.

Welch, D. and Warde, A., 2015. 'Theories of Practice and Sustainable Consumption'. In: L.A. Reisch and J. Thogerson, eds. *Handbook of Research on Sustainable Consumption.* Cheltenham: Edward Elgar Publishing, 84–100.

Wertheim-Heck, S.C.O. and Spaargaren, G., 2015. 'Shifting Configurations of Shopping Practices and Food Safety Dynamics in Hanoi, Vietnam: a Historical Analysis'. *Agriculture and Human Values*, 33 (3), Online First.

Chapter 2

Practice theory as flat ontology

Theodore Schatzki

Introduction

Ontologies are an ineliminable part of social theory. By 'ontologies' I mean accounts, or simply ideas, explicit or implicit, about the fundamental nature, structure, dimensions, or elements of some phenomenon or domain thereof. Because social theories concern things social, the ontologies that imbue them are accounts of, or just ideas about, the fundamental nature of social life or social phenomena. The present chapter discusses the kind of social ontology that is promulgated in theories of the practice sort and emphasizes one particular feature of this ontology, namely, its 'flat' character. My claim is that practice theory as social ontology holds that the realm of the social is entirely laid out on a single level (or, rather, on no level). Practice theories are not the only theories to advance flat social ontologies. Nonetheless, their version of this idea is unique and has significant implications for investigation and explanation.

Practice theory

The introduction to this volume has already demarcated the domain of practice theory. I want briefly to revisit the boundaries of that domain to point out the ontological character of what unifies practice theories.

There are many different ways of demarcating the domain of practice theory. One way is to count as practice theories all theories that either claim the label or upon which it is regularly pinned. On that criterion, practice theories include the work of Elizabeth Shove, Stephen Kemmis, Robert Schmidt, and myself as well as Pierre Bourdieu, Anthony Giddens, Andreas Reckwitz, and Silvia Gherardi. Amid the significant differences in these theorists' ideas, three commonalities, which are therefore central to practice theory, stand out. A first, lexical commonality is that the term 'practices' is central to their theories and analyses of social phenomena. A second commonality is that they understand practices as social in character, at least in the sense of being something carried out by indefinitely many people. A third commonality is the thesis that (important) social phenomena such as organizations, power, science, education, and transportation are understood as constellations of, aspects of, or rooted in practices. The second and third of these commonalities are ontological ideas about the fundamental nature of something. The unity that defines practice theory as demarcated above is, thus, ontological.

Of these three claims, the second and, above all, the third are contested in social thought. Indeed, the third claim demarcates practice theory as a social ontology from other families of social ontology, including those that hold that social phenomena are to be understood by reference to individuals, systems, wholes, structures, or flows. It is important in this context to stress the internal diversity of the family of practice theories and ontologies. Not only do practice theories sport different conceptions of practices, but just how social phenomena are to be understood as constellations of, aspects of, or rooted in practices varies depending on how theories construe the determination of action, what binds activities into practices, the organization of practices, and relations among them. For example, Giddens (1979) conceptualizes practices as collections of action that are governed by sets of rules and resources. Such sets bind actions together into practices and govern the extension of practices over space-time. Practices, moreover, form systems which are shaped by the interconvertibility of rule-resource sets, by causal loops that entrap the unintentional consequences of actions, and by reflexive self-regulation. And institutional sectors such as economy, polity, law, and discourse are distinguished by which of the three structural types of rules and resources (signification, domination, legitimation) a given sector organizes. By contrast, Shove *et al.* (2012) construe practices as persisting sets of materials, meanings, and competences that are brought together in performances of actions. Elements of these three sorts circulate, resulting in the creation, dissemination, and dissolution of practices. Practices, moreover, form bundles when they connect in situations of copresence, and they form complexes as they become interdependent over time and space. Bundles and complexes alike are maintained by processes of monitoring and cross-referencing. This account then provides the material for analysing social life. Despite differences such as these, practice theories are joined in the belief that social phenomena should be analysed by reference to practices, actions, and the organizations of and relations among practices.

Flat ontology

Practice theories are not just ontologically unified through the above propositions. Their ontologies share an additional general feature: flatness. A flat ontology holds that everything there is to phenomena of some general sort is laid out on one level of reality. In the philosophy of science, levels of reality are conceived of as domains of entities between which systematic relations of causality or supervenience exist. The existence of such relations establishes domains as higher and lower levels. Prominent causal theses that are regularly raised in this context are that mental phenomena (systematically) arise from neural phenomena and that social phenomena (systematically) arise from mentality and activity or themselves (systematically) engender mental states and actions. The relation of supervenience exists, meanwhile, when changes to entities in one domain cannot occur without (corresponding) changes to entities in another domain. Supervenience differs from emergence, which exists when the causal interactions and processes that befall entities in a given domain give rise to new phenomena that are at least partially autonomous from these entities (Sawyer, 2005). As with causality, the direction of the supervenience relation, whenever it obtains, establishes domains as higher and lower levels. Typical supervenience claims are, 'No mental change without a (corresponding) neural change' and 'No change in a social institution or system without a (corresponding) change in individuals'.

A third possible relation between domains is constitution: entities in one domain consisting in entities in a second domain. Constitution does not establish the two domains involved as levels. Rather, it entails that there is nothing more in the world to entities in the one domain than features and arrangements of entities in the other, in other words, that there is – substantially – just one domain. Familiar philosophical claims in this vein are that mental events consist in, are nothing but, neurological events and that social phenomena consist in patterns of actions. The existence of a constitutional relation does not establish a hierarchical relation between domains.

In social investigation, the two most familiar alleged levels are: (1) a lower level composed of individuals together with their actions and interactions; and (2) a higher level that encompasses such entities as social structures, systems, institutions, and the like. These two levels are sometimes called the 'micro' and 'macro', though phenomena other than those just mentioned can be treated as the principal constituents of the micro or macro levels (e.g. situations, on the micro level). Like all alleged levels, these domains are in fact levels of what populates the alleged higher level – structures and the like – systematically arising from or systematically supervening on what populates the alleged lower level (individuals and their activities), or if they themselves exert systematic causal effects on individuals and individuals' activities (or are that upon which individualist phenomena supervene – a position no one advocates). If none of these situations are obtained, the two domains of entities do not form levels, regardless of whatever relations hold between entities in them, between individuals on the one hand and structures, systems, institutions on the other. If, moreover, structures, systems, and institutions systematically consist of sets of individuals and their actions, then these social entities are ontologically 'reduced' to individuals, and it turns out that just one level exists: that of individuals. This is, in fact, the contention of the position known as ontological individualism, which holds that social phenomena are *nothing but* sets of (1) actions and mental states of individuals and, maybe, (2) relations among individuals. According to ontological individualists, social phenomena are nothing but complicated agglomerations of individuals and their properties, though most ontological individualists have not typically thought of the domain of individuals as a level.

Notice that explanation does not number among the above mentioned sorts of relation by virtue of which domains of entities comprise distinct levels. If entities on a putative higher level can be systematically explained by the activities of entities on a putative lower level, entities on the higher level explanatorily are reduced to entities on the lower level. Explanatory reduction does not entail ontological reduction but only that higher level entities can be exhaustively explained at the lower level. I set aside explanatory reduction and autonomy in the present context because they raise considerations that go behind ontology.

The plenum of the social

Practice ontologies are flat because (1) they treat practices as the central element in the constitution of social phenomena; and (2) practices are laid out on one level. This characterization holds whether practices are thought of as forming sets of homologous fields as in Bourdieu (1980), systems that uphold regularized relations of dependence between individuals and groups as in Giddens (1979), bundles and complexes as in Shove *et al.* (2012), or a plenum as on my account. One mark of the flatness of these ontologies is that they analyse social phenomena as arrays of the components of fields, systems, bundles/complexes, or plenum and as lacking any substantive or distinct existence beyond this. Giddens's notion of virtual structure is not an exception to this rule, since this structure is the structure of practices and systems thereof and not something distinct from these. I thus disagree with Robert Schmidt's (2012: 236) claim that practice theory treats macrophenomena as emergent in character, that is, as arising causally from but not explainable by microphenomena. As I will explain, not only does practice theory deny that what 'micro' and 'macro' designate fall into distinct levels, but it problematizes the ontological significance of this distinction. I will now elucidate the idea of practice theoretical flat ontology by reference to my own ideas. (For an earlier flat ontology building on these ideas, see Marsten *et al.*, 2005.)

Bundles of practices and material arrangements make up sites of the social (Schatzki, 2002). What I mean is that social life, i.e. human coexistence – which I construe as the hanging-together of human lives – inherently transpires as part of such bundles. The sum of such bundles thus marks out a plenum in which all social affairs transpire. Note that the hanging-together of lives is not the same as their interdependence. Lives hang together through the full range of connections that exist among them, not just through those connections that foster states of interdependency. For instance, people might share ends, a rich variety of action chains might connect what they do, and the settings in which they act might be linked by built infrastructures or telecommunication systems. Their lives hang together through these and other connections, regardless of whether and how interdependent these lives are. Note also that in using the term 'plenum' to denote all the bundles there are, I indicate that the basic ingredients of all social phenomena are of a piece. Social affairs display a certain high-level ontological sameness: every social phenomenon consists of slice(s) or aspect(s) of the plenum of practice-arrangement bundles.

By 'practices' I mean open spatially-temporally dispersed sets of doings and sayings organized by common understandings, teleo-affectivities (ends, tasks, emotions), and rules (Schatzki, 1996). By 'material arrangements' I mean linked bodies, organisms, artifacts, and things of nature. To say that doings and sayings are organized is not to say that anyone organizes them, let alone intentionally. It is instead to say that doings and sayings are governed by elements of a common pool of understandings, teleo-affectivities, and rules. Moreover, because social existence transpires as part of bundles of practices *and* material arrangements, it is a mistake to shear off the material dimension of society and to reify it as a relatively hard form that shapes social life. Not only is this dimension quite malleable, but it continually evolves as a form or facet of changes in bundles.

The idea that practices and arrangements form bundles implies that practices and arrangements interrelate. Practices and arrangements form bundles in that (1) practices affect, alter, use, and are directed toward or are inseparable from arrangements; while (2) arrangements channel, prefigure, and facilitate practices. There are six principal types of relation between practices and arrangements: causation, use, constitution, intentionality, constraint, and prefiguration. Most bundles of practices and arrangements encompass relations of all these sorts. As bundled, furthermore, practices and arrangements connect not just to one another. Practices also link to other practices in the bundle, whereas arrangements link to other arrangements. Practices, for instance, can share ends and projects and be connected by varied chains of action, whereas arrangements can be linked by causal relations, physical structures, and contiguity. Bundles also range in complexity from pairs of practices and arrangements (e.g. a particular ritual in a particular office) to compounds of multiple practices and arrangements (e.g. a company) to linked compounds of practices and arrangements, which I call 'constellations' (e.g., an economy). These bundles vary in the mix, density, and numbers of practices, arrangements, and relations of the above sorts that compose them. Indeed, it is the existence of these relations – or of a far-flung pattern of them – that makes it the case that a bundle – or a constellation – exists. Note that a constellation is simply a large and possibly complex bundle, a large and possibly complex linkage of practices and arrangements.

The site of the social is a mass of linked practices and arrangements that is spread out across the globe and constantly changing through time. All social phenomena are slices or aspects of this mass. Social phenomena differ in the practices and arrangements that compose them and in the density, continuity, and spatial-temporal spread and shape of their constituent.

Practices, arrangements, and bundles extend over objective time and space. I mention this because it is sometimes said that practice theory is best at analysing local or micro phenomena (Brand, 2010). The spatial-temporal extension of bundles entails that the thesis, that bundles form a plenum, grants no priority to (face-to-face) interactions or the local situation. The activities, entities, rules, understandings, and teleologies that are at work in any interaction or local situation are elements of phenomena – practices, arrangements, and bundles thereof – that stretch over time and space beyond such situations. Indeed, these items often come to be at work in interactions and local situations *because* they are components of practice-arrangement bundles. This ontology, therefore, must be distinguished from interactional, ethnomethodological, and phenomenological ones, which highlight interactions or local situations (Schutz, 1974; Goffman, 1983; Garfinkel, 2002).

Similarly, analysing 'macro' social phenomena such as institutions and economies as constellations of bundles or as slices or features thereof does not imply that macro phenomena are composed of 'micro' or 'local' phenomena (as theoretical micro-sociologists claim). As indicated, not just macro phenomena, but micro/local ones, too, are composed of practice-arrangement bundles or of features or slices thereof. The category of bundle, accordingly, is not inherently micro or local in character: bundles are a sort of third thing that make up both macro and micro phenomena. This is also the sense in which, as noted, macro and global phenomena, on the one hand, and local and micro phenomena on the other, have the same basic composition. Bundles, moreover, do not fall into two classes, micro and macro. Rather, they form, among other things, a spectrum from smaller to larger. In fact, so-called 'macro' social phenomena are simply composed of practice-arrangement bundles that are larger – more spatially temporally extensive – than are the bundles that constitute what are called 'micro' phenomena: it is the scalar distinction between smaller and larger that chiefly distinguishes phenomena classified as micro or local from those dubbed macro or global (see Largeness). Whether, however, a given bundle counts as large versus small depends on the relevant universe of comparison. As a result, it is misleading to equate micro/macro with small/large.

To close this section, I return to the topic of flatness. I noted that the two most prominent putative levels of social life are individuals and structures, systems, institutions. The plenum of practices and arrangements is not composed of these two levels. Nor is it itself one or the other of them. In fact, practice theory generally holds that significant features of both individuals and their activities and structures and institutions are products, elements, or aspects *of* practices (i.e. practice-arrangement bundles). What's more, the objective spatial-temporal spread of the plenum of practices and arrangements defines the boundaries of the possible objective spatial-temporal extensions and shapes of social phenomena. Hence, as Bruno Latour argues, there is nothing social, no level of social phenomena, 'above' this mass: no structure or system that collects, encompasses, holds, or determines practices, arrangements, bundles, and constellations. What there is to social life is entirely played out in the practice-arrangement plenum. Hence, social life does not admit levels. Or rather, it encompasses just one level: the plenum of practice-arrangement bundles. It also follows from these considerations that 'macro' and 'micro' cannot designate distinct levels of society.

Contrasting ontologies

This section further elucidates the flat practice theoretical ontology just outlined by contrasting it with two other ontologies, one flat and one layered.

Just as I claim that all there is to social affairs are linked practices and arrangements, Latour holds that all there is to such affairs (and anything else) are associations and more associations, all linked. An association is a set of connected entities such as humans, artifacts, and things. The entities involved are experiential (e.g. 'visible', Latour, 2005: 174; for discussion, see Schatzki, 2002: 185–8), and Latour refers to them collectively as actants, entities that do things. Entities that do things come to be part of associations via processes Latour collectively dubs 'enrollment' or 'transmission.' Any state of affairs having to do with humans, thus any human social state of affairs (however this is defined), encompasses an association of humans and nonhumans.

Latour's associations bear an obvious resemblance to what I call 'arrangements'. I hold, however, that social phenomena are slices or aspects, not of a plenum of arrangements alone, but of a plenum of linked arrangements and practices. Latour's account recognizes no pendent to practices and construes social affairs as composed of associations alone. This difference is tied to different attitudes toward human activity. On my analysis, human activities are the activities of individual people, but they are also essentially members of organized sets of activity (Schatzki, 1996). For Latour, by contrast, human activities, like activities more broadly, are only contingently related to one another.

A wide variety of ontologies conflict with the flat ontology of practice theory in attributing two or more levels to social reality. These ontologies typically embrace the familiar distinction between a level of social structures, systems, or institutions and a level encompassing individuals and their actions and interactions. For instance, microfoundationalists (Coleman, 1990; Little, 1998) hold that first social structures and institutions systematically arise causally from actions and interactions and second that any causal relation among structures and institutions must be effected by causal pathways in the realm of action and interaction. By contrast, Durkheim (1964) famously claimed that social facts, which are distinct from facts about individuals, systematically exert a constraining causal effect on individual thought and behaviour. A contemporary parallel is critical realism (Bhaskar, 1979; Archer, 1995), which holds that social structures or properties of certain types causally constrain the behaviour of individuals. In the following paragraphs, I want to consider a recent, less theoretically famous example of a multilevel social ontology, namely, the so-called 'multi-level perspective' (MLP) on sociotechnical development. This perspective is prominent in the current transitions management approach to such development (Grin, Rotmans, and Schot, 2010). I choose to discuss this particular ontology in some detail, partly because it departs from the aforementioned two-level view of social reality but more so because its specific empirical detail and richness provide an excellent opportunity to illustrate what it is to flatten levels.

According to this perspective, sociotechnical developments involve three levels of phenomenon. On one level lie sociotechnical regimes. A sociotechnical regime is a 'relatively stable configuration of institutions, techniques, and artifacts, as well as rules, practices, and networks, that determine the 'normal' development and use of technology' (Smith *et al.*, 2005: 1493). Examples are steam ship transportation, the coal industrial generation of electricity for customers, and the assembly line organization of manufacturing. Sociotechnical regimes such as these embrace technologies, practices, meanings, infrastructures, industry structure, policy, and knowledge (Geels, 2002). The level that such regimes occupy, moreover, is a 'meso' one intermediate between micro and macro levels. The micro level is composed of unique niches, 'protected spaces for the development and use of promising technologies by means of experimentation...' (Kemp *et al.*, 1998: 186). Examples are start-up enterprises, heavily subsidized demonstration projects, lead markets, and small communities of early adopters of new technologies. In contrast to meso level regimes, which embrace relatively solidified configurations of practices, norms, and institutions, micro niches are spaces for innovating and experimenting with technologies that might eventually become key ingredients of regimes or the kernels of new ones. The macro level, finally, is composed of a mix of pervasive social phenomena such as political and cultural attitudes, worldviews, macro economies, demographic states of affairs, and the natural environment. Much like the durating material structures that Braudel (1973) discerned, the macro landscape tends to evolve slowly if at all and is largely impervious to intentional transformation.

These three levels are ontologically suspect. To begin with, the concept of a niche comes into question as denoting entities that lie on a level only when it is paired with a second concept that designates 'spaces' that exist on the same 'level' as niches but in which – instead of innovations being nurtured – extant practices and the uses of extant artifacts are perpetuated. This supplement is necessary because spaces of innovation are too few in number, and not the right sort of thing, to compose a domain of entities that bears systematic causal or supervenient relations to entities allegedly populating meso or macro levels. In spaces of this second sort, the past and present are maintained. An example of a concept that designates such spaces is the concept of tradition as Shils (1981) and Gadamer (1989) use it (though the word 'tradition' is commonly reserved for a narrower range of such spaces). In the context of sociotechnical development, however, the concept of spaces of maintenance is more or less coextensive with – covers the same range of social situations, set-ups, and phenomena as – that of a sociotechnical regime. In short, what the MLP distinguishes as the micro and the meso 'levels' are really just different components or sectors of a *single* plenum embracing spaces of innovation and spaces that perpetuate the past and present.

The 'macro level' suffers a parallel fate. Political and cultural attitudes are features of both niches and spaces of continuity. They inform activities in many corners of life. Macro economies are simply larger practice-arrangement constellations that encompass smaller ones, and demographic states of affairs are statistical measures of properties of people acting in niches, regimes, and elsewhere. These so-called 'macro' phenomena are actually elements, sectors, or measures of the plenum of practices and arrangements. Indeed, these macro phenomena, which the MLP collectively dubs the 'sociotechnical landscape', do not form a distinct context in which social processes proceed. This landscape is a motley abstraction, and the phenomena populating it are varied slices, features, or measures of the plenum of bundles and constellations. An 'economic system', for example, is a particularly extensive constellation of practices and arrangements (alternatively, the sum of measures of and patterns appearing in this constellation), whereas cultural values and worldviews are features of multiple bundles and constellations. Analysing the sociotechnical landscape in these flat ontology ways robs it of its separateness from, and assumed stability relative to, what is intended with the terms 'niche' and 'regime'.

The one macro phenomenon that differs from these in character is the natural environment, or as I would prefer to dub it, nature. Nature is not inherently a slice or feature of bundles and constellations, but a collection of events, entities, and states of affairs, unformed by human activity, that can connect with (or be part of) bundles and constellations in various ways. Nature also includes the physiochemical composition of people, artifacts, organisms, and things in so far as this is not formed through human activity. Nature, consequently, is something like a supportive and intervening background amid which social life proceeds (see Schatzki, 2010). Apart from nature, however, what the MLP calls the 'macro level' is composed of features, measures, and larger sectors of the very same plenum of practices and arrangement, slices and features of which constitute what they call 'micro' and 'meso' phenomena. What chiefly distinguishes micro from meso phenomena and meso from macro ones are differences in spatial extension.

Largeness

An important implication of flat ontology is that none of the familiar contrasts between micro and macro, local and global, or even activity and structure lie at the core of social analysis. Far more central is the scalar contrast between larger and smaller. Other key dimensions – though I cannot discuss them here – are density, duration, shape, and qualitative complexity.

I claimed above that social phenomena should be analysed, not as denizens of multiple levels, but as sectors, slices, and aspects of a single plenum of practices and arrangements. This plenum exhibits variations in the thinness and thickness and directness and circuitousness of the relations whereby practices and arrangements form bundles (see the plenum of the social). As described by these variations and gradations, practices and arrangements form bundles and constellations of smaller or larger spatial-temporal spread. A central dimension of variation in the social plenum, therefore, is smaller and larger, i.e. extension in objective space-time. Because, consequently, bundles and constellations provide the stuff of social entities, smaller and larger is also a key dimension of variation in social phenomena (Tarde, 1899; Collins, 1981).

What do contrasts between micro and macro or local and global amount to for an ontology that construes the site of the social as a flat plenum of practices? Consider the micro-macro relationship. However micro and macro are defined, any micro phenomenon and any macro phenomenon equally consist in slices and aspects of the same one plenum of practices and arrangements. The 'relationship' between the micro and macro will thus vary according to how the terms are interpreted and what specific micro and macro phenomena are at issue, and it will encompass all the relations between the slices and aspects of the plenum that compose the particular micro and macro phenomena in question. These relations will hold between the less spatially extended cluster of slices and aspects that compose the micro phenomenon and the more spatially extended cluster that composes the macro one. These relations will also be diverse, contingent, and lack the systematic character attributed to relations between micro and macro when the latter are construed as levels.

Consider the purchase of a fast food hamburger and the encompassing economic system as examples of micro and macro phenomena respectively. No systematic relations of causality or supervenience link these two phenomena. Rather, a bevy of different relations link the event of the purchase and the spatially far-flung (slices and aspects of) bundles and constellations that make up the system. For example, the counter where the transaction takes place is part of a material set-up at the restaurant that is linked to parking lots and roads, on the one hand, and the material infrastructures of credit card companies and the chain's corporate headquarters on the other. Purchases might be the target of various corporate policies aimed at maximizing what is purchased or at enhancing ambience in restaurants. A variety of action chains, possibly originating at great distances, converge on or support the transaction, for example, those embracing the advice of friends, the transmission of corporate rules and innovations, and the delivery of supplies. Intentional relations, meanwhile, likely link the consumer, on the one hand, and the corporation, the particular restaurant, or a particular employee at that restaurant on the other. These relations indicate part of the person's reasons for favouring this chain or going to this particular restaurant. The counter, moreover, is understood both in consumption and economic practices broadly as a place to conduct transactions. And the purchase likely links with other spatially extended economic phenomena that embrace other purchases by this consumer, other places in town, and local companies just as corporate bundles link with those of other corporations, government enforcement agencies, financial markets, and so on. This spatially (and temporally) far-flung totality of relations is what the relationship between the micro and macro amounts to in this case. Different, possibly similar nets of far-flung relations link other micro and macro phenomena.

There is, however, no 'the micro-macro relationship'. Nor is micro-macro equivalent to smaller-larger, even though micro phenomena tend to be smaller than macro ones. Any given phenomenon is larger or smaller than myriads of other phenomena of different sizes, and whether a given phenomenon is small or large is relative. What there are, are endless clusters of relations among the slices and aspects of the plenum that compose particular micro and macro phenomena.

According to a flat ontology such as mine, size and scale are produced. Latour claims this, too. For him, sites (local associations where interactions take place) are linked via material conduits and vehicles, through which actors and sites 'scal[e], spac[e], and contextualiz[e] ... other[s] through the transportation in some specific vehicles of some specific traces' (Latour, 2005: 184). Latour also holds, however, that this linking of sites to bring about larger entities is chiefly effected by actions performed in sites of a particular general type, namely, those connected to many others. One prominent subtype is oligoptica: sites that are able to see a narrow band of other sites very well. An example is the field head-quarters of an army division. Others subtypes are centres of calculation and pan-oramas (ibid.: 178–84). A panorama is a site that is able to dimly see a broad band of other sites; an example is a fast food chain's corporate headquarters. Both field headquarters and corporate headquarters are tied via various media (fax machines, secure communications systems, couriers, roads) to many other sites. Latour claims that size and scale are achieved only via connections that work through sites such as these.

A larger phenomenon embraces a more spread out network of relations (among practices, arrangements, and bundles) than a smaller one does. Latour (and Tarde) is right, moreover, that larger phenomena 'arise from' smaller ones, in my scheme, from smaller bundles of practices and arrangements. As Latour puts it, 'we should not consider that the macro encompasses the micro ... but that [t]he small holds the big ... the big [can] at any moment drown again in the small from which it emerged and to which it will return' (ibid.: 243). However, the actions of oligoptica, centres of calculations, and panoramas do not always have priority in how larger phenomena arise from smaller ones. In the first place, larger phenomena 'arise from', in the sense of being constituted by, *all* the aspects of and relations among bundles and constellations by which bundles form constellations and constellations form larger ones. Similarly, large phe-nomena are brought about by *all* the activities and events that compose these bundles and constellations, whichever events and activities these are and which-ever bundles are involved. The constellations formed by networks of bundles that extend far over space and time need not centre on, or be anchored in, bundles that are particularly rich in connections. The constellation of a fast food corporation joins a large number of practice-arrangement bundles, and the oligoptica and panoramas included are no more constitutive of, and only a little more causally responsible for, the corporation than are the other bundles and relations involved.

Stability and change

A further notable characteristic of bundles, constellations, and the larger phenomena built out of them is the absence of stability, equilibrium, or closure. Largeness and patternness do not imply stability or closure (Shove and Walker, 2010). Since the previous section engaged with transition theory in some detail, let me draw on it again to illustrate opposed ideas. As noted, transition theorists treat sociotechnical regimes as stable entities. Berkhout (2002: 2), for example, describes technological regimes – defined as 'assemblages of technical artifacts organized in co-evolving market and regulatory frameworks' – as stable and continuous entities, attributing stability and continuity to such matters as the prevalence of particular knowledge and problem-solving heuristics, the interrelatedness of technical systems, economies of scale, and institutional, political, and economic commitments. These matters constrain innovation and novelty and confine change to particular paths. Of course, in reality these determinants of stability and continuity themselves unevenly develop and shift, and the combined and cumulative effect of changes in them is continually evolving technological regimes with unevenly developing components and links. A similar presumption of stability leads Geels and Schot (2007: 406) to base their typology of four transition pathways on the 'zero proposition' that 'if there is no external landscape pressure ... the regime remains dynamically stable and will reproduce itself'. These authors conceptualize macro landscapes largely as semi-inert, only occasionally rapidly changing material infrastructures that offer 'gradients of force' that facilitate or hinder actions. They add that 'radical niche-innovations may be present, but have little chance to break through as long as the regime is dynamically stable'. These propositions obscure the possibility that sudden dislocations and significant changes can arise *within* regimes – or, rather, within constellations of practice-arrangement bundles – even in the absence of 'landscape pressures'. Novelty and innovation can burst forth anytime and, although inextricably tied to the past and present, set developments in new directions unanticipated by present actors. Indeed, any large social phenomenon, even a macroeconomic system, can in principle collapse precipitously.

Even when they do not trigger precipitous changes, events are perpetually happening in and to practices, arrangements, and bundles. Bundles and their components thereby undergo halting, uneven, but not necessarily infrequent, and sometimes rapid, changes. Whether such changes are significant and amount to the emergence of changed or different bundles varies from case to case and depends on the perspectives of observers. Geels and Schot (2007: 406) acknowledge this turbulence in conceding that 'stable regimes still experience dynamics'. They overly narrow the scope of this dynamics, however, by restricting it to changes that are permissible within the rules that govern regimes and by claiming that it 'proceed[s] in predictable directions (trajectories)'. The uneven, jagged front of change that characterizes a bundle or constellation often does take the form of gradual, cumulative, even predictable developments. It can also, however, upend practice organizations and bundles and unpredictably, even suddenly lead to larger-scale dislocations and transformations. All the more so since changes of all magnitudes from incremental to dislocative can result from, or be reactions to, dramatic biophysical events (e.g. viral invasions, earthquakes, droughts) and social affairs (e.g. revolutions). At the same time, some things stay the same for shorter or longer periods. Social life is not in constant flux even as it continually develops unevenly. In picturing a flat society, consequently, we do best not to prioritize either stability – as transition management theorist do – or metamorphosis – as theorists of becoming do today – but to depict social life as a complex and developing mosaic of continuity and change.

Conclusion: taking ontology seriously

I have suggested that practice theories share a general approach to social ontology that highlights practices, analyses social phenomena by reference to practices, and is flat in the sense that the plenum – or fields, systems, or bundles/complexes – of practices is laid out on a single plane. What role do and should these ontologies play in practice-based investigations? Stances on this issue vary according to the roles scholars believe ontology plays in social investigation generally. Scholars sometimes advocate an ontology but ignore it when investigating particular phenomena. Doing this amounts to not taking ontology seriously. In my view, a major contribution of ontology to empirical work is the provision of concepts and ways of thinking with which topics and objects of study can be conceptualized, and descriptions, explanations, and interpretations be formulated. To take ontology seriously is to use ontological concepts thus. For practice-based research, doing this requires acknowledging the plenum of practices and arrangements, declining to subsume the plenum under conventional and possibly familiar categories, and devising concepts that capture features of and processes in this plenum. The power and scope of practice theory will become more apparent as progress is made down this path.

References

Archer, M., 1995. *Realist Social Theory: The Morphogenetic Approach*, New York: Cambridge University Press.

Berkhout, F., 2002. 'Technological Regimes, Path Dependency and the Environment', *Global Environmental Change*, 12, 1–4.

Bhaskar, R., 1979. *The Possibility of Naturalism*. Atlantic Highlands, NJ: Humanities Press.

Bourdieu, P., 1980. *The Logic of Practice*, trans. Richard Nice. Cambridge: Polity Press.

Brand, K.W., 2010. 'Social Practices and Sustainable Consumption. Benefits and Limitations of a New Theoretical Approach'. In: M. Gross and H. Heinrichs, eds. *Environmental Sociology. European Perspectives and Interdisciplinary Challenges*, Dordrecht: Springer, 217–36.

Braudel, F., 1973 [1969]. *Capitalism and Material Life*, trans. Miriam Kochan. London: Weidenfeld and Nicholson.

Coleman, J.S., 1990. *The Foundations of Social Theory*, Cambridge, MA: The Belknap Press.

Collins, R., 1981. 'On the Microfoundations of Macrosociology'. *American Journal of Sociology*, 86, 984–1014.

Durkheim, É., 1964 [1895]. *The Rules of Sociological Method*, trans. Sarah A. Solovay and John H. Mueller. New York: The Free Press.

Gadamer, H.G., 1989 [1960]. *Truth and Method*, second, revised translation, trans. Joel Weinsheimer and Donald G. Marshall. New York: Crossroad.

Garfinkel, H., 2002. *Ethnomethodology's Program. Working Out Durkheim's Aphorism.* Edited and Introduced by Anne Warfield Rawls. Lanham, MD: Rowman and Littlefield.

Geels, F.W., 2002. 'Technological Transitions as Evolutionary Reconfiguration Processes: a Multi-Level Perspective and a Case Study'. *Research Policy*, 31, 1257–74.

Geels, F.W., 2010. 'Ontologies, Socio-Technical Transitions (to sustainability), and the Multi-Level Perspective'. *Research Policy*, 39, 495–510.

Geels, F.W. and Schot, J., 2007. 'Typology of Sociotechnical Transition Pathways'. *Research Policy*, 36, 399–417.

Giddens, A., 1979. *Central Problems in Social Theory*. Berkeley: University of California Press.

Goffman, E., 1983. 'The Interaction Order'. *American Sociological Review*, 48 (1), 1–17.

Grin, J., Rotmans, J. and Schot, J. in collaboration with Geels, F. and Loorbach, D., 2010. *Transitions to Sustainable Development: New Directions in the Study of Long Term Transformative Change*, London: Routledge.

Kemp, R., Schot, J. and Hoogma, R., 1998. 'Regime Shifts to Sustainability through Processes of Niche Formation: the Approach of Strategic Niche Management'. *Technology Analysis and Strategic Management*, 10, 175–96.

Latour, B., 2005. *Reassembling the Social. An Introduction to Actor-Network Theory*. Oxford: Oxford University Press.

Little, D., 1998. *Microfoundations, Method, and Causation*, New Brunswick, NJ: Transaction Publishers.

Marsten, S.A., Jones III, J.P. and Woodward, K., 2005. 'Human Geography without Scale'. *Transactions of the Institute of British Geographers*, New Series, 30, 416–32.

Sawyer, R.K., 2005. *Social Emergence. Societies as Complex Systems*. New York: Cambridge University Press.

Schatzki, T.R., 1996. *Social Practices: A Wittgensteinian Approach to Human Activity and the Social*. Cambridge: Cambridge University Press.

Schatzki, T.R., 2002. *The Site of the Social: A Philosophical Account of the Constitution of Social Life and Change*. University Park: The Pennsylvania University Press.

Schatzki, T.R., 2010. 'Materiality and Social Life'. *Nature + Culture*, 5 (2), 123–49.

Schmidt, R., 2012. *Soziologie der Praktiken*. Frankfurt am Main: Suhrkamp.

Schutz, A., 1974 [1932]. *Der sinnhafte Aufbau der sozialen Welt*. Frankfurt am Main: Suhrkamp.

Shils, E., 1981. *Tradition*. Chicago: University of Chicago Press.

Shove, E. and Walker, G., 2010. 'Governing Transitions in the Sustainability of Everyday Life'. *Research Policy*, 39, 471–6.

Shove, E., Pantzar, M., and Watson, M., 2012. *The Dynamics of Social Practice: Everyday Life and How It Changes*. Thousand Oaks: Sage.

Smith, A., Stirling, A., and Berkhout, F., 2005. 'The Governance of Sustainable Socio-Technical Transitions. *Research Policy*, 34, 1491–510.

Tarde, G., 1899 [1898] *Social Laws. An Outline of Sociology*, trans. Howard C. Warren. New York: Macmillan.

Chapter 3

The methodological challenges of practising praxeology

Robert Schmidt

Introduction

In recent years the debates on praxeology gradually led to a bifurcation, following the beaten pathways of the division of scientific work. On the one hand, praxeological approaches were received in social theory and comparative theoretical studies. They were seen as theoretical innovations, and assessed and classified accordingly, with regard to their intersections and differences to other theoretical approaches (Reckwitz, 2002; Schatzki, 1996). Most of the foundational approaches to praxeology are closely connected to empirical studies. This applies to Harold Garfinkel's ethnomethodology, to Erving Goffman's studies of interaction, to Pierre Bourdieu's praxeology and to Bruno Latour's actor-network-theory (ANT). This dominant theoretical strand of practice theory however hardly accounts for the practical problems linked with using praxeological approaches in empirical research. On the other hand, just recently the relevancy and the affordances of praxeology for consulting, advising and policy interventions have been called for and emphasized (Nicolini, 2012; Shove *et al.*, 2012). In the light of this prevailing divergence between theoretical endeavours on the one hand, and applied organizational and political objectives on the other hand, we now run the risk of losing sight of the epistemological and methodological issues at the core of praxeology.

To address such issues, this chapter focuses on the methodology of praxeology. It suggests a procedure of praxeologizing the objects of inquiry. This procedure is depicted in three steps: First the chapter comes up with the empirical example of academic practices of writing, especially of writing social theory. This serves to point out the methodological tasks and empirical challenges of praxeology. It is shown how praxeologizing theoretical writing can highlight particular and novel aspects of this practical and epistemic activity. By empirically studying academic writing practices, praxeology helps to question prevailing approaches in writing studies. Second, the epistemological aspects of praxeology are pointed out. It is argued that praxeology, first of all, is concerned with the misrepresentations of doings and practical activities in the theoretical models designed to grasp and to explain them. Referring to Pierre Bourdieu's discovery of the praxeological mode of epistemology in his ethnographic studies in Algeria, this 'negative' and reflexive perspective on social practices is highlighted. In a third step, the chapter proceeds to provide a conceptual tool kit for praxeologizing. It is argued that praxeologizing implies changing perspectives, in order to access and understand the objects of inquiry in the process of their ongoing social production, transformation and destruction respectively. This is done mainly to open up new possibilities of describing and understanding. Praxeology observes and illuminates the observations, interpretations, shared understandings, and ratifications of participants and seeks to reconstruct their practical and meaningful constructions of social reality.[1]

Doing social theory: practices of academic writing

Empirical praxeological studies of science, which have focussed on laboratory work in the natural sciences mainly, have convincingly demonstrated how scientific knowledge is accomplished in ongoing practices of writing (Lynch, 1993). In reference to sociology and the social sciences, Niklas Luhmann has pointed to the contingency of academic writing practices:

> Scientists also have to compose sentences when they wish to publish. However, the choice of words necessary therefore is governed by a degree of contingency, unthinkable for most of the readers. Also scientists themselves rarely realize this. Most of the texts by far could also be phrased differently and they would be formulated differently, if they would have been written on the next day.
>
> (Luhmann, 2008: 10, authors translation)

In doing writing, we rely on routine ways of doings and understandings on how to practise this practice. But following Luhmann, there also is a contingency and processuality of phrasing and formulating. This demonstrates that the practice of construction of social theory for instance, should be made accessible not merely with regard to the theoretical texts that are produced as its result. Above all, social theories could also be illuminated and deciphered by referring to the situated practices of producing them, which is by studying the epistemic social practices of academic writing.

Writing, although rarely considered and mostly unnoticed, is at the core of doing theory, bridging theoretical thinking and theoretical texts (which usually are reckoned to be merely thinking put into written form). Praxeologically, studying epistemic and academic writing practices is to reject the hierarchical dualism of thinking and doing. This implies not to marginalize writing and consider it a subordinated and external activity of 'merely writing down' antecedent theoretical thoughts and ideas. Undermining the dualism of thinking and doing is to refer to writing as the observable gestures of theoretical activities and to put them centre stage when doing empirical analysis.[2] In doing so, praxeology at the same time questions and empirically destabilizes prevailing 'cognitivist' approaches in writing research which depict writing as a form of problem solving brain work while being preoccupied with constructing mental models of accomplishing tasks.[3]

Writing as a practical mode of thinking

Theorizing thus cannot be understood as a purely cognitive or intellectual activity governed by mental models and schemes. Rather, to theorize is to activate specific incorporated competencies of writing, reading and communicating.[4] They become manifest in observable and situated collaborations of theorists, texts, artefacts, media and technologies.[5] Thus, writing, in its practical, processual and situational dimensions by far exceeds merely the 'writing down' or 'putting on paper' of entities already produced and fixed by thinking before. We know not least, as and because we are writing. By writing we come to conclusions, discover ideas, modify and validate them, put them into perspective, dismiss them and write on. Contrary to hand writing on paper, word processing software and other digital artefacts afford specific support for such preliminary and tentative moves. They help to keep what has just been written in permanent temporariness. What is more, there also is an explorative dimension to writing. As Howard Becker (2007: 43) pointed out, it is not before the process of writing, that we discover what we wish to say or state.

In such processes, scribbling and notes are generated that may obtain the status of epistemic things (Rheinberger, 2012). Academic or epistemic writing can be seen as a practical mode of thinking, conceiving, structuring, recognizing, composing and arranging, mediated by things and artefacts. At the same time, it includes mental, cognitive and intellectual skills as well as bodily, materially embedded and technologically mediated processes. Social practices of writing are composed of movements of fingers and hands, monitored by the eyes and guided by a specific practical, intellectual, academic or theoretical knowing how, as well as pencil, keyboard, computer screen, paper, data carriers, and other materials and artefacts. Thus it appears that methodically praxeologizing the production of social theory provides for a novel empirical understanding of this crucial academic activity. Such an understanding originates from observing and illuminating actual empirical processes of writing.

With the help of praxeological methodologies, the teleological bias of many studies in textual scholarship that aim at specifying the formation of classical works, could be overcome. Such studies are set to work predominantly on the written and already accomplished work and try to reconstruct the process of text formation. In doing so, they seek to reconvert the work into the actual processes of writing. They thereby retroactively attribute far too much rigour and finality to the actual practices of writing. When writing is too closely associated with its products and results, all the forms and epistemic modes of writing that do not lead to some definition of text, tend to be excluded and ignored (Grésillon,

2012). In seeking to overcome this teleological bias, praxeologizing social practices of academic writing should seek to centre on writing as it happens, while also capturing its ephemeral aspects.

Praxeologizing implies focusing on the dynamic and process-related aspects of writing. They in fact are of epistemic value but they are not forthrightly tied to the production of outlasting texts and they cannot be made accessible by textual analysis only. Empirical studies of academic writing practices therefore should not be constrained to text formation. They should focus on the situated and practical processuality, where in the very moment of writing the conditions of 'writing on' are realized. Scribbling, notes, drafts, fragments, versions, revisions and other traces of writing practices – the preferred type of data in ex post analysis prevalent in literature studies – do not warrant immediate access to the writing process (Gréssilon, 2012: 153). They only provide incomplete evidence for ex post reconstructions of this process and therefore should be complemented by observational and process-related data.[6]

Academic writing practices are collectively accomplished

Although they are coined by individualistic views and beliefs, practices of academic writing are socially organized. Writing practices themselves are continuously recruiting participants, who enter the practice and gradually acquire and share foundational principles and criteria regarding the aims, orientations and common understandings as well as the specific problems and difficulties of certain writing practices. In academic discourse for example, accuracy, precision or originality of an argument constitute shared criteria for attributing quality and goodness to practices of writing social theory. What is more, those criteria stand in close relation to a collectively held ethical norm of being good (Jaeggi, 2014: 175). Similar to the specific knowing-how as related to literary writing practices investigated praxeologically by Tasos Zembylas and Claudia Dürr (2009), theoretical literacy could also be seen as personal knowledge (Polanyi, 1958). In fact it is about a personal competency which is nevertheless not to be considered private knowledge because it is being generated in collectively shared practices of theorizing.

Communities of practice constitute collectives, whose participants continuously interact in various ways and attentively and reciprocally observe their productions. Therefore the social organization of writing social theory at the same time is the result of and the precondition for continuous collaboration and cooperation.[7] This encompasses citing, reading, reviewing and criticizing by peers, anticipating shared expectations of theoretical communities, reciprocal acknowledgement in ritual gatherings like conferences or workshops and joint attention constituting a basic principle of the publicness of social practices (Schmidt and Volbers, 2011).

In this respect it is especially interesting to account also for reading and the relations to reading publics as aspects of the collective character of writing practices. Reading and writing are not distinct activities, because every writer always acts as her own first reader. So the relations of reading and writing on the one hand include reading of what has just been written by the reader herself, when she is adopting the perspective of a generalized other, related to the community of practice she is participating in. On the other hand, also remote readers who are absent, spatiotemporally dispersed and connected by technical media are addressed, included and thus take part in the social practices of writing.

The different spatial and temporal expansions of academic writing practices may be illuminated empirically. This could for instance lead to assessing and mapping the trans-local associations and translations signifying the actor-networks of certain strands of social theory in fields of academic discourse. It could be especially instructive to trace the empirical globalization of practices and networks of doing social theory as well as their specific relations of domination and subordination. Dominant networks of theoretical practices can be envisioned as expansive, marked by their size and 'geographical' spread and enacted at many levels at once. They accumulate symbolic resources, control access to academic positions, journals and publishers, and they specify topics, paradigms, subject areas and fields of study which are widely recognized, acknowledged and regarded as legitimate. There are relations of conflict and antagonistic cooperation with smaller fields, islands and networks of dominated intellectual production, engaged in redefining dominant discourse as orthodox doctrine and at the same time struggling to establish and legitimate their own heretical paradigms.[8]

Academic writing practices as subjectivization

In being involved in the interactions, collaborations and the shared normativity of communities of academic writing, the production and practical self-fashioning of the academic subject is carried out. In this respect, doing social theory for instance can also be seen as a process of subjectivization. Participants are obliged to invest and involve themselves in the social practice of academic writing to a substantial extent. Such investments can be analysed and illuminated in terms of Foucauldian analyses of power. The peculiar and fruitless writing practices for instance, which mainly novices and junior scientists in the social sciences and humanities are participating in with persistent engagement, resemble practicing spiritual exercises or forced and continuous work out in subjectivization.

Since only a steadily decreasing fraction of submitted manuscripts is published by the leading review journals, while the number of submissions is steadily on the rise, addressing and obtaining readers cannot be considered a realistic goal of such academic writing practices. Mass-writing of academic texts without chances of being read, amounts to a continuous commitment, indolent and resistant to constant denial and rejection. Such commitment is continually being inspected and tested and has to be manifested time and again in specific monitoring procedures embedded in academic life: workshops, conferences, meetings, colloquia and the like. Everything here, it seems, is about practising and rehearsing a certain academic style, demonstrating recognition of certain theoretical authorities, following and reproducing certain conventions. Compliance with such rules, manners and customs is observed and controlled by only a few reviewers, surveyors, supervisors and editors. In this perspective, academic writing reveals itself to be a rather conformist practice, directed not only to publishing but also to conserving certain theory traditions as well as to the tedious bodily as well as mental formation of an academic habitus.

According to the study of Zembylas and Dürr (2009), related models of discipline and subjectivization are also to be found in literary writing practices. Here participants get involved to such an extent, that writing might grow into a whole way of life. Over long periods of time a tough work schedule is maintained, a certain self-discipline of keeping on is being cultivated, accompanied by stages of loneliness and quietness. Writing in this context amounts to a byword for excluding oneself from ordinary life and creating situations of 'presence of mind', in order to achieve ultimate concentration for the writing process. This condition of inwardness and interiority, compared by some writers to spiritual practices, at the same time is an ascetic situation of turning away from the hustle of the everyday (ibid.: 88).

The epistemic value of praxeologizing academic writing

As the preceding remarks have shown, praxeologizing academic writing allows for sketching out certain epistemic, process-related, practical aspects and dimensions of writing practices in order to counterbalance prevailing misconceptions. Studying academic writing practices as the site of academic theorizing helps to broaden and deepen the understanding of this epistemic activity. As has become clear, practices of theorizing as they happen exceed the mere construction and formation of theoretical text. What is more, theoretical knowledge is not to be conceived of as necessarily preceding and instructing acts of writing. It is in fact, and first and foremost, being generated within the very practices of writing themselves. Thus, knowing and theorizing are not purely mental and unobservable occurrences that take place 'in the head' of writers. Rather they are overtly public and observable practical procedures that involve mental activity as well as bodily movements, gestures and material components, up to the subjectivization, incorporation and tedious bodily formation of an academic and theoretical habitus. Forming intersections with other bundles of practices, practices of academic writing and theorizing may eventually constitute a normatively integrated and governed form of life (Wittgenstein, 1967).

Praxeology's negative epistemology

In view of the fact that *praxeologizing* objects and phenomena of research may lead to an empirical critique of scientific, academic or 'scholastic' misconceptions, I would like to further elaborate on this distinctive epistemic and methodological feature of praxeology. I will do so by referring to Bourdieu's discovery of the praxeological mode of epistemology in his ethnographic studies in Algeria. According to Bourdieu's *Outline of a Theory of Practice* (1977), praxeology first of all is concerned with the misconceptions and prevailing misrepresentations of the practical logic of social occurrences, events, doings and activities in the theoretical models designed to explain them. In Bourdieu's praxeology, social practices first of all are spotlighted in this 'negative' and critical perspective.

This implies that praxeology is not just another theoretical vocabulary. Rather, praxeology refers to an empirical and reflexive modus operandi. Its focus is on situated, observable and meaningful social occurrences that are not only performed linguistically but also by tacit bodily movements and by the agency of material artefacts. Furthermore, praxeology is in search of a new understanding of 'theory' and aims at reconsidering the relation between theory and empirical data.

The conventional view assumes that theories are scientific only, if they can be scrutinized and checked against empirical reality. But there are different and contradictory ideas about the procedures of empirical checking and scrutinizing. The most widespread are the positivist concept of verification and Popper's principle of falsification. Both rest on the assumption 'that the level of empirical observation and that of theoretical interpretation or explanation may be clearly distinguished, and thus that purely theoretical statements may be tested against separate, purely empirical observations' (Joas and Knöbl, 2009: 8). Accordingly, empirical observations that are supposed to falsify theories must not contain theories themselves. In Bourdieu's praxeology this separation is being undermined and destabilized. 'Theory' and 'empirical data' are considered to permeate each other.[9]

Algeria revisited

This understanding is grounded in a particular praxeological epistemology, which Bourdieu developed in his ethnographic studies in Algeria. In the late 1950s, the colonial situation of Algeria provides an extensive field of observation and experiment for Bourdieu. The Algerian field keeps at hand considerable surprises and substantial irritations – irritations that are questioning and destabilizing the theoretical concepts which Bourdieu had brought with him from the world of French academic philosophy. The Algerian field disorients the theoretical constructions. For that very reason, Algeria in the 1950s provides a particularly salutary context for seminal scientific discoveries. Such discoveries take centre stage in Bourdieu's *Outline of a Theory of Praxis*. They are heralded by the ethnographic style of epistemology that is prevalent in the whole book.

However, these discoveries do not become apparent offhandedly. This is because this book is still a work in progress. In its textual and interdisciplinary variety it results from an unfinished process of research, writing and reflection. Bourdieu's Algerian experience is the experience of a fundamental difference: a difference between an empirical reality and practical logic of practice studied by participant observation, and a distorted relation to the objects of study that characterizes the theoretical concepts and models that Bourdieu brought along. The ethnographic and explorative style of the *Outline of a Theory of Practice* therefore is not directed towards Algerian culture in a period of transition or the like. In fact, Bourdieu's ethnography is all about another analytical finding. He discovers the praxeological mode of epistemology for social science and cultural analysis.

The distinctive epistemology of Bourdieu's conception is shaped by the crisis-laden course, which determines the discovery of social practices, their properties and their creative potentials. The discovery of the logic of praxis is accomplished negatively. The argument starts with criticising the theoretical concepts available for comprehending the practices Bourdieu observed.

Praxeology's negative epistemology

Exploring the limitations and projections of so-called 'scholastic' concepts and theories is crucial for Bourdieu's critical epistemology. This procedure illuminates, albeit negatively, properties of the logic of practice that theoretical knowledge misses. A 'positive' concept would merely veil and thereby perpetuate the basic epistemological problem that Bourdieu encounters in his Algerian ethnography: that is, the difference between practical activities grasped from the outside, seen as external objects and functioning as 'projection screen' for detached 'scholastic' views on the one hand, and the everyday perspectives and practical orientations and reasoning of participants being involved in those activities on the other hand.

These insights come close to ethnomethodology's understanding of social practices. Ethnomethodology also rejects attempts to construct a general and 'positive' theory of the logic of practice. Accordingly, such endeavours would merely conceal and overlook the fundamental divide between situated performances of practices and abstract accounts of those practices. Thereby, they necessarily would not confront and solve the fundamental epistemological problems and limitations of the theoretical mode of knowledge, but rather carry those limitations forward and perpetuate them, preferably in methodological debates on appropriate empirical methods for representing social practices.[10]

In his 'negative' approach, Bourdieu first of all discovers social practices to constitute all that, what the competing theoretical and scholastic concepts are not able to grasp, because they are not reflecting on their relations to their objects. Accordingly, Bourdieu develops his 'theory of practice' to constitute a critical epistemology, opposed to 'scholastic fallacies' (Bourdieu 2000: 49–84) of 'subjectivist' as well as of 'objectivistic' theoretical approaches. There are nevertheless subtle properties of social practices being illuminated in this 'negative' procedure. Properties that the praxeological mode of epistemology seeks to account for.

The practical logics and temporal strategies in gift exchange

The temporality of practices serves as one example for what a praxeological mode of epistemology can deliver (Bourdieu, 1977: 4ff.). Practices almost always take place under a certain practical urgency and pressure. What is more, they not only unfold in irreversible sequences in time, but they also play with time. As Bourdieu describes, referring to gift exchange, practical temporal strategies of haste, delay, reacting promptly or even anticipating are widespread. They operate within the indeterminate temporal intervals between gift and counter-gift. Acts of giving bind the receiver. She is 'obliged' and expected to show gratitude until she herself has given in return. The moment of giving in return however is variable to some degree. It should not last too long for not running the risk of being accused of ingratitude and it should also not follow promptly for this might 'denounce the initial gift retrospectively as motivated by the intention of obliging one' (Bourdieu, 1977: 6). In the synoptic and 'detemporalized' theoretical models of gift exchange such temporal strategies are rendered invisible. Thus, the difference between those theoretical models of reciprocity and the practical logic of exchanging gifts not least is a difference in temporality. It is significant for Bourdieu's negative approach, that exactly this incongruity is being employed to explore and contour the temporal properties of social practices. Social practices of gift giving and receiving are analysed for the specific ways in which they deviate from the temporal logic suggested by conventional theoretical models and theoretical knowledge.

> Science has a time which is not that of practice. For the analyst, time no longer counts: not only because – as has often been repeated since Max Weber – arriving post festum, he cannot be in any uncertainty as to what may happen, but also because he has the time to totalize, i.e. to overcome the effects of time. Scientific practice is so 'detemporalized' that it tends to exclude even the idea of what it excludes: because science is possible only in a relation to time which is opposed to that of practice, it tends to ignore time and, in doing so, to reify practices (...). In order to understand what practice is – and in particular the properties it owes to the fact that it unfolds in time – it is therefore necessary to know what science is – and in particular what is implied in the specific temporality of scientific practice.
>
> (Bourdieu, 1977: 9)

Instead of producing totalizing and 'timeless' theoretical models, praxeology adheres to the temporal dynamics of streams of practices. Therefore praxeological concepts are rendered process-related and preliminary in principle.

Two negative objectives of praxeological epistemology

This course leads to an assignment of two 'negative' tasks of praxeology. On the one hand, praxeological epistemology seeks to carve out the peculiarities of social practices – this task being pursued negatively and in opposition to theoretical logic. In doing so, praxeology tries to develop a conception of the non-theoretical, practical involvement in social processes and practices. On the other hand, praxeology also seeks to uncover the effects and the systematic failures of theorizing. This second objective is also pursued negatively and in contrast to the practical logic of the processes and phenomena being investigated. In this respect, praxeology aspires to an analysis of the theoretical relations of the social, implied in theoretical practices.

A conceptual toolkit for praxeologizing objects and phenomena?

What conclusions are to be drawn from Bourdieu's 'negative' praxeology? How should this epistemology be practised in research? What kind of instructions can be derived from his approach with respect to the methodology and methods of praxeologizing? Considering my previous remarks, answering those questions poses severe problems and seems to be a hard thing to do. Raising positive rules for the praxeological modus operandi amounts to completely neglecting praxeology's negative epistemology as sketched out above. What is more, the praxeology suggested calls for a unique adequacy of methods in relation to the phenomena. So therefore no rules of procedure can be isolated from the objects of analysis and stated in any general way. Talking about the method and procedure of praxeology in a detached manner thus is like trying to swim without water. When I nevertheless dare to do so in the following, I try to take at least some countermeasures by referring to the example of the social practices of academic writing and by doing social theory in a manner as suggested by the community of authors in this volume.

Towards a praxeological construction of the object

The sociology of social practices, in my view, is not out for elaborating a realistic conception of social practices. Practices should not be treated as an empirical reality, but as a concept for mapping and analytical understanding empirical social reality. In this methodological perspective, the question, whether there really is such a thing like a social practice, is not relevant. More important is the analytical gain provided by seeing an object or phenomenon of inquiry as an ongoing practical accomplishment of different participants and carriers ('Träger') to the practices. This implies changing perspective, in order to understand the object with regard to the process of its perpetual social production or destruction, its construction or undoing respectively. This is done mainly to open up new possibilities of describing and understanding. Analytically focussing upon an object of inquiry this way, means to construct it. What is at stake is to decontextualize it, transform it, translate it or rearticulate it as an object of praxeological research.

Praxeology focuses on the operational and ongoing establishment of social ordering. According to this methodological decision, normative assumptions or *ex ante* definitions of research objects are to be avoided. Unquestioned assumptions, presuppositions and pre-constructions that are often unhesitatingly incorporated in empirical research designs and social theory, should themselves be turned into empirical objects of inquiry in a manner as suggested by Bourdieu.

Praxeological analysis is situating the objects and phenomena in fields of bodily and materially mediated activities and processes. These are regarded as being organized by shared understandings and collective practical knowledge. Specific fields of practices are at the same time considered to figure as parts and details of an overall sociality, understood as 'total nexus of interconnected human practices' (Schatzki, 2001: 2). Praxeologizing an object of inquiry – as I would like to call this constructivist and analytical operation – means to focus on its situated and – at the same time – its transsituative accomplishment.[11] In the remainder of this chapter, I will comment on both aspects.

Observing participant's situated observations and interpretations

Constructing – in a first and important step – the phenomenon in question as an object of praxeological research, refers to the constructions of the participants. This signifies understanding the phenomenon as being members' work, that is, as being naturally organized and accomplished by the participants. Methodologically speaking, in this regard praxeology pertains to second order observation, or 'double hermeneutic', as Anthony Giddens (1984: 284) called it. Praxeologizing is to observe the observations, interpretations, shared understandings and ratifications of participants and to reconstruct their practical and meaningful constructions of their social reality. The research question crucial in this regard reads like this: how is the phenomenon practically accomplished as this particular and intelligible phenomenon by the participants? How is it identified reciprocally and interactively and made accountable? How does it build upon the results of previous social science research as appropriated by the members of the practice?

There are two additional aspects of methodological relevance, which I would like to comment upon briefly. First, I would like to hint at the method of rendering implicit normativity observable. And second I want to emphasize the critical competences of members and practitioners. This latter aspect is important for counterbalancing ethnomethodology's bias towards 'successful' accomplishment of local social order. This bias can be resolved by accounting for the critical, destabilizing and destructive aspects of member's work.

The observability of implicit, tacit normativity

By focussing on ways in which members mobilize their shared understanding and their situated practical accomplishment of a phenomenon as a meaningful social fact, we assume that the phenomenon or practice is organized by a particular normativity.[12] We suppose there is a shared practical sense for doing X in a proper and appropriate way. Therefore there have to be criteria for determining, whether X is and has been done properly or not. According to such criteria, deviations, breaches and violations are noticed on the spot. They are sanctioned, repaired or corrected (Garfinkel, 1984). Those criteria are at the same time implicit and overtly public, which means they can be rendered observable in order to be grasped and reconstructed.

The example of academic writing serves very well to clarify this. There are shareable, reportable, accountable, implicit, normative and public criteria for this activity of writing, and for how it should be done. Academic writing therefore constitutes a broadly intelligible social practice – at least within academia. Nevertheless, writing usually is rendered unobservable to others and performed in the solitude of the study. As becomes clear now, the public nature of social practices – not just practices of academic writing – and their observability have to be distinguished. Both aspects are not to be confounded or equated. There is no observability per se of social practices. Observability is – and has to be – fabricated, established and achieved by suitable methods of observation, like, in the case of academic writing practices, keystroke logging, participant observation, video recording etcetera.

Critical competences of practitioners

My next point is concerned with overcoming ethnomethodology's tendency to overemphasize members' successful accomplishment of local social order. In doing so, it is crucial to also shed light on practitioners' critical competences. There is not only coordinated activity helping to establish social ordering, but there are also competent activities of destabilizing and practical criticism, which have to be taken into account empirically. Praxeology therefore should not only be concerned with member's local accomplishment of social ordering but also with local questioning, ongoing criticism,[13] destabilizing, undoing and deconstructing. In doing so, praxeology can work to expand the ethnomethodological paradigm. Praxeology can tie in with the thinking of Luc Boltanski. In his *Adorno Lectures*, Boltanski (2011) accentuates competent practices of criticizing, reaching from discursive verbal criticism related to regimes of justification, to tacit forms of undermining, subverting, obstructing and rendering reality unacceptable.

Such critical and obstructing activity can also be found within the social practice of academic writing. In this context, frequent plagiarizing could be regarded as practically undermining and critiquing the cultural concepts of authorship, intellectual property and individual merit, and therefore questioning and challenging the normativity incorporated in the socio-cultural practice of academic writing. Plagiarizing is only done successful, if it is not detected as such. It therefore has to be both, disguised and – at the same moment – accomplished competently within the practice of academic writing. This presupposes a specific craftiness and knowing how of the practice of academic writing and its implicit rules. However, in the long run, plagiarizing will destabilize academic writing practices, if it is done by a multitude of participants. This will probably lead to certain countermeasures like designing and using computer software to detect frauds or issuing ethical guidelines of good academic practice. Eventually this will result in the transformation of the social practice of academic writing. From this it follows that praxeologizing should also include focussing on how initially working practices eventually corrode, fail and collapse. Thus, praxeology should adopt a process-oriented perspective and concentrate on how practices continuously turn into something else, how they self-destruct or are being destroyed by their practitioners and participants.

Relating situated and transsituative accomplishments

Praxeologizing the objects and phenomena of research connotes also to relating the situated, local accomplishments of ordering and critique to the transsituative dimensions of their accomplishment. This is to study the associations, connections and networks, of which the local phenomena are nodal points and intersections, and to investigate how these associations emerge, transform, empirically globalize or collapse.

Situated courses of interaction are to be conceived as sites in the sense of local processes and manifestations of multi-locally dispersed social practices. In this regard the philosophical notion of 'site' – introduced by Theodore Schatzki (2002) – can be connected to analytical procedures of siting and locating as prevalent in social and cultural anthropology (Gille, 2002, 2012). Siting amounts to empirically localize complex and global formations, which are simultaneously taking place at different sites, and to render them observable. So-called multi-sited ethnographies have convincingly suggested different research strategies of accessing and connecting different sites, in order to illuminate how multi-sited objects and phenomena are continuously and multi-locally generated (Marcus, 1995).[14]

With respect to academic writing practices, siting could imply to empirically localize a certain discourse in social theory by shedding light on its continuous process of production in local discursive, textual and writing practices and their linkages. In doing so, siting discourse could illustrate the complex networks and associations that are employed in the discursive practices of academic writing. Methodologically this calls for following the linkages and concatenations of texts, topics, journals, institutions, offices, departments, authors, scholars, editors, conferences, etcetera. This also implies to count, calculate and map them, to construct surveys of the spatial and temporal extension of a phenomenon or its trajectory and maybe also to understand its statistical distribution within a population of scholars, in order to reveal the whole picture. At this point praxeology can apply a range of quantitative methods and techniques of 'single hermeneutic' or first order observation like counting and calculating the number of publications and citations, as well as other methods of bibliometrics and scientometrics.

This nevertheless should serve praxeological epistemology. That is to engage in the interpretative project of understanding, picturing and describing the ongoing practical accomplishment of a phenomenon. This always amounts to also illuminating how participants interactively and reciprocally render the phenomenon intelligible. As Aaron Cicourel (2004) convincingly explained, such an interpretative epistemological project fundamentally differs from the methodology and logic of measurement as prevalent in quantitative research. In praxeology siting, mapping, counting and calculating can only figure as subordinated procedures. They are not deployed for testing detached hypotheses and merely may follow preceding interpretative analyses of the practical accomplishment of the phenomena in question through members' work.

For the procedure of praxeologizing social objects and phenomena it is crucial to always consider the symbolic or discursive meanings they have acquired and to investigate how they are observed and understood by the participants. Participants' accounts and interpretations as well as broader discursive embedment are to be treated as (meaningful) aspects of the empirical phenomena themselves (which always also exist – broadly speaking – in and through practices of interpreting and theorizing). Not only members' theorizing, but also sociologists' theorizing may substantially contribute to the practical accomplishment and intelligibility of the phenomena in question. It is – not least – for this reason, that praxeologizing theoretical writing, academic work and discursive practices should be an integral part of the reflexive and explorative project that is praxeological analysis.

Notes

1 Thus *praxeologizing* implies second order observation and comes close to what Anthony Giddens called double hermeneutics (Giddens, 1976, 1984).
2 Vilém Flusser (1991) holds that writing is not an activity of two distinct processes of thinking and subsequent physical activity of hands and fingers, but rather a social and cultural practice of thinking itself:

> To write is thus not a 'clarification' but a realization of ideas, and to have ideas means nothing. It is only when writing them down that one may say, that one 'had them', but then they are no longer like one believed one had them before writing. It is held by some philosophies that 'thought' is the antithesis of 'matter'. The observation of the gesture of writing shows that such philosophies are based on entirely abstract extrapolations. There is no such thing as a pure thought. There is only an intention toward impressing letters upon a paper surface.
>
> (Ibid.: 9)

3 For such a mentalist approach in studies of writing, see Hayes and Flower (1980).
4 Reasoning along similar lines, Randall Collins (2005: 345ff.) portrays academic writing as using shared symbols and ideas that circulate in communities of scientific and theoretical practice. In Collins' view writing is a collectively shared mode of doing thinking.

5 A similar view is at the core of New Literacy Studies (Street, 1995; Mills, 2010). This area of praxeological and ethnographic research on literacies seeks to illuminate different situated practical skills in writing, ranging from writing love letters or user manuals up to programming codes. What is more, academic and theoretical literacies or practical competencies in the theory of students of social sciences are also being investigated (Smith, 2013).

6 Process-related and observational data could be generated by adopting methods developed in didactical and psychological writing research (for an overview, see Alamargot and Chanquoy, 2001). Most useful in this respect are the 'thinking aloud method' (Van Someren et al., 1994) and 'keystroke logging' (Van Waes and Leijten, 2009).

7 In his sociological analysis of philosophies, Randall Collins (2000) emphasizes the social organization of academic writing. In Collins' view philosophies are the results of competing networks of intellectual production.

8 Homo Academicus, Bourdieu's (1988) famous analysis of the academic world, can still be regarded as a pioneering study in this respect.

9 In praxeological approaches 'theory' is rendered empirical, that is, it is deconstructed as an assemblage of theoretical practices. Referring to Thomas Kuhn (1962) as well as to laboratory and science studies (Latour and Woolgar, 1979), theorists' actual doings, their writing practices and modes of operation are investigated and at the same time an explicitly theoretical empirical research is pursued. That is to say that praxeology is not engaged in architecturally building a general theoretical system; praxeology rather pursues methodological objectives, seeks to 'empiricize' theoretical perspectives and strives to empirically unsettle theoretical concepts, that is, to render them empirically insecure.

10 As Michael Lynch argues:

> it is pointless to seek a general methodological solution to 'the vexed problem of the practical objectivity and practical observability of practical actions and practical reasoning', because any abstract account of the logic of practice immediately reiterates the problem. The investigative task for ethnomethodology is therefore to describe how the logical accountability of practice is itself a subject of practical inquiry.
>
> (2001: 146)

11 In a similar approach Annemarie Mol in her ethnographic study of athereosclerosis focuses on the 'practicalities of doing disease' and she suggests a 'praxiography' (2002: 31). She shows how in different sites, different athereoscleroses are enacted and multiple bodies are produced as instable knowledge objects. Those multiple and different contextual manifestations exist and hang together in transsituative networks and associations.

12 According to Schatzki, normativity is closely connected to practice's teleoaffective structures:

> the normativity that characterizes a practice's teleoaffective structure shapes what makes sense to people to do by way of the example, instruction, and sanction to which neophytes (and veterans) are subject and in the context of which certain mental conditions arise in these individuals.
>
> (2002: 81)

13 This could also encompass members' theorizing, which is widely neglected in dominant discourse as well as in sociological analysis. As Joao Biehl suggests, through ethnographic rendering 'people's own theorizing of their conditions may leak into, animate, and challenge present-day regimes of veridiction' (2013: 594).

14 In detail George Marcus (1995) suggests: follow the people (follow scholars along their different positions, appointments and sites of migration in investigating transnational academic discourse practices); follow the things (books, articles and their different reprints and translations); follow the signs, symbols and metaphors, follow the stories, follow the biography and follow the conflict.

References

Alamargot, D. and Chanquoy, L., 2001. *Through the Models of Writing*. Boston/Dordrecht/ New York: Kluwer Academic Publishers.

Becker, H.S., 2007. *Writing for Social Scientists*. Chicago: University of Chicago Press.

Biehl, J., 2013. 'Ethnography in the Way of Theory'. *Cultural Anthropology*, 28 (4), 573–597.

Boltanski, L., 2011. *On Critique. A Sociology of Emancipation*. Cambridge: Polity Press.

Bourdieu, P., 1977. *Outline of a Theory of Practice*. Cambridge: Cambridge University Press.

Bourdieu, P., 1988. *Homo Academicus*. Cambridge: Polity Press.

Bourdieu, P., 2000. *Pascalian Meditations*. Cambridge: Polity Press.

Cicourel, A., 2004. 'I am NOT Opposed to Quantification or Formalization or Modeling, But Do Not Want to Pursue Quantitative Methods That Are Not Commensurate With the Research Phenomena Addressed. Aaron Cicourel in Conversation With Andreas Witzel and Günter Mey.' *Forum Qualitative Social Research (FQS)* 5 (3): *Art.* 41, http://nbn-resolving.de/urn:nbn:de:0114-fqs0403412.

Collins, R., 2000. *The Sociology of Philosophies: A Global Theory of Intellectual Change*. Harvard: Harvard University Press.

Collins, R., 2005. *Interaction Ritual Chains*. Princeton and Oxford: Princeton University Press.

Flusser, V., 1991. *The Gesture of Writing*. www.akbanksanat.com/pdf/the-gesture-of-writing.pdf.

Garfinkel, H., 1984. *Studies in Ethnomethodology*. Cambridge: Polity.

Giddens, A., 1976. *New Rules of Sociological Method*. New York: Basic Books.

Giddens, A., 1984. *The Constitution of Society.* Berkeley/Los Angeles: University of California Press.

Gille, Z., 2012. 'Global Ethnography 2.0: Materializing the Transnational'. In: A. Amelina, D. Nergiz, T. Faist and N. Schiller, eds. *Beyond Methodological Nationalism. Research Methodologies for Cross-Border Studies*. New York: Routledge, 93–110.

Gille, Z. and O'Riain, S., 2002. 'Global Ethnography'. *Annual Review of Sociology*, 28, 271–295.

Grésillon, A., 2012. 'Über die allmähliche Verfertigung von Texten beim Schreiben'. In: S. Zanetti, ed. *Schreiben als Kulturtechnik*. Berlin: Suhrkamp Verlag, 152–186.

Hayes, J.R. and Flower, L.S., 1980. 'Identifying the Organization of Writing Processes'. In: L. Greg and E. Steinberg, eds. *Cognitive Processes in Writing*, Mahwah, New Jersey: Lawrence Erlbaum Associates, 3–30.

Jaeggi, R., 2014. *Kritik von Lebensformen*. Berlin: Suhrkamp Verlag.

Joas, H. and Knöbl, W., 2009. *Social Theory. Twenty Introductory Lectures*. Cambridge: Cambridge University Press.

Kuhn, T., 1962. *The Structure of Scientific Revolutions*. Chicago: University of Chicago Press.

Latour, B. and Woolgar, S., 1979. *Laboratory Life*. Beverly Hills: Sage Publications.

Luhmann, N., 2008. *Schriften zur Kunst und Literatur*. Frankfurt am Main: Suhrkamp.

Lynch, M., 1993. *Scientific Practice and Ordinary Action: Ethnomethodology and Social Studies of Science*. Cambridge. Cambridge University Press.

Lynch, M., 2001. 'Ethnomethodology and the Logic of Practice'. In: T. Schatzki *et al.*, eds. *The Practice Turn in Contemporary Theory*. London, New York: Routledge, 131–148.

Marcus, G.E., 1995. 'Ethnography in/of the World System: The Emergence of Multi-Sited Ethnography'. *Annual Review of Anthropology*, 24: 95–117.

Mills, K.A., 2010. 'A Review of the "Digital Turn" in New Literacy Studies'. *Review of Educational Research* 80 (2), 246–271.

Mol, A., 2002. *The Body Multiple. Ontology in Medical Practice*. Durham: Duke University Press.

Nicolini, D., 2012. *Practice Theory, Work and Organization. An Introduction*. Oxford: Oxford University Press.

Polanyi, M., 1958. *Personal Knowledge. Towards a Post-Critical Philosophy*, London: Transaction Publishers.

Reckwitz, A., 2002. 'Toward a Theory of Social Practices: a Development in Culturalist Theorizing'. *European Journal of Social Theory*, 5 (2), 243–263.

Rheinberger, J., 2012. 'Zettelwirtschaft'. In: S. Zanetti, ed., *Schreiben als Kulturtechnik*, Berlin: Suhrkamp, 441–452.

Schatzki, T., 1996. *Social Practices. A Wittgensteinian Approach to Human Activity and the Social*. Cambridge: Cambridge University Press.

Schatzki, T., 2001. 'Introduction: Practice Theory'. In: T. Schatzki *et al.*, eds. *The Practice Turn in Contemporary Theory*. London, New York: Routledge, 1–14.

Schatzki, T., 2002. *The Site of the Social. A Philosophical Account of the Constitution of Social Life and Change*. Pennsylvania: The Pennsylvania State University Press.

Schmidt, R. and Volbers, J., 2011. 'Siting Praxeology. The Methodological Significance of "Public" in Theories of Social Practices'. *Journal for the Theory of Social Behaviour*, 44, 419–440.

Shove, E., Pantzar, M. and Watson, M., 2012. *The Dynamics of Social Practices. Everyday Life and How It Changes*. London: Sage Publications.

Smith, P., 2013. *Academic Literacy Practices: Plausibility in the Essays of a Diverse Social Science Cohort*. A Thesis Submitted to the University of Manchester for the Degree of Doctor of Philosophy in the Faculty of Humanities, www.escholar.manchester.ac.uk/uk-ac-man-scw:190459.

Street, B., 1995. *Social Literacies: Critical Approaches to Literacy in Development, Ethnography and Education*. London: Longman.

Van Someren, M.W., Barnard, Y. and Sandberg, J., 1994. *The Think Aloud Method. A Practical Guide to Modelling Cognitive Processes*. Amsterdam, London: Academic Press.

Van Waes, L. and Leijten, M., 2009. 'Keystroke Logging in Writing Research. Observing Writing Processes with Inputlog'. *German as a Foreign Language*, 2–3, 41–64.

Wittgenstein, L., 1967. *Philosophische Untersuchungen*. Frankfurt am Main: Suhrkamp Verlag.

Zembylas T. and Dürr, C., 2009. *Wissen, Können und literarisches Schreiben. Eine Epistemologie der künstlerischen Praxis*, Wien: Passagen Verlag.

Chapter 4

Emotional agency navigates a world of practices

Don Weenink and Gert Spaargaren

Introduction

The past two decades witnessed a prolific revival of practice theories. Sociologists and social philosophers such as Davide Nicolini (2012), Andreas Reckwitz (2002), Theodore Schatzki (1996, 2002, 2010; Schatzki, Knorr Cetina and Von Savigny, 2001), Robert Schmidt (2012) and Elizabeth Shove and collaborators (2003, 2012) have elaborated, deepened and refined practice theories that were developed in sociology in the 1970s and 1980s by Pierre Bourdieu and Anthony Giddens in particular. To put it succinctly, practice theories are grounded in the idea that social life consists of socio-material interactions through which people transform their world and themselves. In the words of Schatzki (this volume) these socio-material interactions comprise 'bundles of practices' and 'material arrangements'. The former should be regarded as 'open spatial-temporal manifolds of activity', while the latter consist of 'interconnected human bodies, organisms, artifacts, and things'.

Since the older generation of practice theories had neglected the material dimension of practices, current formulations aim, in critical engagement with material semiotics or actor network approaches, to make practice theory more receptive to the role of material elements and objects, of both human and non-human origin, in social practices. In addition, current practice theories emphasize their potential relevance for the governance of social change while at the same time distinguishing themselves explicitly from some of the prevailing theories of social transformation. At a time when a number of authors seek to reconcile practice theory with transition theory (Grin *et al.*, 2010; Spaargaren *et al.*, 2012; Shove *et al.*, 2012; Hargreaves *et al.*, 2013), Theodore Schatzki (this volume) is keen on pointing out the differences that exist between both kind of theories. The crucial difference in the way they study long term, structural changes is the fact that practice theories reject the claim of transition theories that there are different dynamics at play on different levels of the social. Notions such as large-scale structures, overarching culture, macro-meso-micro distinctions or niche-regime-landscape hierarchies are judged ontologically inappropriate. Instead, practices theories claim that processes of becoming and change unfold at just one level: the level of practices. Hence, the ontology of practice theories is said to be flat (Schatzki, this volume), and allows for understanding processes of change as open ended and at least partly contingent. By emphasizing complexity and contingency, practice theories provide a realistic understanding of the limited possibilities that single (policy or governance-) actors and organizations have when they seek to manage processes of social change in a linear, direct and instrumental way (Evans *et al.*, 2012). The message for those involved in the management of social change is to improve the quality of interventions by connecting policy strategies to the dynamics of practices as sets of interrelated doings and sayings.

Although early formulations of practice theory by Bourdieu and Giddens in particular emphasized the need to go beyond structuralism and instead offer an agency-inclusive formulation of social interaction and reproduction, the relationship between agency and social change remains underexposed in many contemporary practice theories. The ways in which human agents intervene in the ongoing flow of events in the world and their involvement in bringing about changes in their socio-material environments and in themselves, remain insufficiently explored and conceptualized. As a result, the more recently developed practice theories do not provide convincing answers to issues of agency, emotions and power which might help to explain what brings about social change in a flat world consisting of practices. Why do practices appear and disappear, what makes them more or less widespread, stable and mature, and why are some practices more meaningful, attractive and intense for human actors than others? These questions all revolve around the issue that practices (are made to) matter for people. People engage with innovation, reproduction and social change in the sense that they develop a meaningful relation with the practices they help to reproduce and change, they themselves becoming different persons in the process. If we accept the idea that social life is a vast and continuous 'open-ended spatial-temporal manifolds of actions and material arrangements', which individuals experience as sets of more or less relevant, meaningful, coherent, and interrelated doings and saying (Schatzki, 2002: 59–122; Schatzki, 2010), then we must develop notions of agency, power and social change which help us to understand what it is that makes people move through/engage with/find their ways in social life in the first place. Issues of agency and power are about how people navigate a world of practices.

Agency is conceptualized differently in different streams of social theory. In Weberian conflict theories for instance, agency is rooted in the competitive urge for privileged positions. In rational actor theories agency is about optimizing profits, and in symbolic interactionism it revolves around the capacity to give meaning to self and others in social situations. In this chapter we aim to develop a conceptualization of agency that not only remains within the contours of practice theories – practices rather than individuals are the central unit of analysis – but which is also distinct from the ways in which agency is approached in other social theories. To put it in a short and radical formulation, we argue that agency resides in emotions. Emotions are (re)produced in social practices and people experience the world and engage in it emotionally. The focus on emotions helps to explain why practices make individual human agents engage with and actually care about the doings and sayings around them. Emotions are connected to practices in a number of ways, and they provide (positive and negative) valences to both practices and their practitioners. In this way, emotions-in-practices help explain what matters to individuals and how they are set into motion by emotions. On the individual side of the equation, we argue that the human capacity to act (back) upon the world resides in the 'emotional modes of being' (Freund, 1999) of individuals. On the practice side of the equation, we will show how practices produce emotional energy (Collins, 2004).

The concept of power is even more debated and coated with controversies than the concept of agency. When reviewing the concept of power in sociology, Manuel Castells (2009) has suggested that in contemporary network societies the classical concepts of power as for example derived from the works of Weber and Parsons on the one hand and Marx on the other, are in need of revision. The concepts, which organized debates in sociology and political sciences since their inception, need to be complemented with new notions of power that are particularly suited to analyse social change in contemporary, 'horizontally organized' societies, which are composed of networks. One of the dimensions of power that need to be articulated and re-invented has to do with 'the relationships between emotion, cognition and politics' (Castells, 2009: 7). Although the work of Castells does not seem to go along very well with the flat ontology of practice theories,[1] we argue that his discussion of agency and power can be used to highlight dynamics of change in a world of practices.

Outline of the chapter

In the sections to follow, we review the key concepts of agency, emotion and power in more detail, also exploring their relevance for the analysis of social change in (networks of) practices. We start with the concept of agency as it is discussed in theories of practices. Then we seek to explore the concepts of emotions, emotional agency and emotional energy, staying within the framework of practice theories but using insights from neighbouring theories like the sociology of emotions and Randall Collins' (2004) theory of Interaction Rituals. This will be the most extended section of the chapter, since emotions and how they navigate the world of social practices are at the centre of our analysis. A discussion about transitions in (configurations or networks of) practices however cannot do without the concept of power. Again building on authors – Collins and Castells – who are commonly not perceived as social practices theorists, we conclude our chapter with a discussion on power, agency and social change.

Agency in theories of social practices

Practice theories differ from one another in the degree to which they consider human agency (Nicolini, 2012: 44–69). Some forms of practice theory hardly offer a discussion on the key characteristics of agency and its role in social change. This seems to be the case for practice theories that are inspired by science and technology studies and actor network approaches in particular. The analyses offered by Shove et al. (2012) and Reckwitz (2002) serve as two examples. Shove, Pantzar and Watson emphasize the need to decentre the human subject when exploring the overall dynamics of practices. They urge to do so in order to distance themselves from cognitivist views of agency in which individuals are rendered as value-oriented subjects who consciously shape their futures and identities by pursuing lifestyles (Welch and Warde, 2015). In contrast to this cognitivist portrayal, Shove et al. offer a discussion on the performance[2] of practices mainly in terms of combinations being established between the three components of practices: materials, competences and meanings. For the institutional analysis of social change, they offer an extensive and interesting discussion on linkages between (components of) practices. By highlighting the role of components in the processes of (de)linking practices and by emphasizing the embeddedness of practices in larger constellations of adjacent and connected practices, they seem to suggest that the study of social reproduction and change could be conducted mainly with the help of institutional analyses, bracketing the strategic actions, motivations and emotions of individual human agents. As a result, their image of the world of practices is coloured primarily by complexes, arrangements, infrastructures, chains, nexuses and bundles.

We recognize the merits of using concepts like circuits of reproduction, feedback-loops and dominant trajectories since they are instrumental for recognizing the relationships between practices and the ways in which these relationships change over time. By emphasizing interrelations and interdependencies between practices, they bring some flesh on the 'institutional bones' of practice theory, especially vis-à-vis competing neo-institutionalist theories that claim to offer causal explanations of social innovation and change. With the strong focus on institutional analysis of (networks of) practices, Shove et al. certainly help moving away from the individual human subject as the cherished and unique source of social reproduction and change. However, the ways in which this decentring of the individual human subject is to be combined with a discussion of agency, power and social change, remains in the dark. With Shove and colleagues (2012), emotions, motivations, identities, reasons and beliefs, the reflexive monitoring of action, practical intelligibility and practical understanding play a less prominent role in the analysis of social change. In fact, in the perspective offered by Shove et al., individual human subjects are not just decentred but effectively positioned at the periphery of practice theory, so it seems (Welsh and Warde, 2015).

A similar decentring of subjects can be found in Reckwitz's (2012: 256) frequently cited overview of practice theories, where he notes that 'the social world is first and foremost populated by diverse social practices which are carried by agents – body minds who carry and carry out practices'. The term 'carriers of practices' to typify the role of individuals in practices has become common usage amongst theorists in this domain in a rather short period of time. For instance, Nicolini (2012: 4) sees the *homo practicus* as a 'carrier of practices' and also Shove *et al.* (2012) suggest adopting the carrier concept in theories of practices. Although being a carrier does not exclude some form of engagement with that what is being carried, the metaphor of the Greek god Atlas 'eternally carrying the world on his shoulders' brings in associations not just with hard work and punishment but with passivity and repetition as well. When the carrier concept is combined with an emphasis on the routinized, habitual and taken for granted nature of practices (see the overview by Nicolini, 2012), there is a risk of portraying social change in a rather determinist way. Individuals-as-carriers suggest human agents who simply do what others did before them, more or less automatically incorporating a shared history of bodily know-how, understandings, motivations and affects. Reckwitz (2002: 252) comes close to suggest just this as he states that practice theories do not rely on the kind of dialectical reasoning that can be found in what he calls 'intersubjectivism', a branch of theorizing – exemplified by George Herbert Mead's conceptualization of the Self – which he typifies as allowing for 'the interaction-mind-interaction' dialectic. As a result, the position of Reckwitz could be (mis)understood for its mechanistic understanding of social change in ways similar to a reading of Bourdieu's work in which the habitus is depicted as a set of pre-structured dispositions determining the trajectories of social reproduction and change.

In comparison with formulations of practice theories that are inspired by science and technology studies and actor network approaches, the versions offered by Giddens and Schatzki consider the notion of agency in much more detail. We will shortly depict some of their main concepts and ideas that are most relevant for the discussion on agency and social practices. For Giddens (1984), a notion of agency is required to understand where creativity, innovation and social change originate from. He does not stop emphasizing throughout his work that people are knowledgeable and capable actors or human agents, knowing how to go on in everyday life, drawing upon the sets of rules-resources which make interaction possible, and changing the world while reproducing it. Even in situations where power relations are very unequal, there is always some room for manoeuvre left to subordinated human agents who can put their transformative capacities into situational use. The 'could have acted otherwise' phrase, indicating that there is no room for a zombie-concept in structuration theory, belongs to the frequently quoted expressions from Giddens' work. The formulation of practice theory as put forward by Giddens resorts under the category of theories in sociology that Elliott and Turner (2012) labelled 'Society as Creation'. Although structuration theory shares with other theories of practices an emphasis on the routinization of many everyday behaviours, Giddens (1984) makes ample conceptual space for the agency of human actors involved in the reproduction and change of social practices. Three key concepts are important with regard to agency: the reflexive monitoring of action, practical consciousness and transformative capacity. While routinization might bring the suspicion of conducts being enacted on the automatic pilot, the concept of reflexive moni-toring indicates that human actors know about and continuously keep in touch with the ongoing flow of events in the world. When being involved in the flow of events, they are able to shift from going with the flow in a practical manner (a state of practical consciousness) into discursive and deliberative forms of enact-ing practices as soon as situations ask for it (a state of discursive consciousness). Finally, the notion of transformative capacity of individual human agents is used to give agency a central place in the reproduction of social (power) rela-tions within and between practices. Because of the assumption that every human agent possesses the transformative capacity to interact with the material and social environment, Giddens' structuration theory can be said to depart from Marx's notion of species being (Giddens, 1979, 1984). For Schatzki (2002: 105–122) human agency is a crucial topic as well, for example where he – contra actor network theory – argues that only humans carry out practices, not objects. While objects have performative power as they exert influence on the ways prac-tices unfold, they lack intelligibility, intentionality and affectivity. Eventually, 'the world is such that human activity takes the lead in the mesh of practices and orders where human coexistence takes place' (Schatzki, 2002: 119). But then the question is what it makes for human activity to take the lead. We will discuss Schatzki's view on agency, its relationship with emotions and how both con-cepts can be understood as being among the 'drivers' of change in more detail in the next section.

Our short excursion on the role of agency in practice theories illustrates the different ways in which individual human beings are being decentred and human subjectivity is being (re)defined by different authors. What they have in common is the inclination to give conceptual priority to practices rather than individuals, also in matters of human agency. Agency is seen as a result of practices, meaning that the capacity of human beings to understand and to act intentionally upon them 'always results from taking part in one or more socio-material prac-tices' (Nicolini, 2012: 214). They are social practices that provide horizons of practical and general understandings, motivations and affects, and it is by engag-ing in practices that people incorporate these understandings, motivations and affects (see also Reckwitz, 2002: 256). Although practices are in the lead, that does not mean however that acting individuals simply imitate or replicate the practice-bound understandings, motivations and affects. In George Herbert Mead's (1934/1962) conceptualization of the Self, the 'Me' unconsciously pro-jects and consciously reflects upon what is done so far and what might be done in the future, while the 'I', the acting Self, knows what to do, how to do it and when, without projecting or reflecting on these actions.[3] Following Mead, one could argue that the acting I brings spontaneous changes and creativity into social life. Doings may surprise individuals while they 'just do', for example when a lively conversation with participants being engrossed in a creative dia-logue unexpectedly brings about some new, previously unthought ideas, insights or plans. When practices are enacted, also production, innovation and social change are made to happen as an inherent characteristic of society as creation. Change is inherent to social practices, also when they are not being performed and managed with the goal of social transformation in mind, and also when they bring about unintended consequences next to aimed for outcomes. Individual human actors are part of this process and key sources of innovation, even when it is rightfully argued that practices have the lead.

Agency and emotions

Most practice theorists have not been very specific about emotions, although they do not neglect them altogether. The work of Giddens offers an illustration in this respect. While being strong on agency in general, his structuration theory has been criticized for its neglect of bodily experiences and the ways in which people respond to structures on sensual and sensory grounds (Shilling and Mellor, 2001). The main message from prior work in the field of practice theories is that the emotional mood that people experience while engaging in a set of doings and sayings are not a property of themselves but of practices. Practices bring certain affective tones with them. The source of this insight is Heidegger, as Nicolini (2012: 36) points out. Experiencing the world, being in the world, means to encounter objects and other beings. This experiencing of the world is necessarily emotional, in the sense that our engaging in practices is not disinterested or cold, but 'biased' instead. Reckwitz (2002: 254) goes so far to note that 'every practice contains a certain practice specific emotionality. Wants and emotions thus do not belong to individuals but – in the form of knowledge – to practices'. This statement however generates a number of questions. First, it seems ontologically misleading to state that emotions do not belong to individuals since emotions involve complex neuro-endocrinological processes that take place in individuals as a result of their experiencing and engaging with practices. Second, and more importantly for our discussion, the quote can be read in a way that the affective order in practices assumes a homogenous form which is incorporated by each and every practitioner in an equal manner. The 'feeling rules' (Hochschild, 1979, 1983) that are part of practices here seem to function as a code which programs participants' desires, motivations and wants from the outside. In our view, however, it is more realistic to allow for variation in the way participants perceive of, feel about and react upon feeling rules while also recognizing the linkages between emotions and power.

Schatzki in his *The Timespace of Human Activity* (2010) offers one of the more elaborate treatments of the concept of emotion in the field of practice theories. A precursor of this 2010 discussion can be found in his earlier treatment of Heidegger's notion of signifying (1996: 122–123). Here, it becomes clear that the affective dimension of signifying – what matters to people: moods, emotions, feelings, affects and passions – plays a crucial role in activity. For it 'omnipresently structures the stream of behaviour … by affecting what is teleologically signified as the thing to do'. One of the central concerns in Schatzki's later

Heideggerian theory is the teleological character of activity which 'consists in people performing actions for ends' (Schatzki, 2010: xiii). Note that these ends can be determined by cognition (beliefs or perceptions), emotion, moods or desires, needs and wants. They can be conscious and acknowledged, or remain hidden to the individual. In all cases however, ends are inherent to action and to social practices since for Schatzki 'human activity remains centrally and pervasively teleological' (Schatzki, 2010: 111). His treatment of emotions offers a discussion of the ways in which also 'irrational' emotions can be made fit into this teleology. Before we examine the role of emotions with Schatzki in some detail however, we need to shortly discuss his notion of 'practical intelligibility', as this concept is crucial to understand Schatzki's account of human action. Practical intelligibility is the feeling, sense or urge, conscious or not, to do something, to perform an action. The determination of what to do, or, in other words, what action is signified by practical intelligibility, arises from what an individual experiences, believes, perceives, and imagines to be the 'state of affairs', given that it makes sense to perform an action for the sake of a desired, wanted, needed etcetera 'state of being' (2010: 114–115). For Schatzki (2010: 114), practical intelligibility 'animates or informs the frequent redirections and restarts that mark the flow of conduct'. While individuals need not to be consciously aware of it, practical intelligibility is always teleological as it determines what people do next in the flow of daily life.[4]

With this concept of practical intelligibility in mind, we now can turn to his discussion of emotions and how they feed into human action and the realization of ends. Schatzki (2010: 121–130) distinguishes three ways of how emotions determine action. First, emotions play an important role in shaping practical intelligibility. They (co)determine practical intelligibility by selecting and lighting up what matters in a specific situation. Emotions foreground the 'ways of being' and the 'states of affairs' which determine what it makes sense to do at a certain moment (Schatzki, 2010: 121). Second, emotions also indicate which specific actions it makes sense to do, given these states of affairs and ways of being. And because emotions are at play, what it makes sense to do can diverge from what seems rational to do for the actor.[5] Third, emotions may determine action directly, – bypassing the sense-making of practical intelligibility or actions. In these situations, people are 'in the grip of' emotions, their actions just 'happen to them' while they do not sense they want to do it, neither do they sense the purpose of what they are doing – only afterwards. Think of very fast, automatic bodily reactions out of fear, such as braking immediately when a child suddenly runs across the street while you are driving. These emotions are overwhelming and total, in the sense that they take full control over the body. Typically they are also infrequent and of short duration, but of high intensity. Nevertheless, people can and do try to control and manipulate these overwhelming emotions, for instance in military training, with variable degrees of success. For our discussion it is important to note that only the third form of emotional action is causally determined in the sense that emotions are the causes of activity prior to their execution. In the other two cases, with emotions foregrounding state of affairs and indicating the actions that are relevant to do, there is an indeterminate relation; which emotions actually determine practical intelligibility and action is only settled the moment people act (Schatzki, 2010: 176).

With this analysis of practical intelligibility, emotions and their relation with activity, Schatzki shows how emotions bring about actions of individuals who are always caught up in teleologies. Because of this focus on emotions in relation to individual human actors, Schatzki's 2010 account at this point is not very explicit on how emotions should – in line with practice theories – be analytically attributed to and distributed over individuals and practices. It is to this issue that we turn next, making use of insights from the sociology of emotions, the work of Schatzki again, and Collins' theory of interaction rituals.

Emotions and the human body

When discussing how emotions navigate a world of practices, we first discuss how emotions are connected with human bodies. Here we rely on the sociology of emotions (Turner and Stets, 2005; Franks and Smith, 1999; Kemper, 1987). This branch of sociology is grounded on phenomenological theory (Merleau-Ponty, 1945/1962), pragmatic social theory (George Herbert Mead, 1934/1962) and elaborated further on the basis of neuroscientific insights (Damasio, 1994; Ledoux, 1996; Gazzaniga, 1998). To put it very simple here – given the variety and neural-endocrinological complexity of emotional processes – emotions are negative and positive valences that move people into action, including thought. As Franks (2010: 100) notes: 'Without an emotional predisposition, one is left endlessly thinking of alternatives, giving everything equal weight whether they are relevant or not'. Emotions are what matters to us, what we care about. Emotions therefore move us, quite literally: all bodily action systems are closely connected by the emotion processing systems in our brain (Turner and Stets, 2005; Gazzaniga, 1998; Damasio, 1994). Note that this is not only true for the fast, overwhelming and total emotions or impulses we discussed above. All emotional reactions are always bodily reactions, but they differ in intensity and duration. In this respect, Collins refers to undramatic emotions that are long-lasting, the underlying tones or moods that permeate social life, ranging from 'a readiness for contact with the environment' at the high end to 'disinterest and apathy' at the low end (2004: 105–106; and 387, note 11, the reference to Frijda, 1986: 13, 71). Humans are biologically preconditioned to process all lived experience emotionally and it is this relentless emotional processing that directs our acting, thinking and feeling (Turner and Stets, 2005). Indeed, the brain's main activity is to ceaselessly process experiences (Gazzaniga, 1998; Ten Houten, 1999). The emotional processing may encompass parts of the brain (the *neocortex*) where these experiences are mentally projected, thus becoming part of our conscious self. The larger part of the processing however does not take this neural route, and remains hidden to people (Damasio, 1994; Gazzaniga, 1998; Franks and Smith, 1999).

Both neuroscience and the sociology of emotions rely on phenomenological insights to arrive at the notion that human beings are emotional beings: we can only 'be' through the emotional experience of practices (Freund, 1999). Note the double meaning of experience here: it means both undergoing a particular practice as well as the learning (through storage with emotional tags in the brain) of its understandings, motivations and affects. The phenomenological perspective on emotions fits well to the notion of practical intelligibility, which aims to capture the structure of experiential acting, that is, the experience of being in the world as one acts (Schatzki, 2010: 119).

Emotions with individuals and practices

Emotions provide the 'interactive coupling' between individuals and the world of practices (Slaby, 2014: 37). Slaby (ibid.) refers to this coupling as a 'hybrid system' that gives rise to neural and bodily processes that 'the organism "on its own", decoupled from the relevant environmental structure, would be incapable of instantiating'. Obviously, practices would neither emerge 'on their own' without these neural and bodily processes. Connecting this to the issue of agency as discussed above, it can be argued that it is through the relentless interactive coupling of past and immediate experiences, that emotions enable people to direct their actions, both immediately on the spot, but also reflexively. Emotions navigate people through a world of practices and their horizons of opportunities for engagement, significance and meaning.

To say that individuals engage in practices as emotional modes of being does not mean that people are in a constant state of intense emotional arousal however. What it does mean is that all our actions, including decision-making and planning, is based on emotional valences. Since practice theories often emphasize that practices are routinized, habitualized patterns of doings and sayings in which actors rely on tacit knowledge and practical understanding, one could expect motivation and emotions being remote or absent in these behaviours for most of the times (Giddens, 1984; Warde and Southerton, 2012). Recurrent and routinized practices however are not without emotions and could be interpreted as having a rather neutral feel for the participants. Participants in routinized performances may experience either low intensity positive (feeling confident, at ease, satisfied) or negative (feeling bored, dull) emotions. When interpreted in this way, recent insights from the sociology of emotions allow to connect emotions to agency in a manner that fits the ontological commitments of the practice approach. This means reasoning from the sets of doings and sayings and how they matter to the human actors involved in social practices. When describing emotional agency from a practice theoretical perspective, there is no separate level of the 'individual personality', where agency must be located. That means that our conceptualization of emotional agency remains flat, while allowing for a dialectical relationship to exist between individual human bodies, emotions and practices. Let us now be more specific on what emotions do for practices and the ways in which they are performed.

Emotions and the 'hanging together' of practices

When discussing how emotions contribute to the integration of practices, we follow Schatzki's (2002: 59–122) conceptualization of how practices hang together and then consider in some detail how the hanging together is related to emotions or emotional agency. Schatzki distinguishes four integrative elements of practices: practical understandings, general understandings, rules and teleo-affective structures. All elements connect to emotional agency in a particular way.

First, practical understanding is a notion that captures the very heart of every practice. It comprises a feel for the game, the visceral, ingrained ways of 'knowing' of how to do things on the spot, in the middle of the action. It concerns routine, non-reflexive and habituated behaviours in ways that are expressed by Giddens' concept of practical consciousness and Bourdieu's concept of feel for the (practice-)game.[6] Furthermore, it is through practical understanding that the participants are able to mutually align their actions in split seconds, thus creating coherent and recognizable sets of doings and sayings. As the learning process that produces practical understanding consists of interactive coupling with the environment, such know-how necessarily involves emotional processing. In fact, these experiences can only be stored as visceral memories *because* they capture emotional loadings in ways as discussed above (Gazzaniga, 1998; Turner, 2007). While the emotions that are attached to practical understanding are most often not consciously manifest, they provide strong bodily-emotional dispositions and inclinations that direct individuals' everyday doings and sayings.

The second integrative element is termed general understandings. General understandings are conceived as projections – what we think, dream, fantasize, feel – of what a set of doings and sayings entails. General understandings provide an answer to the question about 'what we are doing', to understand that a series of actions belongs to, for example, cooking, fishing, biking or moving house. These projections thus tie the various activities of the participants together into a coherent set of doings and sayings as they give the participants a shared sense of what is happening, and what they can expect to happen next. However, individuals can also project a practice while doing something else, like thinking about a meeting while gardening, or imagining to play football while driving. They can even project practices they have never engaged in, or practices they most likely never will engage in. The ability to project practices allows individuals to act intentionally upon practices because they are always already emotionally charged: even without actually executing a practice, the projected practice matters to them, provides them with the energy to engage in them, change them or avoid them. Like the actual practices people engage in, such emotionally infused projections offer a flow of images that carry them along, navigating the stream of daily practices.

The third integrative element of practices mentioned by Schatzki refers to rules. With Schatzki, rules are explicit guidelines and instructions for the practice that specify what should be done at a certain moment. In this way, rules provide a diachronic order in the tasks and activities that are carried out in practices. Rules help to orientate participants (even when they do not agree with the rules) to what should happen or should be created in the course of the practice. Rules thus provide a focus on the future. The enforcement and enactment of rules in practices cannot be understood without considering the inherent relationship of rules with power and normative sanctions. Rather than using coercive force, however, the ones in power more efficiently seek to rely on the emotional arousal that goes along with (not) complying to the rules. They make use of the inherent connection that Goffman and Giddens claim to exist between rules and normative sanctions. The rules as guideline become the normative rules of compliance. Power then rests on the threat of being 'out of face' (Goffman, 1967) and of being exposed to shaming and blaming in public. In most practices it is impossible for the powerful to enforce adherence to all the rules for all the participants all the time via direct surveillance. For practices to be sustained and not fall apart, it is for that reason important that rules, even those of the explicit and formalized kind, are internalized by the participants to a certain extent. The execution of the internalized normative rules operates through the mechanisms of (both positive and negative) emotional arousal. Massey (2002) argues that it is only possible for normative rules to influence behaviour when they are stored with emotional tags. A norm should invoke emotional arousal for it to have an impact on behaviour. The most important form of emotional arousal concerning norms is fear.[7]

Fourth and final, Schatzki outlines the teleoaffective structure as an integrative element. The teleoaffective structure comprises a set of ends that participants should or may pursue, a pattern of shared expectations considering the future situation that the practice will bring. These expectations are not neutral, they have some compelling or even coercive force, both in the negative (fear) and in the positive (enthusiasm) form. In the words of Nicolini (2012: 166), the teleoaffective structure comprises direction and oughtness. Not just with regard to the aim the participants should be pursuing and how the various tasks should be executed, but also concerning the kind of emotions which go along with the enactment of practices. The affective structure thus concerns Hochschild's (1983) feeling rules, prescribing which emotions – both positive and negative – participants should experience and how they should express them in a certain practice. Feeling rules may become manifest when saying and doings are maladjusted and seem to bring out a different future than was anticipated. As with Goffman's embarrassment, Schatzki's normative emotions in this case are expected to sustain the situational order. Feeling rules can however also be revealed via positive emotions, as when practices are being enacted successfully.

To conclude, emotions are implied in the successful performance of social practices by serving the integration of the practice. They help integrate sets of doings and sayings in four circumscribed ways. First, they play a crucial role in practical understanding through the execution and memorizing of bodily know-how. Second, they provide the (positive and negative, strong and neutral) valences attached to the general understandings of what is going on in a practice. Third, they tag and enforce rules through emotional arousal, thereby securing the impact of the rules on behaviours. Fourth, emotions make people execute practices in a certain way and toward a certain goal through following, experiencing, reproducing and innovating the positive or negative feeling rules which belong to specific practices.

Emotional energy as generated in and through practices

We have argued above that emotions provide valences, hence enabling people to direct their actions. Furthermore, we have indicated that these emotions emerge through the interactive coupling of individuals and practices. In this section, we will be more specific about how exactly emotions come about in and through the reproduction of practices. The question we will try to answer is how practices produce the emotional energy that allows people to navigate their worlds of practices. Here we rely on Randall Collins' (2004) *Interaction Ritual Chains*. Interaction rituals, when they are successful, are emotionally intense practices and they can be more formal or natural in character. A moving funeral or an exciting pub conversation might serve as respective illustrations of both types. These examples also indicate that a successful interaction ritual can be connected to both negative (sadness, sorrow, anger) and positive (excitement, joy, arousal) emotions. Collins uses the term interaction ritual in reference to both Durkheim and Goffman. In Durkheim's (1912) theory of religious life, rituals are crucial. Rituals are gatherings of people who mutually adjust their actions and attention toward a single focus. Durkheim mentions the example of the religious meetings of Aboriginals, who dance and sing themselves into a trance before their totem. However, such rituals are not restricted to the Aboriginals. Durkheim (1912/2001: 322) writes that:

> no society can exist that does not feel the need at regular intervals to sustain and reaffirm the collective feelings and ideas that constitute its unity and its personality. Now, this moral remaking can be achieved only by means of meetings, assemblies, or congregations in which individuals, brought into close contact, reaffirm in common their common feelings...

If the focus is strong, a great enthusiasm flows through the participants. At these peak moments, 'effervescence' emerges, the experience of strong feelings of group membership (Durkheim 1912/2001: 157–158; 285). Goffman (1967: 57) used the term interaction ritual to denote situations where the presence of an object with 'special value' (the self, in Goffman's analyses) requires people to 'guard and design the symbolic implications' of their acts. In this definition, Goffman not only highlights that the situation rather than individual propensities or motives determines behaviour, he also points to the focus of attention and mutual alignment towards the object of special value. Building upon Goffman and Durkheim, Collins' theory specifies how interaction rituals produce feelings of group membership, symbols of group membership and also emotional energy for their practitioners. Collins' theory advances earlier work as it specifies the bodily emotional attunement processes involved, introduces the concept of emotional energy and because it allows understanding that the Durkheimian and Goffmanian objects of special value are brought about by interaction rituals, rather than a given.

Collins (2004: 42) describes emotional energy as 'feelings of confidence, strength, enthusiasm, and desire for action'. Thus if we understand agency as the capacity to intervene in and navigate through the world, for Collins then agency resides in emotional energy. In discussing emotional energy Collins is in line with practice theories, since his interaction ritual theory gives priority to situations rather than individuals. While it is individuals who experience emotional energy, it 'arises in interactions in local, face-to-face situations, or as precipitates of chains of situations' (Collins, 2004: 6). Following Collins (2004: 48), for an interaction ritual to bring about emotional energy, a gathering of participants should start to develop a shared focus of attention as well as a common emotional mood. Feedback loops intensify the group feelings: the attention and actions of the participants become more and more oriented toward the common focus, and as they become increasingly aware of their mutual attunement, they experience the sharing of their emotions more intensely, which in turn reinforces their common focus. The experience of these intense group feelings, of being absorbed in the group action, generates confidence, strength, enthusiasm and elation to engage with their environment; it gives people a boost of emotional energy.

Navigating the world of practices with Collins is about individuals seeking emotional energy as it is being (re)produced by the interaction rituals they take part of (Collins, 2004: 157). In everyday life, people move from interaction ritual to interaction ritual, not unlike bees and flowers. The navigating brings them variable amounts of emotional energy. The more emotional energy they gain from an interaction ritual, the more attractive the interaction ritual is to them and the more likely they will try to experience them again in the future (Collins, 2004: 44). Alternatively, if people are trapped in interaction rituals that generates low or even negative emotional energy, their navigating through social life can be oriented to reduce losses in emotional energy, rather than seeking maximum positive emotional energy (Summers-Effler, 2002). When depicting the emotional dimension of the social, it is the flowering plants and not just the bees that provide the better picture of the overall structure and distribution of emotional energy. So both practice theories and interaction ritual theory adhere to Goffman's adage 'Not, then, men and their moments. Rather moments and their men' (1967: 3). Individuals, in the sense of (lifestyle-specific) personalities that consist of unique combinations of preferences, disposition, urges, inclinations, needs and desires, are the result of their prior involvement in (chains or nexuses of) practices. They are 'transient fluxes charged up by situations' (Collins, 2004: 6) who carry chains of interconnected interaction rituals that form their personality (the history of all emotionally charged practices they participated in), and shape their preferences for future involvement in social practices.

In summary, when analysing how emotional agency and emotional energy navigate the world of social practices, we have to decentre the individualized human subjects without losing sight of the crucial role of subjectivity in the reproduction and transformation of the social.

Emotional energy, symbolic objects and linkages between practices

So far, our analytical lens has been zoomed in on situated practices and the human actors involved in their performances. When we now start considering linkages between practices, we are zooming out (Nicolini, 2012). What we then 'see' is an enormous vibrant web of interconnected practices. Practices always intermesh, overlap and connect to other doings and sayings in different ways and to various degrees. Consequently, Nicolini (2012: 180) warns that asking questions such as: 'Where do practices end?' and 'What are the boundaries of a practice?' can be misleading since practices are never impermeable and discernable as neatly bounded units in clearly defined networks. When we view practices in the zoomed-out modality, we also use other analytical tools and ask different kind of questions. To prevent the risk of reifying practices – for example in terms of categorizing neatly defined practices after mapping and classifying their components – Nicolini's suggestion is to 'start with processes and to take the emergence and creation of provisionally identifiable units as the thing to be explained'. While participants may experience a practice as a coherent set of doings and sayings, the researcher should always keep in mind first that coherence is brought about by the intermeshing of the doings and sayings of participants and the material arrangements and second that such a set of doings and sayings is always in many ways necessarily and inextricably connected to other practices. Nevertheless, the tasks and actions that belong to some sets of doings and sayings may be more distinctively expressing the hanging together of that set than the tasks and actions of others sets. Practices thus vary in the degree of connectedness and openness, not unlike the hanging together of ecosystems and their being embedded in wider sets of ecosystems. It is this openness, connectedness, stability and change of sets of socio-material practices that we want to explain and analyse in more detail with the lens zoomed out.

When discussing interconnections between practices, we again argue that the emotional processes and factors as described above play an important role and deserve to be taken into account when researching social change from a practice theoretical perspective. However, it should be clear that we are not arguing that the reproduction of practices and their linkages are exclusively brought about by emotions. As Shove *et al.* (2012) have convincingly argued, competencies and material elements are crucially involved in both the reproduction of and the linkages between social practices. We do think however that the role of emotions in this respect is underestimated in practice theories so far. One obvious way to move forward from an emotional agency point of view is to look at objects and symbols travelling between practices while being charged up with emotional energy.

Objects occupy an important role in most versions of practice theory. Objects are the focus of the transformative efforts of human beings. Through the teleo-affective structures that integrate the doings and sayings of the participants, these objects are worked upon and transformed into collectively projected outcomes. Objects appear in both material (artefacts, natural things, hybrids) and ideational (symbols and signs to interpret the world) form. Practices are object oriented in the sense that they focus the attention of the participants toward the projected transformation of the object (Nicolini, 2012: 110). Objects in the context of social practices bring alive the transformational capacity of human beings, and this arousal can be regarded an emotional process. The question is then how do objects manage to become attractive targets for the transformational capacity of human beings. The answer again must be found in practices or – with Collins – in interaction rituals.

The process of emotional and bodily attunement in interaction rituals not just produce emotional energy in the participants, but emotionally charged symbols as well. The symbolic objects represent the group of actors involved in the inter-action ritual. Collins describes these symbols or sacred objects in terms of 'emblems or other representations (visual icons, words, gestures) that members feel are associated with themselves collectively' (Collins, 2004: 49). The situational solidarity that emerges from intense interaction rituals is what generates the charged-up symbols of group membership. The charging happens when an object becomes the focus of the bodily and emotional attunement processes in intense interaction rituals. Peak moments of solidarity raise an object above normalcy. Now charged with feelings of group membership, they become special (sacral, in Durkheim's analysis) and subject to rules about how they should be treated, by whom and at which moments (Collins, 2004: 95–101). Any object can be turned into a symbol, be it scientific ideas, fast food, slow food, butterflies, houses, football matches, computers, celebrity stars, dogs, money, cows, books or cars. Collins (2004: 81–87) notes that people use these symbols to revive feelings of group membership. The objects or symbols – loaded with emotional energy – are important bridges or linkages between different, both present and future interaction rituals. People 'celebrate' their symbols again in subsequent practices in order to invoke the group feelings again and to realize the increase in personal levels of emotional energy they are looking for.

To discuss how symbols and their emotional energy are involved in making linkages between practices, Collins (2004: 95–101) distinguishes between three forms of symbol circulation. First order circulation of symbols refers to the original interaction rituals which generated the symbols. What kind of practices coined the symbol or object in the first place, and when and how did it happen?

Second order symbol circulation refers to the traveling, reproduction and uses of symbols outside the settings in which they were originally produced. People start using the symbols in situations that follow-up on the original ones. People involved in other practices start taking up the symbols and try to integrate them in practices that differ from the original context of the symbol. They may talk about the symbol or act toward it in various ways (such as worshipping, exhibiting or carrying the symbol around). In terms of practice theory, second order distribution is not only about the travelling of the original object to other practices, but also about the transfer of the integrative elements of the original practice in which that object became an emotionally charged symbol. The symbolic object brings practical understanding of knowing how to deal with the object, the general understanding of the meanings of the doings and sayings related to that object, the rules of proper treatment, and finally the teleoaffective structure that provides both a future orientation and the implicit feelings rules that are associated with engaging with the symbol. In this way, the circulation, travelling and distribution of symbols infuse new elements in existing practices and connects them to each other in novel ways, spreading new understandings, motivations and affects through the plenum. Collins also mentions a third order circulation, whereby people use symbols in their thought processes, reminding them of and reviving feelings of group membership. In practice theory, this concerns general understandings, which enable participants to project the practice in which they act upon the symbol. When people think, dream or fantasize about such symbols they may feel enthusiasm and pride and/or they may be reminded of something good and worthy they had been undertaken with others. In this way, symbols that carry group feelings in them provides people with emotional energy, without the need for direct participation in the practice in which these symbols emerged. Individuals carry various emotionally charged general understandings with them, and these stocks of symbols provide the emotional map through which they make their way in a world of practices (Collins, 2004: 151–158; Maller and Strengers, 2012). From the viewpoint of the individual, some practices allow for the successful meshing of their package of generalized understandings/symbols, resulting in an interaction ritual that provides them with high levels of emotional energy. But in other practices, their stock of symbols does not connect to that of others very well, so that they are not able to contribute to the bodily/emotional attunement process, with the result of less emotional energy being generated. This happens when one feels in the wrong place, not knowing what to say, unable to switch the group's focus to a topic that is related to one's emotional resources (Collins, 2004: 151–158).

As noted by Durkheim in 1912, the peak moments of high intensity rituals are sources of social change. It is in these situations of collective effervescence where new ideas are born or where existing ideas are strengthened or brought to live again. The emotionally charged symbols and the related practical and general understandings they generate then spread through the vast intermeshing of practices, reverberating changes in each of them. In this way, the rise of, for example, new social movements, collective political action on a massive scale, or the worldwide uptake of eco-labels can be grounded realistically on the emotional and bodily attunement processes in interaction rituals where new symbols are created. However, the emission of these emotionally charged understandings, motivations and affects through the plenum will never be emulated and imitated exactly in other practices, as they will be confronted with already existing understandings, motivations and affects as well as existing material arrangements. The existing constellations differ in the degree to which they are open to and match with the new elements, thus resulting in different patterns of social change (Geels *et al.*, 2015).

Throughout this lengthy section we have discussed several aspects of the relationship between human agents, practices and emotions. We started by discussing the relevance of the body and its brains for understanding the processing of emotion by human agents. We then discussed emotions as part of a hybrid system of human actors and practices, arguing that in practice theories emotional agency must be analysed as always being distributed over human agents and practices. Our practice theoretical perspective on emotional agency was further elaborated by exploring what emotions do to practices (being involved in their integration in different ways) and what practices do to emotions (generating them through interaction rituals). We concluded with a discussion on how emotions affect the linkages between social practices. Our discussion aimed to show that emotional agency in all these dimensions deserves to be investigated and discussed more often by practice theorists since emotions help explain innovation and social change. Participants of practices navigate and are navigated through a world of practices while being guided by emotions. Navigating a world of practices also refers to the flows of emotional energy that are running through chains and networks of practices. These flows are being carried along both by human agents and objects. The nature of the emotional energy flows determines the likelihood that new practitioners, symbols, objects and understandings will become part of the practice-arrangement bundles in the future.

While emotional agency must be considered a crucial factor for explaining the dynamics of social change in a world of practices, a comprehensive analysis of social change cannot do without looking at the relationship between (emotional) agency and power. It is to this topic that we turn in the next section.

Agency, power and dynamics of change in networks of practices: some preliminary remarks

Agency has the connotation of creation, innovation and change (Elliott and Turner, 2012). Emotional agency can be regarded as a driver of change, a motivating factor for finding your way in the world of practices. With the concept of power, the associations are most of the time not on the enabling but on the constraining aspects of the social. Think about the disciplining dynamics as described by Foucault, or the Weberian approach to power which emphasizes the restrictions for realizing ones goals by the ambitions and strivings of other actors. In theories of practices, power has not been a central issue so far. Giddens' structuration theory might be regarded as one of the more explicit attempts to give power significant analytical weight regarding social reproduction and change (Giddens, 1979). With Giddens, power is given two faces: an 'agency face' in the form of transformative capacities of human agents, and an 'institutional face' with power as structures of domination. While Giddens seems to distribute power over individuals and an apparent overarching structure, we position the former 'face' of power in situated practices and the latter in the chains or networks of practices in our discussion of power below.

Agency and power in situated practices

Power manifests itself as a relevant factor in the performances of social practices in a number of ways. First, there are differences in competences between practitioners in a certain practice. The concepts of capital (Bourdieu,1986) or transformative power (Giddens, 1979) are referring to what an agent can do in a specific practice given her access to and mastery of the rules and resources relevant for the practice and for the specific tasks and projects the actor aims to realize. We have already discussed extensively how emotions are co-determining what an agent can do. Emotions bring a certain state of affairs and modalities of action to the attention of the actor, they tag experiences and rules in ways that make them have an impact on future doings and sayings of the actor, and they are implied in the energizing of peoples and objects during intense interactions.

Collins (2004), and in a more explicit and elaborate manner Theodore Kemper also (2011), discuss how emotional factors, power and status go together in the reproduction of interaction. The actors and objects with most emotional energy tend to be the energizing factors in the reproduction and innovation of social practices. High emotional energy-actors take the lead, position themselves and other sacred objects in the centre of the process, show themselves to be experts in the (feeling) rules and resources to be applied, and because of all this, they find themselves in a position to receive status and to give orders. At the other end of the status-power matrix we find actors receiving orders and paying proper tribute to those claiming high status. The status-power relations within practices help explain why actors with high levels of emotional energy are in a position to further enhance their power, while those with low levels of emotional energy end up in a position that makes them lose even more energy. Positive and negative valences are distributed unevenly both among and within practices.

Agency and power in networks of practices

With the lens being zoomed out and targeted at the clusters, networks or bundles of practices, the agency performed by human actors is temporarily put in between brackets. The focus is on the specific ways in which practices are embedded in wider networks, arrangements, bundles or complexes. The more institutionalized the relationships, the more visible and stable the patterns are in time-space, with structures of domination reflecting the distribution of power throughout the network.

Because of the methodological advice to bracket performances when doing institutional analyses, there is the danger of re-constituting the micro-macro and agency-structure dualism when doing actual empirical research with the help of practice theories. Power structures, dominant circuits of reproduction, value chains, practice complexes etcetera are then being discussed without constantly bearing in mind that there are human agents involved in the reproduction and change of these institutions. Some socio-technical systems and relations are so firmly anchored in time and space that it seems almost natural to refer to them as social structures in the mode of reification, as if they have a life on their own.

The main achievements of Castells' (2009) analysis of power in the global network society is the fact that he provides an elaborate analysis of the reproduction of power structures without losing sight of the agency dimension involved in the making and breaking of linkages between social practices. In the language of Giddens' structuration theory, he balances social- and system-integration when analysing social change (Giddens, 1977: 76). Power for Castells is about connections and connectivity: the more connected, well embedded and integrated in (global to local) networks, the more power in terms of transformative capacity. The worst thing that can happen for an organization, a country, a particular social class, or a region is to be left on your own, to be judged irrelevant for the network, to not being connected. Connectivity is key to power, innovation and social change. Networks strive to connect with new nodes or practices which are instrumental for the further increase of the power of the network. Once a node/set of practices in the network is no longer performing well in terms of empowering the overall network, attempts will be made to disconnect or decouple the practices. This gatekeeping and decoupling work is done by specialized groups of actors who are trained to exert 'networking power'. They know about the gains and losses which are likely to result from new connections being made and obsolete relationships being done away with and they know how to create and break connections. Next to gatekeepers, Castells also distinguishes groups of 'switchers' and 'programmers' as being specialists in the making and breaking of links between networks. They know about the (importantly emotional) codes, standards, general and practical understandings and how to create them. Switchers and (re)programmers are employing 'network-making power', a new form of agency and power that Castells claims to be the most important in the network society. Note that we can ground this form of power and agency in emotions as well: both switchers and programmers seek out the network opportunities that generates most emotional energy to them. Moreover, emotionally dominant switchers and programmers manipulate and transform their network environment such that it offers opportunities for interaction rituals to develop in which they themselves or their creations are the focus of attention.

While not being developed in the context of a theory of practices, Castells' analysis of agency and power in the network society can be valuable for practice theorists who aim to investigate the practice-work involved in the making and breaking of linkages between (sets of) practices and thereby for the reproduction and change in wider complexes or networks of practice-arrangement bundles.

Conclusion

Our analysis of emotional agency, power and social change has been short and selective, as the topics are widely discussed in the social sciences. The criteria for selecting the topics and concepts we put under scrutiny are derived from our aim of contributing to the further conceptual development of practice theories in a way that makes them applicable to the analyses of social change in contemporary societies. For practice theories to offer an original and practice specific account of the dynamics of change in (networks of) practices, we argued that two challenges had to be confronted. First, the relationship between agency and emotions had to be explored in connection with social change. Second, the concept of power has to be invented anew in the context of practice theories. We conclude the chapter by summarizing the results of our preliminary investigation of these two topics, indicating as well the work that still has to be done.

First of all, if we account for agency as emotional experience, new research questions appear on the agenda of practice theories, in particular with regard to social change. We can start to formulate questions about why some practices generate many followers, whereas others perish in terms of the emotional experiences they generate. Also, if changes in the participation patterns in certain social practices reflect changes in emotional agency, we may trace these changes in the history of emotionally charged practices the followers have been participating in. We would like to highlight that when analysing emergence and decay in practices, emotional experiences need to be given separate treatment. Emotions do interact with material elements and competences in many different ways, and cannot be reduced to one of the components or elements of practices as distinguished in contemporary theories.

Second, when investigating the going together of agency and emotions, it is important to profit from the agency-structure debate that has been connected to practice theories from their inception. We suggested studying the agency-emotion theme with the analytical lens switching between different – zoomed in and zoomed out – modalities. Emotions do reside in bodies and need to be studied on that level, but what makes a practice approach distinct is the focus on how emotions and practices go together. We discussed what emotions do to practices and what practices do to emotions. Finally, with the lens zoomed out, we investigated how emotions contribute to the making and breaking of linkages between (network of) practices.

Third, while emotions are important drivers of innovation and change, they need to be connected to issues of power to prevent being naive on dynamics of change in a world populated with practices. Power analyses with the lens zoomed out very easily make us forget the 'agency-dimension' of change in networks of practices. Castells' concept of 'networking power' and 'network-making' power were offered as a starting point for reflecting on ways to connect practice theories with other theories of change (for example transition theory) without doing away with the 'flat ontology' and 'human agency' assumptions that are crucial for practice theories.

Fourth and final, we have been venturing an approach to navigating a world of practices in which some theories and authors were newly introduced to the family of practice theories. Although both Collins and Castells are commonly not perceived as practice theorists, we argued that parts of their work can be meaningfully connected to the body of practice theories. By deepening our understanding of the agency – emotion relationship (Collins) on the one hand and the agency – power relationship (Castells) on the other, we might improve practice-based approaches to the dynamics of change in contemporary network societies.

Notes

1 This is not because of the central place of the concept of network in his analyses, since network analyses seem to connect very well with the flat ontology of practice theory. The differences in analysing social change stem from Castells' crucial distinction between the 'space of places' versus the 'space of flows'.

2 The concept of 'performance' is used by Shove *et al.* (2012) to refer to a mode of analysis that focuses on the ways in which the practices are being enacted and reproduced through combining three constituting components. With Giddens, this modality of analysing practices is called the 'analysis of strategic action'. The concept of performances seems to be preferred by Shove *et al.* over the concept of strategic action in order to make room for analysing 'acting objects' and 'fitting competences' without the need to constantly consider the related actions of situated human actors who make the practice possible.

3 See below for a further explanation and discussion of 'practical intelligibility' and 'understandings', based on Schatzki, 2002: 74–76).

4 With his formulation of practical intelligibility Schatzki distinguishes himself from Giddens' notion of practical consciousness on the one hand and from Bourdieu with his 'sens pratique' on the other. With Schatzki, the teleological character of action can and should be discussed without fear for voluntaristic or deterministic reasoning.

5 Schatzki points out that what makes sense to an actor can diverge from what is 'rational' to do for that person given his or her particular perspectives, goals and circumstances. People can be 'taken by emotions' and act in certain (dangerous, stupid etcetera) ways since at that particular moment (of being angry, drunk, etcetera), it makes 'emotional sense' to do so (Schatzki, 2010: 126).

6 Practical understandings differ from practical intelligibility, which indicates for the individual actor a sense of *what* to do next, rather than the referring to the know-*how* of doing it. Practical intelligibility governs practical understanding, as it singles out what actions individuals execute because of their practical, embodied understanding (Schatzki, 2002: 74–76, 79). This explains why practical intelligibility is not included in the list of factors that make for the hanging together.

7   Perhaps most crucial for the integration of practices is the fear of the loss of a social
    bond (Scheff, 2003), as norms indicate the moral boundaries of the group. Not follow-
    ing the norms thus means running the risk of being perceived as an unworthy group
    member.

References

Bourdieu, P., 1986. 'The Forms of Capital'. In: J. Richardson, ed. *Handbook of Theory and Research for the Sociology of Education*. New York: Greenwood, 241–258.

Castells, M., 2009. *Communicating Power*. Oxford: Oxford University Press.

Collins, R., 1993. 'Emotional Energy as the Common Denominator of Rational Choice'. *Rationality and Society*, 5, 203–230.

Collins, R., 2004. *Interaction Ritual Chains*. Princeton: Princeton University Press.

Franks, D. and Smith, T., eds, 1999. *Mind, Brain, and Society: Toward a Neurosociology of Emotion*. Stamford, CT: JAI Press, 157–182.

Damasio, A., 1994. *Descartes' Error: Emotion, Reason and the Human Brain*. New York: Putnam.

Durkheim, É., 1912/2001. *The Elementary Forms of Religious Life*. Oxford: Oxford University Press.

Elliott, A. and Turner, B.S., 2012. *On Society*. Cambridge: Polity Press.

Engeström, Y., Miettinen, R. and Punamäki, R.L., eds, 1999. *Perspectives on Activity Theory. Learning in Doing: Social, Cognitive and Computational Perspectives*. Cambridge: Cambridge University Press.

Evans, D., McMeekin, A. and Southerton, D., 2012. 'Sustainable Consumption, Behaviour Change Policies and Theories of Practice'. In: A. Warde and D. Southerton, eds. *The Habits of Consumption*, Helsinki: Open Access Book Series of the Helsinki Collegium of Advanced Studies, 113–129.

Franks, D., 2010. *Neurosociology. The Nexus between Neuroscience and Social Psychology*. New York: Springer.

Freund, P., 1990. 'The Expressive Body: a Common Ground for the Sociology of Emotions and Health and Illness'. *Sociology of Health and Illness*, 12: 453–477.

Frijda, N., 1986. *The Emotions*. Cambridge: Cambridge University Press.

Geels, F.W., McMeekin, A., Mylan, J. and Southerton, D., 2015. 'A Critical Appraisal of Sustainable Consumption and Production Research: The Reformist, Revolutionary and Reconfiguration Positions. *Global Environmental Change*, 34, 1–12.

Gazzaniga, M., 1998. *The Minds's Past*. Berkeley, CA: University of California Press.

Giddens, A., 1979. *Central Problems in Social Theory*. Berkeley, CA: University of California Press.

Giddens, A., 1984. *The Constitution of Society*. Cambridge: Cambridge University Press.

Goffman, E., 1959/1990. *The Presentation of Self in Everyday Life*. London: Penguin Books.

Goffman, E., 1967. *Interaction Ritual; Essays on Face-to-Face Behavior*. New York: Pantheon Books.

Grin, J., Rotmans, J. and Schot, J., 2010. *Transitions to Sustainable Development: New Directions in the Study of Long Term Structural Change*. New York: Routledge.

Hargreaves, T., Longhurst, N. and Seyfang, G., 2013. 'Up, Down, Round and Round: Connecting Regimes and Practices in Innovation for Sustainability. *Environment and Planning A*, 45 (2), 402–420.

Hochschild, A.R., 1979. 'Emotion Work, Feeling Rules, and Social Structure'. *American Journal of Sociology*, 85, 551–575.

Hochschild, A.R., 1983. *The Managed Heart. Commercialization of Human Feeling.* Berkeley, CA: University of California Press.

Houten, W. ten, 1999. 'Explorations in Neurosociological Theory: From the Spectrum of Affect to Time Consciousness'. In: D. Franks and T. Smith, eds. *Mind, Brain, and Society: Toward a Neurosociology of Emotion.* Stamford: JAI Press Inc, 41–80.

Katz, J., 1999. *How Emotions Work.* Chicago: Chicago University Press.

Katz, J., 2010. *Emotion's Crucible*, unpublished paper, UCLA Sociology.

Kemper, T.D., 1987. 'How Many Emotions Are There?' *American Journal of Sociology*, 93, 263–289.

Kemper, T.D., ed., 1990. *Research Agendas in the Sociology of Emotions.* Albany, NY: State University of New York Press.

Kemper, T.D., 2011. *Status, Power and Ritual Interaction; A Relational Reading of Durkheim, Goffman and Collins.* Surrey: Ashgate.

Lawler, E.J., Thye, R.S. and Jeongkoo, Y., 2014.'The Emergence of Collective Emotions in Social Exchange. In: C. von Scheve and M. Salmela, eds. *Collective Emotions. Perspectives from Psychology, Philosophy and Sociology.* Oxford: Oxford University Press, 189–203.

LeDoux, J., 1996, *The Emotional Brain: The Mysterious Underpinnings of Emotional Life.* New York: Simon & Schuster.

Maller, C. and Strengers, Y., 2012. 'The Global Migration of Everyday Life: Investigating the Practice Memories of Australian Migrants'. *Geoforum*, 44, 243–252.

Massey, D., 2002. 'A Brief History of Human Society: the Origin and Role of Emotion in Social Life: 2001 American Sociological Association Presidential Address'. *American Sociological Review*, 67, 1–29.

Mead, G.H., 1934/1962. *Mind, Self & Society from the Standpoint of a Social Behaviorist.* Edited and with an Introduction by Charles W. Morris. Chicago: University of Chicago Press.

Merleau-Ponty, M., 1945/2002. *Phenomenology of Perception.* Abingdon: Routledge.

Nicolini, D., 2012. *Practice Theory, Work & Organization. An Introduction.* Oxford: Oxford University Press.

Reckwitz, A., 2002. 'Toward a Theory of Social Practices. A Development of Culturalist Theorizing'. *European Journal of Social Theory*, 5, 243–263.

Schatzki, T., 1996. *Social Practices. A Wittgensteinian Approach to Human Activity and the Social.* Cambridge: Cambridge University Press.

Schatzki, T., 2002. *The Site of the Social. A Philosophical Account of the Constitution of Social Life and Change.* Philadelphia: Penn State University Press.

Schatzki, T., 2010. *The Timespace of Human Activity. On Performance, Society, and History as Indeterminate Teleological Events.* Plymouth: Lexington Books.

Schatzki, T., 2016. 'Practice Theory as Flat Ontology'. In: G. Spaargaren, D. Weenink and M. Lamers, eds. *Practice Theory and Research: Exploring the Relevance for Social Change.* Routledge: Abingdon, UK.

Schatzki, T.R., Knorr Cetina, K. and Von Savigny, E., eds, 2001. *The Practice Turn in Contemporary Theory.* London and New York: Routledge.

Scheff, T., 2003. 'Shame in Self and Society'. *Symbolic Interaction*, 26, 239–262.

Shilling, C. and Mellor, P.A., 2001. 'Embodiment, Structuration Theory and Modernity: Mind/Body Dualism and the Repression of Sensuality'. In: C.G.A. Bryant and D. Jary, eds. *The Contemporary Giddens; Social Theory in a Globalizing Age.* New York: Palgrave, 130–147.

Schmidt, R., 2012. *Soziologie der Praktiken. Konzeptionelle Studien und empirische Analysen.* Berlin: Suhrkamp Verlag.

Shove, E., 2003. *Comfort, Cleanliness + Convenience; The Social Organization of Normality.* Oxford: Berg.

Shove, E., Pantzar, M. and Watson, M., 2012. *The Dynamics of Social Practice; Everyday Life and How It Changes.* London: Sage.

Slaby, J., 2014. 'Emotions and the Extended Mind'. In: C. von Scheve and M. Salmela, eds. *Collective Emotions. Perspectives from Psychology, Philosophy and Sociology.* Oxford: Oxford University Press, 32–46.

Spaargaren, G., Oosterveer, P. and Loeber, A., 2012. *Food Practices in Transition; Changing Food Consumption, Retail and Production in the Age of Reflexive Modernity.* New York: Routledge.

Summers-Effler, E., 2002. 'The Micro-Potential for Social Change: Emotion, Consciousness, and Social Movement Formation'. *Sociological Theory*, 20, 41–60.

Turner, J.H., 2007. *Human Emotions: A Sociological Theory.* London: Routledge.

Turner, J.H. and Stets, J.E., 2005. *The Sociology of Emotions.* Cambridge: Cambridge University Press.

Vygotsky, L.S., 1978. *Mind in Society: The Development of Higher Psychological Processes.* Cambridge: Harvard.

Warde, A. and Southerton, D., eds, 2012. *The Habits of Consumption; Studies across Disciplines in the Humanities and Social Sciences 12.* Helsinki: Helsinki Collegium for Advanced Studies. www.helsinki.fi/collegium/e-series.

Welch, D. and Warde, A., 2015. 'Theories of Practice and Sustainable Consumption'. In: L.A. Reisch and J. Thogerson, eds. *Handbook of Research on Sustainable Consumption.* Cheltenham: Edward Elgar Publishing, 84–100.

Part II

Zooming in on practices as performances

Chapter 5

Handling things at home

A practice-based approach to divestment

Andrew Glover

Introduction

In developed world economies, goods are ubiquitous. As Douglas and Isherwood observed, material consumption stands as the 'arena in which culture is fought over and licked into shape' (1979: 57). In this way, goods are constitutive of contemporary forms of sociality, not merely accompanying artefacts. They are 'social relations made durable' (Miller, 1998: 19).

Yet the manner in which durable household goods are used has changed over time. Cooper (2010), for instance, contends that structural elements within the economy, as well as consumer expectations, have re-oriented themselves toward material goods having ever shorter life spans. The sustainability impacts of this shift are widespread, from more material resources used in their production, as well as more waste generated when they are (more quickly) disposed of.

Similarly, Rifkin (2000) argues that regimes of economic activity are increasingly shifting away from long-term ownership of goods. However, he views this as a more fundamental shift toward 'The Age of Access', whereby consumers will come to own less durable goods than in the past. Instead, consumers will engage in short-term leases, rentals, memberships, and other service agreements to fulfil their material needs. In such an economy, objects are valued primarily for their contribution to enabling certain experiences and practices, rather than being valued in and of themselves. Whilst one could argue that this situation already exists, or even that it has for some time, Rifkin sees an acceleration of this trend at the expense of long term ownership of material objects.

One example of this trend lies in the maturing concept of 'collaborative consumption'. The advent of online communication (particularly mobile devices) and peer-to-peer channels for exchanging goods and services has facilitated new forms of commerce and sociality:

> We are now able to match 'haves' with 'wants' online, reducing geographical boundaries. This has the potential to create an opportunity for efficient exchanges and generates the social glue to build trust between strangers, eliminating the need for middlemen and bureaucratic barriers.
>
> (Botsman, 2010: 29)

This has significant implications for how we deal with durable material objects, since there are increased opportunities for households to find recipients for unwanted goods. In this sense, collaborative consumption provides a platform to preserve value in material objects, by facilitating the exchange of used goods and thereby reducing the extent to which they enter the waste stream.

While these digitally mediated forums provide a platform for more sustainable forms of divestment that focus on reuse rather than disposal, this does not necessarily guarantee that the platforms will be used. It will be argued in this chapter that it is rather the specific practices of how material objects are engaged with throughout, and toward the end of, their use-life that can lead to more or less sustainable product-life cycles. For example, those practices that preserve value by prolonging an object's use-life are likely to be more sustainable than those practices that render goods as waste once an owner no longer uses it.

This requires an understanding of how objects are being (re)used, and how this reuse and exchange is embedded in everyday life. To address these issues, this chapter attempts to describe several use and divestment practices that can be viewed as more sustainable than disposal and its associated waste creation. It does this by engaging with literature of practice theory generally, and specifically Schatzki's concept of 'teleoaffective structures' to differentiate between these practices.

Theoretical framework and research design

Reckwitz (2002: 249) defines *practice* as that which emerges from 'forms of bodily activity, forms of mental activity, things and their use, background knowledge in the form of understanding, know-how, states of emotion, and motivational knowledge'. More concisely, Shove *et al.* (2012) argue that practices are constituted by three types of elements: competences, meanings, and materials. While these definitions have subtle differences, the emphasis is the same: practices decentre the individual by focusing on socially mediated phenomena: skills, norms, arrangements, infrastructures, and so on, rather than individual beliefs and choices.

Practices can also be conceptualized as entities in themselves, to which people who 'carry' the practices are recruited. In this way, practices can be considered as the object of research, rather than merely the 'carriers' (individuals or groups) themselves (Shove *et al.*, 2012). This chapter describes and analyses three distinct practices of divestment (Gregson *et al.*, 2007; Wieser *et al.*, 2014) that do not engage with traditional waste management services: 'making do', 'passing on', and 'selling'.

These practices will be discussed using Schatzki's concept of teleoaffective structures. As Schatzki defines it, 'a teleoaffective structure is an array of ends, projects, uses (of things) and even emotions that are acceptable or prescribed for participants in the practice' (2005: 471). Given this, a teleoaffective structure for divestment entails the knowledge and ends ('teleo') for divesting something in a certain way, as well as an emotional, or motivational ('affective') aspect to the practice. With the help of these concepts suggested by Schatzki, it is possible to analyse in some detail the differences in reuse divestment practices, and thereby explain why certain divestment practices are preferred over others in a given context.

Practice theory should be regarded as an approach that opens up new possibilities for conceptualizing social change rather than prescribing specifically how those changes occur (Shove, 2010). In this way, research that takes a practice theory approach can also be largely 'data driven' (Glaser and Strauss, 1967), since many of the specific characteristics of practices and the way they interrelate will be unique to the context in which they are present.

This research was undertaken through 17 in depth, semi structured interviews with households (eight in Australia, nine in the Netherlands). The approach of practice theory was reflected in the interview questions concerning what divestment practices were being undertaken (practised), not merely what respondents valued about divestment. Recruitment was by way of a letterbox drop of approximately 300 information and 'invitation to participate in research' leaflets in Sydney, Australia, and Amsterdam and Utrecht, the Netherlands. Leaflets were distributed in the week prior to a bulk kerbside waste collection (where appropriate), to capitalize on the likelihood that households may have been engaging in divestment around the time of the interview. It was reasoned that recent or imminent divestment would assist participants in recalling particular instances of divestment during the interview. Investigating cultural variation in practices between Australia and the Netherlands was not the goal of the research, but noted where it was pronounced. The relatively similar standards of living between the research locations served to ensure that these were not grossly different pools of participants. Interviewing households in both Australia and the Netherlands therefore provides a more thorough understanding of the types of practices undertaken in developed world economies.

Interviews were transcribed and subject to coding in a qualitative data analysis program (NVIVO). In this process, a participant's testimony is reviewed line-by-line, and broken into phrases or sentences called 'incidents' (Charmaz, 2006). From this, it was possible to distinguish between transcript material that was tangential, or unrelated to divestment practices. Following this, a focused coding process was undertaken, which was more directed, selective, and conceptual than line-by-line open coding (Glaser, 1998). These codes turned out to be many of the elements of social practices, such as particular actions they described, or meanings they attributed to certain phenomena – albeit isolated at this stage and as yet unable to be integrated in theory. These focused codes were then subject to coding themselves – a process of relating codes to each other around an 'axis' of commonality (Strauss, 1987). This process gave rise to many of the descriptions of discrete practices, such as 'making do' and 'passing-on'.

As mentioned previously, the notion of object reuse – while necessary in an overarching sense – does not capture the nature of what specific practices are being carried out throughout the life of an object. Getting to know these practices and developing a thorough understanding of the kind of actors, understandings, motives, projects, and ends that are at stake, is critical to (re)designing and promoting more sustainable ways of engaging with material objects. Sustainability in this context is argued to refer to ways that preserve value and limit the creation of unnecessary waste. For present purposes, I use the term 'waste' to refer to objects that are disposed of while they still retain some use or exchange value.

Throughout this chapter, practices of use and divestment will be framed in terms of a 'subject-object relation'. This term signifies my contention that neither the human agent – nor the material object – is exclusively 'responsible' for a practice being enacted. This ensures that in any given case of object use and divestment, causality is not attributed to either a human agent 'choosing' an outcome on the one hand, or a material object 'forcing' an outcome on the other. This is also consistent with the claims of some versions of practice theory, which argues that materials (objects, infrastructures) act as 'scripts' of human behaviour, directing activity toward certain outcomes (Shove and Walker, 2007).

What follows is a depiction of divestment and reuse practices that do not directly involve public waste management services, or other institutions that are traditionally known to accept redundant goods (such as charities). In providing detailed descriptions of divestment practices, I hope to elucidate how objects are divested as part of an ongoing sociality, and how newly emerging technologies, motives and symbols can offer novel routes of reuse for sustainability. The practices primarily focus on the occasions in the life course (both of the owner and the object), when an object is faced with the prospect of divestment. In some cases, this may result in an object being retained – as is described in a practice of 'making do' – while in other cases objects are divested by way of 'passing on', or selling.

'Making do' – retaining and reusing when divestment beckons

A subject-object relation may be threatened by breakages, wear and tear, technological innovation, or obsolescence. These are not merely conditions of the object itself, but also of one's capability and willingness to maintain an object in the face of its divestment. Drawing on Schatzki, we could say that what happens in the divestment practices crucially depends on the teleoaffective structure present. There remains the potential for not acquiring new things to replace existing ones. In many cases, this is a practice of 'making do' with existing possessions.

In the case of breakdowns in frequently used objects such as white goods and household appliances, the window of opportunity for competing practices to capture people can be narrow. In other words, the necessity for everyday life to resume as it was means that those practices that are the most prepared, rehearsed, or convenient, are likely to be the ones that become enacted. The occasions where the option arises to make do with an object already in possession may be relatively infrequent. Indeed, normal everyday life rests on a relatively stable set of infrastructures that allows for the development and sustaining of habits and routines. When materials fail, and the subject-object relation is threatened, acute episodes of object maintenance and repair may be necessary in the practice of making do.

A lack of knowledge and capability for repair and reuse prior to breakdown events can often precipitate divestment and replacement. However, while knowledge of an object's functioning, possession of the skills and equipment necessary for maintaining usability, and confidence in one's ability to achieve the desired outcome facilitate a practice of 'making do' when everyday life is disrupted, it is not always the case that such competencies must have been acquired beforehand.

Evelyn (35) and Larry (31, Utrecht) found themselves in this position when their otherwise reliable washing machine had broken down. With both of them lacking experience in this type of repair, they were initially sceptical of their ability to fix the problem. However, Evelyn searched for solutions on the internet, where she discovered that only a small rubber o-ring needed replacement. The practice of fitting the o-ring itself took less than 15 minutes – a fraction of the time that would have been necessary to acquire a new washer, or to pay for a repairman. Evelyn herself was surprised at the ease with which she was able to solve the maintenance task. This also provided a sense of satisfaction in being self reliant and thrifty – 'affective' elements in the teleoaffective structure of making do. Lacking any specialized expertise herself, she was able to utilize the advice and practical knowledge of others who were willing to share it.

Stories such as Evelyn and Larry's demonstrate that teleoaffective structures should be defined much more broadly than individual capabilities and emotional orientations. Shared knowledge about practicing thrift and repair with materials leads to much more diffuse and transferable forms of divestment practices (with different teleoaffective structures) than may have been available in the past. The website iFixit[1] has taken on the ambitious task of developing user generated repair manuals for all household objects. Manuals are catalogued according to their make, model, and the problem faced in proper functioning. Users can upload their successful repair endeavours, for subsequent viewers to browse and gain information and inspiration from. In this way, iFixit not only provides information about the procedures of making do, but also provides a rationale for why this is a worthwhile pursuit to undertake. The ultimate goal of iFixit appears to be an ongoing catalogue of repair solutions for consumer electronics and appliances. The step-by-step manuals, and problem-solution posts are pragmatic sources of both what is possible, and desirable, in the practice of 'making do'.

Of course, not all attempts to make do with existing things are successful. Objects with a higher threshold for skill-based repair – where repair or refurbishment require more sophisticated skills and equipment – may be less conducive to making do. These may require the involvement of the manufacturer or a specialist repair service, which is often then weighed up against the option to simply purchase a replacement. This is particularly the case for computerized devices, where the sheer complexity of materials and circuitry makes making do less attractive for people to attempt their own repair. Tracey (28, Amsterdam) recalled her experiences at being disheartened by not being able to fix her digital camera, since she frequently mended and modified clothing and textile furniture with relative ease. This difficulty in the repair of computerized equipment is likely to become more widespread in the future, as more consumer objects (such as appliances, cars) have complex electronic circuitry built into their functionality.

The affective meanings that underlie the practice of making do with existing objects may be grounded in an ethics of environmentalism, with an aim to reduce the need for new objects to replace existing ones. Such a meaning sits in contrast with what has been called 'green consumerism' – where goods tend to be replaced with more efficient and environmentally benign ones, in favour of retaining existing ones. Practitioners of 'making do', who have a practice understanding, competencies, and a know-how which all revolve around environmentalism, therefore follow a teleoaffective structure in which it is evaluated as to whether the efficiencies gained from purchasing greener products are worth additional resources, if an existing solution can be found in the form of making do. As the message from eBay's recent 'green team' initiative claims: 'the greenest product is one that is already made'.[2] A motivation rooted in ethics of environmentalism in this particular case may result in prioritizing certain tasks or projects contained in the practice of making do over other tasks and projects. Making do, however, also affords a more general expression of anti-consumerism, minimizing the need to participate in the market economy except where essential. By making do with existing objects, one can step off the 'treadmill of production' (Mol and Spaargaren, 2005), resisting the relentless acquisition of material goods that are promoted in contemporary market economies. In that case, the practice of making do, its understandings and teleo-affectivities are assessed against the background of a wider set of (sustainable consumption) practices.

'Passing on' – how objects find life beyond their owners

In cases of divestment where goods retain a perceivable use-value, the practice of 'passing-on' was found to be used to redistribute these goods for at least partially altruistic purposes. Items passed on to others are generally seen to no longer serve the needs of the divestor and, through direct or third party communication, an arrangement is made to transfer possession without any significant monetary exchange.

Karin, who had recently fallen pregnant and was subsequently inundated with offers of baby-related clothing and equipment by friends and acquaintances, described practices of 'passing-on':

There's a lot of trade that goes on in the pregnancy area. Whenever I tell someone I'm pregnant they say 'Oh, do you need things?', because they have clothes, or a cot, or a bed for later on. Anything I can get anything borrowed. And the interesting thing is they don't want them back. They say just 'Pass them on to the next person you meet who's pregnant'.

(Karin, 39, Utrecht)

The passing-on of baby-related items is illustrative of a broader point about this type of exchange that pertains to the subject-object relation. Often it is the changing circumstances of the owner that renders an object unusable, rather than any particular defect or degradation inherent to the object itself. Clothes may become torn or soiled, toys may break, and games may lose their pieces, and thereby become unwanted. Yet, as Karin experienced, often it is simply that the objects become irrelevant to their owners. Families that no longer have babies, no longer have a need for baby 'stuff'. Yet they are acutely aware of the needs of families with new-borns, having been through the process of acquiring baby-related items themselves. Thus, the practice understandings, the motives, and teleoaffective structures involved in the practice of 'passing on' are notable and distinct for their attention to the needs of those receiving the goods, and the satisfaction of assisting those who would benefit from the divestment.

In passing material goods on to others, the life of goods is extended through subsequent 'careers of use' (Gregson *et al.*, 2007). Passing-on capitalizes on existing social bonds, at specific junctures when someone's needs for divesting an object can be matched to another's needs for acquiring that same object. The possibilities for successful passing-on would thus appear to be limited to existing acquaintances – or at most, with an intermediary 'matcher'. However, there are initiatives that have attempted to promote this type of divestment and acquisition for a broader audience.

One of the crucial aspects to passing-on is communication between those divesting and those acquiring. In the past, communication between two interested parties was largely reliant on existing acquaintance, with little possibility for passing-on outside of these relationships. Community notice boards and newspaper classifieds offered limited potential for passing-on, often with a specific declaration that items were being given 'for free', as opposed to being sold for a cost.

Online exchange forums have the potential to substantially extend the scale and scope of the 'audience' for goods to be passed-on. The implications of such a transformation are evident for the practice of passing-on material goods as described above. There are many forums designed to facilitate the direct exchange of goods and services between individuals.[3] For the purposes of this analysis, reference is made to the one that is most closely aligned to the social practice of passing-on: 'Freecycle'. Freecycle is an online forum for exchanging goods at no cost:

> Our mission is to build a worldwide gifting movement that reduces waste, saves precious resources and eases the burden on our landfills while enabling our members to benefit from the strength of a larger community.[4]

This closely parallels the motives, understandings, and teleoaffective structures of 'analogue' passing-on to friends and family, in its ability of this type of divestment to match needs with wants, reduce waste, and also to strengthen social bonds in doing so. The service itself is searchable by item type and location, with item listings offering a basic description and an indication of whether it is being 'offered' (divested) or 'wanted'. Goods are traded on a first come first served basis, with transport or pick-up arranged between the two parties. In this way, Freecycle demonstrates how emerging online communication can extend the scope of the practice of passing-on to those outside one's immediate social context. With a broader 'audience' for divested material goods, there is increased possibility of re-use by another party.

There are several parallels to be drawn here between making do and passing on. In both these practices, the role of information and communication technology (ICT) platforms does not necessarily give rise to new practices, but significantly enhances and extends the possibilities of the 'analogue' practices. This is achieved by drawing on the experiences and capabilities of online communities that assist in making do on the one hand, or by providing a broader network of divestors and recipients to engage in passing on, on the other.

'Getting something for it' – the practices of selling as divestment

This section continues to make the case that divestment practices are embedded in everyday life, both as day-to-day activities, and as punctuated divestment events. In this vein, it distinguishes between distinct selling events such as garage sales and flea markets, as well as more routinized selling as part of divestment.

Garage sales, flea markets, and the potential of digitisation

Ross (67) and Madeline (66) had recently made the decision to move to a smaller unit nearby in the northern suburbs of Sydney. They had made this decision on the basis that their children had recently left home 'for the last time' and that their house was simply too large to justify their continued habitation:

> It just feels empty with the two of us here. When you've got three kids running around then you don't notice … but it's quite an old house, and we just have so many rooms that we don't even use anymore.
>
> (Madeline, 66, Sydney)

When a new unit had been purchased, and the decision to 'down-size' finally materialized, Ross and Madeline decided to hold a garage sale. They attached posters to power poles and street signs in their neighborhood, and placed a classified advertisement in the local weekly newspaper. They placed large items in their driveway, and smaller items on their front porch, with stickered price tags on each item. Some items were moderately priced, such as books for $1, whilst other more precious items had more ambitious price points — $50 for a tray-mobile, $70 for a crystal glassware set, and $70 for a lawnmower. The sale on Saturday morning started well, with a few dozen people turning up at the publicized start time of 8:00 a.m. Ross thought that at least some of these were professional traders, looking for items to resell. They sold some of their additional silverware to these people, but claimed that few other things took people's interest over the course of the morning. They recognized a large proportion of patrons as people from their own street, or that they knew lived nearby.

The preparation and execution of Ross and Madeline's garage sale appears to be largely typical of weekend garage sales as they have been carried out in the past. The methods of notification were primarily local, unlikely to be seen by those outside their neighborhood, perhaps with the exception of seasoned traders. As a result, the majority of attendees lived close by, limiting the audience for their sold objects to a small, localized market. Ross and Madeline held their sale independently, with no coordination sought elsewhere. Its timing on a Saturday morning was rationalized on the basis that this would be the time of the week that most people would be likely to attend. This traditional 'analogue' form of the Australian garage sale as a more or less isolated, localized, and independent event persists to this day.

However, similar forms of selling directly from the home are practised elsewhere in ways that are more public, integrated, and broader in scale. An example of such a practice is the flea market held on Koninginnedag – 'Queens Day'[5] – in the Netherlands, at which I conducted participant observation in April 2010. On this day of the year, residents are permitted, and so tradition has it, to sell unwanted items directly from the front of one's house or in areas in the village, town, and city centres assigned as free market areas. This practice has become a cultural fixture in the festivities of a national public holiday, as the pavements become crowded with makeshift stalls in the cities and larger towns throughout the country. Those that live outside the cities may also set up temporary stalls in available spaces in the city centre. Concerts, food stalls, road closures, and a party atmosphere contribute to the event's notoriety among Dutch residents and tourists alike.

The Queen's Day sales appear to follow a similar trend to garage sales, with professional traders and second hand goods enthusiasts combing the streets earlier in the morning, and more casual buyers perusing stores later in the day. However, as practices of divestment and reuse these markets are temporally concentrated as they are only permitted to occur once per year. This enables a high intensity of practice, as, unlike the traditional Australian garage sale, all practitioners must hold their sales at the same time. For many households that divest goods in this way, goods are retained (stored) to sell on this occasion, rather than trickling out of the home throughout the year. The medium to high-density terrace housing that is so prevalent in the Dutch streetscape also means stalls are in close proximity to one another. These characteristics, of temporal and spatial concentration, result in a veritable flurry of divestment and reuse.

The cultural significance of the Queen's Day flea markets ensure that practices of divestment by selling and reuse become central to the public consciousness for a brief period of time once a year. With many streetscapes literally taken over by practices normally constrained to market squares and second hand shops, exposure and participation in these forms of divestment and reuse becomes much more widespread. The flea market occurs on a national scale, with more goods divested and exchanged on this single day than any other throughout the year. Estimates of the value of exchanged goods range up to €290 million, with over half of the national population indicating some intention to purchase something on the day.[6] In having this practice so widely participated in, and so closely tied to the festive atmosphere of a national holiday, it seems likely that it is seen as a socially accept-able – and therefore normal practice; more so than if sales were scattered, inde-pendent, and easily avoided. One of my Dutch interviewees acknowledged this as a widespread practice, although she had not sold anything herself on the day:

> Oh yes, it's quite fun to go and see what everyone is selling. It's a good atmosphere – and so Dutch.
>
> (Karin, 37, Utrecht)

This sentiment captures what Schatzki refers to as the general understanding of the flea market with a specific teleoaffective structure of the buying and selling at Queen's Day: keeping to the time schedules, participating in the festive atmo-sphere, perhaps satisfying a curiosity at what other people are selling, and being part of the ongoing formulation of a national identity. In other words, divesting in this way is not simply an individual 'choice', but part of a broader set of cul-tural practices.

The two practices of selling described in this section – traditional Australian garage sales and the Dutch Queens Day market – clearly differ in terms of how widespread they are, their potential for exchange and reuse practices, and their presence in the local culture. However, as is the case with previous sections of this chapter, the role of ICT is enabling innovations in these practices in a way that increases their potential as occasions for divestment and reuse.

Whereas garage sales such as Ross and Madeline's had previously been iso-lated, independent, and localized, the 'Garage Sale Trail'[7] attempts to reinvent the garage sale into a more social, integrated, and broad scale practice. The establish-ment of an Australia wide 'garage sale day' on a Saturday specific day in the year coordinates the numerous dispersed enactments of the practice into a temporally specific, cultural event. The official website describes the initiative as:

a program that enables the peer-to-peer exchange of assets, resources and money on a hyper local level but with a national scale … [Garage Sale Trail] is about sustainability, creativity, community, and micro-enterprise … a perfect way to discover treasure, de-clutter, have fun, make money, make a positive contribution and make neighbourhood connections.

(Garage Sale Trail, 2012)

Registered participants are given information and promotion material similar to what councils have provided in the past. In coordinating numerous garage sales onto one day, and positioning the initiative as a cultural and community building event, Garage Sale Trail imports many of the elements of practice from the Queen's Day markets in the Netherlands. Simultaneous, nationwide practices of selling goods channel a larger market of potential buyers into a single occasion, and use the occasion as an opportunity for community building. While the kind of practice understanding and teleoaffective structures of the Garage Sale Trail may not have yet developed into the feeling of supporting a national cultural event to the extent that Queen's Day has, the focus on community building is present.

In these three distinct practices – traditional 'analogue' garage sales, Queen's Day flea market, and the digitized Garage Sale Trail – we see both cultural variations in traditional selling practices, but also how emerging online technologies are fostering new configurations of practice that may contribute to object reuse and exchange.

The day to day business of selling

In the past, 'analogue' forms of the day to day selling of household goods would tend to involve placing advertisements on community message boards or classified sections of the print media. However, this practice has undergone a rapid transition in recent years, primarily reflecting the rise of ICT and e-commerce.

Popular avenues for selling household goods currently include web-based exchange sites such as eBay, Gumtree, Craigslist, and Marktplaats (Marketplace) in the Dutch context. Items are posted according to different criteria, depending on the particular website being used. They may be posted at a fixed asking price, mimicking traditional classified posting where a seller wishes to obtain a certain return. Indications of price flexibility can also be advertised ('price negotiable', 'or near offer'), potentially signalling a stronger desire to be rid of the object than to achieve a specific price for the sale. Alternatively, goods may be posted in an auction format, where buyers engage in open bidding for the item until a specified end time is reached. Items may also be sold in a combination of these two formats, where they are offered with a price to purchase outright, alongside an open auction.

However, it is important to recognize that the rise of online selling as a divestment and reuse practice is due to a confluence of factors that go beyond the emergence of the particular forums themselves.

In the past, newspaper or magazine classified sale advertisements were usually posted with minimal detail. This was largely a function of the cost required to print large and detailed advertisements, as expensive advertisements could negate the return from all but the most valuable sales. Thus, the more extensive availability of online advertising 'space' has increased expectations of what an advertisement must include. Along with the type of object, desired price, and sale location, online sales are often expected to include photographs of the sale item. This expectation has come about in concert with the rise and democratization of the practice of digital photography, as the necessary materials (cameras, memory cards, photo management software) have been acquired and used by larger proportions of households. Competition has been further intensified by the aggregation of items in the viewable digital online 'space'. As online sales can be drawn from a much larger geographical area than a local community paper or message board, and are often selling to a nationwide or worldwide market, competition is undoubtedly more pronounced. Such broad bodies of potential purchasers also greatly increases the probability of a divestor of a more specialized product finding someone else interested in such specialized goods.

With photographs providing visual detail about an item's appearance and condition, the ability to prepare and present items for sale becomes another valuable skill in selling. Objects may be cleaned and repaired to be more attractive to potential buyers; however this is not the only dynamic of their preparation. While something is more likely to be sold if it is photographed favourably, defects may also be deliberately shown to indicate that a seller is not trying to mislead a potential buyer. This element of trust between participants in online selling is crucial to the practice (Botsman and Rogers 2010). It is also an important element of the practice understanding and the teleoaffective structure of the practice, since the ability and willingness to trust strangers – and to act upon this trust – is required for this type of divestment practices to take place.

Some trading sites have codified and translated this social trust into specific indicators, providing additional means to establish and maintain trust between participants. Systems such as eBay's 'feedback' allow buyers and sellers to rate other users with whom they have traded in terms of their favourability. In this way, a user can generate a reputation as to their trustworthiness, based on the nature of past transactions. The establishment and maintenance of this reputation can be crucial to ongoing divestment through selling, as buyers may be wary of purchasing items from unfavoured users, particularly because these transactions may take place without the seller and buyer ever making direct contact. A lack of trust may result in an unwillingness to purchase, or a general lower price paid for items from sellers without a positive online reputation (Resnick et al., 2006). Situations such as this undermine the sellers ability to 'get what they can' out of a divestment sale.

Nathan (25, Wollongong) is a bike enthusiast, who has practised various forms of cycling since his childhood. His evolving cycling practices demand an ongoing throughput of bicycle equipment, from riding bicycle cross as a teenager, to competitive cross country mountain biking, downhill riding, and his current enjoyment of fitness-focused road cycling. Nathan has become adept at buying and selling bicycle frames and components to suit his current practices. He can easily identify 'bargains' if they appear on line, and is quick to purchase them even if they are not useful to him in their entirety. His proficiency at bike maintenance allows him to swap components, to build complete bikes from parts that he acquires 'on the cheap', and to resell complete ensembles, often for a profitable return. His knowledge gained from online bike trading means that he is confident at selling other unwanted items, such as old computers and unwanted furniture.

While the rise of online markets would suggest that they have a relatively low barrier to participation, many of the competencies discussed above are based on skills for interaction with information technology and a general familiarity with online navigation. It is unsurprising then, that younger participants tended to engage in this form of direct selling more so than the elderly. Wariness about deception, difficulty with set-up conditions, and a general lack of procedural experience were clear barriers to participation in online selling for older people.

These deficits in practical knowledge are not insurmountable however. Jeff (78, Sydney) lacked many of the skills for navigating online services until his son assisted him in setting up his personal computer for video conferencing while he was travelling overseas. Having become confident in the basic skills for online navigation, he sought his son's advice for selling some excess garden tools that were cluttering his shed. These were surplus to his immediate needs, but he felt that someone should 'get good use out of them', since he had maintained them well over the years. His son walked him through the practice of online selling, clarifying his reservations about seller feedback, the bidding process, and secure payment. Having overcome those initial barriers to selling, Jeff was able to successfully divest his tools for a modest return.

This section has discussed several practices of selling as divestment. Whether these are centred around particular personal (garage sales) and cultural (Queen's Day flea market) events, or just part of everyday practice, they are characterized by a broad teleoaffective structure of wanting to get something in return for the goods divested, and satisfaction in completing a sale that is mutually beneficial. In this respect, sold goods are commonly thought to be 'too good to just give away', and selling allows the divestor to 'get something for it'. In cases where divestors and recipients are unknown to each other, such as selling through online forums, the establishment of trust is crucial for the practice to take place. Here, specific trust and reputation indicators such as eBay's feedback, allow for transactions far beyond one's own immediate community.

Conclusion

This chapter has argued that numerous organizations and practices already exist that are directly involved in mediating material divestment. Yet most of these would not be formally considered in the realm of waste management, despite playing a significant role in the reduction of materials entering the waste stream. As this research has pointed out, these practices are able to extend the use-life of material goods, reducing the rate at which many household objects are likely to be disposed of.

These practices vary in the extent to which they require centralized infrastructure, or are distributed through existing institutions and ways of living. In many of these practices, the influence of recent ICT innovations is significant, enhancing existing practices to expand significantly from their past incarnations. In many cases however, the traces of earlier practices continue to be employed without significant alteration. Our discussion of the general and practice understandings, the competences, and the teleoaffective structures of the practices of 'making do', 'passing on', and 'getting something for it' captures the emotional and procedural rationales of digitally mediated forms of divestment as much as analogue. Nor are these innovations in practice occurring in isolation, since they reflect more widespread innovations in practices, such as the proliferation of internet connectivity, e-commerce, and digital photography.

Even the practice of 'making do' with an existing object, through repair and refurbishment, can potentially be enhanced by ICTs. While skills and know-how for engaging in such repair have always been communicated across individual practitioners, the potential for widespread 'shared competence' is enhanced greatly by the proliferation of 'how to' websites. These sites enable practices of 'making do' to extend beyond those with specialized knowledge. In this case, it is not the objects themselves that are shared but the knowledge to maintain them. Throughout this, the understandings and teleoaffective structures of these practices tend to remain similar between their analogue and digital incarnations.

However, one should refrain from focusing excessively on ICT enhanced forms of divestment, since these practices still retain substantial 'offline' aspects, where friends and family members exchange objects directly. In this respect, the platforms for these forms of divestment are existing social institutions such as the family and personal relationships. Similarly, the Dutch tradition of the Queen's Day Market accomplishes this widespread material reuse at a cultural level without a significant online component. In doing so, they are potentially more inclusive of people whose access to online communications is compromised, either through poverty or lack of a practical knowledge for online navigation (such as the elderly).

Shove's concepts of meanings and competences together with Schatzki's concepts of general and practice understanding, and teleoaffective structures were shown to be instrumental for the recognition of what ends a divestment practice is being pursued for, what emotional and affective aspects are present, and how specific forms of know-how facilitate the realization of these things. Next to our empirically guided description and comparison both of old, traditional divestment practices and newly emerging practices for the buying and selling of surplus domestic goods, our analyses have drawn attention to the ICT dynamics of change in divestment practices and to the ways in which divestment practices are connected to wider changes in the networked society.

Future agenda

Durable household objects have a significant embedded environmental footprint. Given the emissions associated with their material extraction, production, distribution, use, and disposal, there is an imperative to find sustainable forms of dealing with our material goods. While the practices described here may not constitute a truly 'Cradle to Cradle' economy (McDonough and Braungart 2002), they do point to how our consumption practices can be made less resource intensive, and less waste creating. They also point to how these post-divestment routes and circulation of materials is largely unquantified by waste management authorities.

In large part, this is because the practices themselves aren't formally considered in the realm of waste management. Second-hand trading and gifting mechanisms are examples of alternative divestment practices of which there is little to no acknowledgement in formal waste management policies or practices. The extent to which these practices contribute to the reduction in the amount of material that would otherwise be directed to landfill is therefore largely unknown at this point. This would require extensive survey and interview data of households (divestors) and reusers, and the various practices they engage in to divest their objects. Households would need to be asked to record estimates of their divested material (size, weight, number of items, materials) as soon as it is placed kerbside, and a follow-up estimate of the amount immediately prior to final collection. This would give a basic set of metrics associated with diversion from kerbside bulk waste collection.

Delving further into the household should also be a goal of future research seeking to understand practices of divestment. Using Schatzki's concept of practice understanding and teleoaffective structures could inform more detailed research into the practices of household divestment. Understanding common 'sayings and doings' of reuse, for instance, could assist waste policy in engaging with more households to undertake this type of divestment rather than disposal. Likewise, assisting households in developing the skills and know-how of object reuse – or where to find them – may reduce the amount of material that waste management services receive from households overall.

The future research agenda proposed here would allow for a more sophisticated understanding of the material trajectories that are 'post-use' but arguably 'pre-waste'. Research such as this may go some way to exploring how changes in practices of divestment and reuse come about, persist, or fade over time. This provokes broader questions concerning how 'cultures' of sustainable divestment and consumption are established, particularly in the realm of stewarding material objects.

Attempting to integrate these household practices into future waste management policy arrangements would go some way to filling the gaps in policy to make actual practice more consistent with an emphasis on reduction and reuse over recycling and disposal. This necessarily involves reconceptualizing the role of formal waste management authorities as the sole provider of these services. Instead, a more integrated approach to waste management is advocated. Such an approach must recognize the active role of non-state actors in effective governance for sustainability – consistent with Biermann's argument that agency must come from 'beyond the state' (Biermann, 2007: 332).

Notes

1 www.ifixit.com accessed on 2/8/2015.
2 www.greenbiz.com/blog/2010/02/16/why-ebay-green-giant accessed on 2/8/2015.
3 See www.collaborativeconsumption.com/the-movement/cc_antenna/ for a comprehensive list.
4 www.freecycle.org/about/missionstatement accessed on 2/8/2015.
5 'Queens Day' has since been renamed Kings Day after Queen Beatrix was succeeded in 2013 by her oldest son and present King Willem Alexander.
6 www.ing.nl/nieuws/nieuws_en_persberichten/2011/04/nederlanders_rekenen_op_290_miljoen_op_vrijmarkt.aspx accessed on 1/9/2012.
7 www.garagesaletrail.com.au accessed on 2/5/2012.

References

Anon., 2012. Garage Sale Trail. Available at: www.garagesaletrail.com.au [Accessed May 2, 2012].
Biermann, F., 2007. '"Earth System Governance" as a Crosscutting Theme of Global Change Research'. *Global Environmental Change*, 17 (3–4), 326–337.
Botsman, R., 2010. 'The Everyday Entrepreneur'. *RSA Journal*, (Winter), 29.
Botsman, R. and Rogers, R., 2010. *What's Mine Is Yours: The Rise of Collaborative Consumption.* New York: Harper Collins Publishers.
Charmaz, K., 2006. *Constructing Grounded Theory: A Practical Guide through Qualitative Analysis*, London: Pine Forge Press.
Cooper, M., 2010. 'Turbulent Worlds; Financial Markets and Environmental Crisis'. *Theory, Culture and Society*, 27 (2–3), 167–190.
Douglas, M. and Isherwood, B., 1979. *The World Of Goods*, New York: Basic Books.
Glaser, B.G., 1998. *Doing Grounded Theory: Issues and Discussions*, Mill Valley, CA: Sociology Press.
Glaser, B.G. and Strauss, A.L., 1967. *The Discovery of Grounded Theory: Strategies for Qualitative Research.* Chicago: Aldine.
Gregson N., Metcalfe, A., Crewe, L., 2007. 'Moving Things along: the Conduits and Practices of Divestment in Consumption. *Transactions of the Institute of British Geographers*, 32 (2), 187–200.
McDonough, W. and Braungart, M., 2002. *Cradle to Cradle: Remaking the Way We Make Things*, New York: North Point Press.
Miller, D., 1998. *A Theory of Shopping.* New York: Polity Press.

Mol, A.P.J. and Spaargaren, G., 2005. 'From Additions and Withdrawals to Environmental Flows: Reframing Debates in the Environmental Social Sciences'. *Organization & Environment*, 18 (1), 91–107.

Reckwitz, A., 2002. 'Towards a Theory of Social Practices: A Development in Culturalist Theorizing'. *European Journal of Social Theory*, 5 (2), 243–263.

Resnick, P. *et al.*, 2006. 'Peripheral Vision: The Value of Reputation on eBay: A Controlled Experiment'. *Experimental Economics*, 9 (2), 79–101.

Rifkin, J., 2000. *The Age of Access*, London: Penguin.

Schatzki, T.R., 2005. 'The Sites of Organizations'. *Organization Studies*, 26, 465–485.

Shove, E., 2010. 'Beyond the ABC: Climate Change Policy and Theories of Social Change'. *Environment and Planning A*, 42 (6), 1273–1285. Available at: www.envplan.com/abstract.cgi?id=a42282 [accessed on 24/02/2014].

Shove, E. And Walker, G., 2007. 'CAUTION! Transitions Ahead: Politics, Practice and Sustainable Transition Management'. *Environmental Planning A*, 39, 763–770.

Shove, E., Pantzar, M. And Watson, M., 2012. *The Dynamics of Social Practice, Everyday Life and How It Changes*. London, Sage.

Strauss, A.L., 1987. *Qualitative Analysis for Social Scientists*, New York: Cambridge University Press.

Wieser, H., Tröger, N. and Hübner, R., 2014. *The Practices of Using and Disposing Things*. Paper presented at the Conference 'An Inquiry into Theories of Practice', 24–25 September 2014, Utrecht, the Netherlands.

Chapter 6

Praxeologizing street violence

An attempt to understand the teleological and normative-affective structure of violent situations[1]

Don Weenink

Introduction

Many studies of violence focus on factors – features of perpetrators and some-times victims or neighbourhoods – to assess the likelihood for violence to occur. This work tends to overlook what is actually happening in violent incidents, and it has been noted that one way to advance social scientific insight in this domain is to put the situation centre stage (Collins, 2008; Katz, 1988; Athens, 1980/1997). Practice approaches, with their focus on the actual doings and sayings, might be well equipped to this task. However, it seems awkward to regard destructive acts of violence as a practice. Without denying that conflict, antagonism or opposition occur in all practices, most practice approaches depart from the idea that people work towards a common goal, mutually adjusting their doings and saying in the light of that aim. Also, most work in this tradition con-siders practices as routine, repetitive activities in everyday life. While the notion of violence is used to capture a great variety of human action, ranging from sym-bolic or structural violence to the intentional physical harm doing (Spierenburg, 2009), most notions of violence neither regard it as routine action nor as a form of mutual alignment toward a common goal. Nevertheless, practice approaches claim to offer an encompassing perspective on social life as a vast intermeshing of a great manifolds of doings and sayings (Nicolini, 2012; Reckwitz, 2002; Schatzki, 2010). Consequently, there is no good reason why the ugly and awful doings and sayings among them should be excluded from the domain of study.

This chapter aims to answer three questions. First, can violence be regarded as sets of doings and sayings in which people mutually attune their actions toward a shared goal and if so, how? Second, how are these teleological actions related to material arrangements, more specifically human bodies and weapons? Third, what can be learnt from approaching violence in this way? By attempting to answer these questions, the chapter also attempts to evaluate how a practice approach may contribute to the study of violence, in particular vis-à-vis interac-tionist (Luckenbill, 1977; Felson, 1982; Felson and Tedeschi, 1993) and micro-sociological (Collins, 2008) perspectives that also give analytical priority to the situation rather than to individuals.

To answer the above questions, this chapter offers a re-analysis of empirical data that were collected for a project on youth street violence (Weenink, 2014, 2015). The analysis follows Schatzki's (2002: 59–122) conceptualization of practices. More specifically, I will consider whether and how street violence can be regarded as integrated sets of doings and sayings. Furthermore, I will consider the role of weapons and the targeted. Schatzki outlines several elements that contribute to the integration of practices so that they are experienced as coherent sets of doings and saying by the participants. I concentrate on just one of these elements: the shared ends and normative emotions, which are part of what Schatzki calls the teleo-affective structure of practices. A full-blown analysis of violence that applies all of the four integrative elements which Schatzki outlines deserves and requires a book rather than a chapter. Moreover, some of these integrative elements require specific data in order to analyse them in full detail – while this chapter relies on textual information about the interactions only (see further below). Finally, given the importance that Schatzki (2010) gives to teleology in theories of action, it seems justified to consider the integrative element in which goal-orientedness is most explicitly conceptualized. Note that in the most narrow definitions of violence, goal-orientedness is also explicitly mentioned, in the form of intentional harm-doing.

The data originates from judicial files of Dutch juvenile courts. The average age of the attackers was 17 years at the time the violence was committed. The files comprise interrogation reports of witnesses, defendants, victims and reports of the courts and the public prosecutor. Based on these files, a textual database was set up, with cases containing detailed descriptions of the violent interaction. The sampling of case files was based on all sections of Dutch penal law considering violent offences: public bodily harm, battery or bodily harm, grievous bodily harm, (attempt to) manslaughter and (attempt to) murder. Case files were drawn from archives of four judicial districts. In sum, the sample consists of 159 violent interactions (more information concerning the sampling and the analytical procedures can be found in Weenink, 2014, 2015). In this chapter, I use only two cases of the data set. These two cases exemplify two of the most common forms of street violence in my dataset, together amounting to 84 per cent of all cases.

In this chapter, a distinction is made between instigators and victims. Instigators are persons who started the physical harm-doing and who often also dominate the interaction. This does not mean that instigators are necessarily the only ones bearing moral responsibility, even if they are seen as offenders by judicial institutions.

The plan of the chapter is as follows. The next session discusses Schatzki's (2002) conceptualization of how practices are integrated, with specific attention given to their teleo-affective structure, and how these integrative elements relate to the targeted body parts and weapons. The empirical sections that follow aim to identify whether and how specific normative emotions and goal-orientedness appear in youth street violence. The chapter concludes by evaluating this attempt to praxeologize street violence in the light of the aim formulated above.

The integration of doings and sayings through teleo-affective structures

Before explicating the term teleo-affective structure, I will first shortly consider the other integrative elements of practices that bring about the 'hanging together' of sayings and doings, as outlined by Schatzki (2002: 59–122). The first element comprises practical understanding or action understanding. This is the embodied or visceral know-how to do things on the spot. This knowing how to perform an action most often proceeds automatically and unthinkingly. General understandings, the second element, are the sets of broader ideas and meanings that are attached to a practice, which allow participants to communicate to themselves and the other participants how the things that they are doing relate to the rest of their world. The third integrative element of practices mentioned by Schatzki are rules; these comprise explicit guidelines and instructions that specify what should be done at a certain moment. Finally, the fourth integrative element comprises the teleo-affective structure, a set of ends that participants should or may pursue. The teleological part seems to be of particular importance with regard to the integration of practices as it allows mutually adjusting series of actions that participants carry out as they work toward a shared goal. There are two aspects related to this teleological part. The first aspect concerns the purpose of the acting, or the shared idea of a future situation that the individuals aim to bring about. Individuals can be consciously aware of such future-in-the-making or not. They can think, feel, dream, fantasize, want, desire or imagine such future. Having a sense of the purpose of the acting gives coherence and meaning to sequences of little tasks or body (including mental) actions, that follow up on one another to bring about the thought, felt, dreamed, fantasized, wanted, desired or imagined etcetera end. Schatzki (1996: 122–123) calls these subsequent series of tasks 'signifying chains', in which each task is tied to the previous one, working toward the purpose. The second teleological aspect, 'practical intelligibility' follows from this. Practical intelligibility is the sense, conscious or not, to do something, to perform an action. Precisely what to do, or what action is signified by practical intelligibility, arises from what an individual experiences, believes, perceives, imagines etcetera to be as the 'state of affairs', given which it makes sense to perform an action for the sake of a desired, wanted, needed etcetera 'state of being' (2010: 114–115). In the course of pursuing body actions in a signifying chain, practical intelligibility provides individuals with a sense of what to do next given the purpose (Schatzki, 2002: 74–76; Schatzki, 2010: 114–115). For practices to be experienced as coherent and recognizable sets of doings and sayings by the participants, the purpose, the signifying chains and the practical intelligibility to bring the purpose about, must be shared, at least to a large extent, among the participants. This enables the mutual alignment of the actions of participants and the situational going-on in practices. The mutual alignment and the situational going-on are strengthened by the affective part of the teleo-affective structure. This is because the shared purpose, the signifying chains and the practical intelligibility are not neutral, they have some compelling or even coercive force. In the words of Nicolini (2012: 166), the teleo-affective structure comprises 'direction and oughtness'. The 'oughtness' not just concerns the end that the participants should be pursuing, the manner in which they should do so, as well as the order in which the various tasks should be executed, but also the kind of emotions participants should experience as well as the manner in which they should express them. In Hochschild's (1979, 1983) terms, each practice brings its own set of 'feeling rules'. There is thus a normative-affective order in practices that buttresses the integrative tendency of the teleological part.

The teleology and normative-affective order may differ in various forms of violence. Relatedly, the role and the type of material arrangements in these doings and sayings may differ as well. Thus, I will consider whether the role of weapons and targeted body parts differs in relation to the end that is pursued in violent action.

At this point, the questions formulated above can be specified. First, the question whether and how violence can be regarded as a practice can now be more precisely put as: How do ends, signifying chains, practical intelligibility and the normative-affective order (feeling rules) appear in violent interactions? Second, how are these elements related to the use of weapons and targeted body parts? The third question is then: what can be learnt from analysing violence in these praxeological terms?

Praxeologizing street violence: an analysis of teleological and normative-affective structures

In this section, I will describe two cases of youth street violence. These cases each represent two forms of street violence, which I called 'contesting dominance', 'performing badness' elsewhere (Weenink, 2015). After each case, I will indicate how the teleological and affective aspects appear empirically.

Contesting dominance

This case revolves around two groups of boys. The group of Johan played football when the group of Anton appeared. Johan and Anton were the main antagonists, who engaged in a contest of daring looks.

JOHAN: When we were playing football, I saw four boys walking up to us. We looked at them, to know who they were or whether we knew them. One of those boys [Anton] started shouting: 'What are you looking at?'. Then we went on playing football. I was a bit annoyed because they were loud-mouthed. Then those boys sat down on the stairs at the dike and watched us playing. Again one of them said: 'Don't you look that way'. I did not respond to that. I saw they wanted to walk away and I followed them with my eyes. Again, they told us we should not look at them. Then the two largest boys came down, up to me.

ANTON: While we passed these boys, I saw one of them [Johan] looking conspicuously at me. When I looked back at him and asked what they were
looking at, I heard him saying: 'Have I got something of yours on me?'
[translated literally from Dutch, meaning: what do you want from me?]. We
then walked to the dike and sat down. The other boys started to play soccer
again. Suddenly, the ball was kicked in my direction. The boy whom I had
spoken to went into my direction to get the ball. Again he was looking at me
conspicuously. I said to him: 'Look just a bit longer!'. He was annoying me.
After I had told him that, that boy put the ball on the ground and kept on
looking at me. Then he picked up the ball and turned back to his game. I
walked down to him and started to unfold my knife, and Machiel jumped on
him to kick him in his back. The contest of challenges was extended even
when attacker Anton showed his knife to Johan, who did not seem to be
impressed and tried to get a hold on the knife. This resulted in getting his
tendon cut by the knife. His hand now bleeding heavily, he finally gave up
and ran away.

I will first point out the central features of contesting dominance as they are
exemplified in the above case. In the fragment, Johan's looking at Anton was
readily taken as a provocation by Anton's group. They perceived his looks as a
challenge that required a response: 'What are you looking at?' In turn, Johan
responded defiantly by asking what they wanted from him. Prolonging the
sequence of provocations now set into motion, Anton's group positioned itself at
the dike to watch the others play. Johan's defiant attitude resulted in their subsequent command 'Don't you look that way'. However, Johan did not give in to
this claim for dominance – as one of the members of Johan's group reported:
'He will not give in, he is strong and is never afraid'. When Anton challenged
Johan 'to look just a bit longer', the latter did not back up and the confrontational tension increased. To conclude: in dominance contests, both parties perse-
vere in a quest for situational dominance and as they do so, they create an arena
in which the focus of attention is on the mutual exchange of threats, insults,
provocations and challenges.

Is it possible to identify a teleo-affective structure, practical intelligibility and
signifying chains in this form of violence? First, the goal of these sets of doings
and sayings is to establish situational dominance at the cost of the opponent, and
this end is attained through an aggressive contest, a competitive struggle in
which antagonistic tension is being build up. Note that the end of attaining situational dominance at the cost of the other party is shared among the participants,
as both parties engage in sequences of provocations, of moves and counter-
moves, claims and counterclaims to the superordinate role. Contesting dominance thus requires some form of 'working agreement' (see also Polk, 1994,
1999; Copes *et al.*, 2013; Jackson-Jacobs, 2014) between both parties to continue the confrontation. Part of the working agreement is that one should not
back up a bit or leave the scene in a situation of increasing tension. Such

working agreement is not entirely voluntarily, given the emotional costs of acting against masculine honor. Especially in the presence of peers, opponents may try to exploit the other's fear of displaying passivity or pusillanimity (Polk, 1994, 1999; Copes *et al.*, 2013; Spierenburg, 1998; Winlow and Hall, 2009).

As they share a purpose, the antagonists also share practical intelligibility. While the data does not allow to offer an accurate description of how the participants perceive the current state of affairs (for instance participants may feel their peers are evaluating their worth or perhaps they may feel angry about something that happened before). However, at the very least it can be said that the antagonists mutually experience the presence of another party that offers an opportunity to engage in a contest. And they also at least share a desired, urged, felt, needed, sensed etcetera state of becoming to dominate the other. Given these situational state of affairs and state of becoming alone, it makes sense for them to throw insults, reproaches, degradations, challenges etcetera to the other party, to stare at the other impudently and to move daringly toward the other's direction, also in response to what the other party is doing. To engage in a dominance contest, the following series of subsequent body actions that make up a signifying chain need to be performed (the list is far from complete, but it indicates that work must be done to set the dominance contest in motion): finding an opponent, launching impudent provocations like staring or scolding or bumping at the other, and then persevering in series of provocations and challenges.

Note that emotional dominance precedes violence, it is not a result of it (Collins, 2008). Situational asymmetry plays and important role in Randal Collins's micro-sociological theory of violence. In the theory, attaining emotional dominance is crucial for violence to occur because it offers a way to overcome the barrier of confrontational tension that normally keeps people from using violence. Two important pathways that circumvent that barrier of confrontational tension are supportive groups and the weakness of the victims.[2] As I have demonstrated elsewhere (Weenink, 2014, 2015), instigators start the actual violence when they feel that ultimate dominance is within reach, either because their supportive group is larger than that of the other party, they outnumber the victim, they carry a knife or because the victims attain a vulnerable position, and most importantly, when they show signs of emotional submission.

The normative emotions involved with contesting dominance are indignation, anger, and self-righteousness rage. These emotions are associated with a moral claim, that enables the opponents to arouse these emotions. Even though many of the contests in my data are actually fabricated, contrived or sought for, just for the sake of engaging in aggressive competition — for the sake of seeking dominance — instigators claim to be affronted, abused, offended, aggrieved etcetera by the other party. In so doing, they express the feeling rules that are attached to contesting dominance. All in all, this form of violence exhibits the important integrative elements that make for a set of doings and sayings that is perceived as coherent and recognizable for the participants, even though they are antagonists.

Finally, let us consider the use of weapons and human body parts. In the fragment, Anton produces a knife, because he considers Johan too large to take on with his fists only. This means that the weapon is used to gain dominance. Weapon and body parts are teleological material as they contribute to the attainment of the end. This is less obvious than it seems, as most youth report they carry a weapon for the sake of self-defense rather than to attain dominance. If weapons can be regarded as objects that sustain the specific teleology in dominance contests, it is not surprising that weapons are used much more often in contesting dominance as compared to the case of performing badness: in 21 out of 86 cases (24.4%) versus 2 out of 48 cases, a significant difference (one-sided chi square test $p=0.002$). With regard to the targeted body parts, the fragment demonstrates that eyes play a central role in the building up of provocations. In addition, the provocative staring is highlighted by verbal provocations that revolve around the impudent looks of the other. In other cases of contesting dominance, eyes and tongues play an equally important role in the building up of the tension. As with the use of weapons, the face is used teleologically. In fact, eyes and tongues are perhaps the most important means to attain dominance at the cost of the other. Thus, in older Goffmanian interactionist work (Felson, 1993; Luckenbill, 1977; Polk, 1994, 1999; Felson, 1982), street violence is often seen as 'saving face' (Goffman, 1967/2005: 5–46). These are 'character contests' (Goffman, 1967/2005: 39–58, 217–218), confrontations between opponents who stand steady, as they try to save face at the other's expense in sequences of provocations and challenges (Felson and Tedeschi, 1993: 109). For this reason, it is understandable that the face of the opponent becomes an important target, because it is the source of the antagonists' attempts to claim dominance. Thus, compared with performing badness, in 42 of the 82 (51.2 per cent) cases of contesting dominance, the head was the only body part targeted, while this was 15 of 48 (31.3 per cent) cases in performing badness.[3] This difference is statistically significant (one-sided chi square test $p=0.021$). As the face and notably the eyes are probably the most important markers of personhood in a human body (see Katz, 1999, Chapter 3 on the importance of seeing to be seen), it seems plausible that attacks against the person of the opponent aim at the face more often in contesting dominance.

Performing badness

In the following case, two girls, Chantal and Esther had agreed to 'get someone', and readily found a victim in Monica, because Chantal thought she had heard Monica scolding Chantal's mother one year before. Esther however had never met Monica before. After a first round of slapping Monica's face, a group gathered and started to cheer and yell.

Lars, friend of attacker Chantal: After they had slapped her, they let Monica run away, went after her and hit her again. She was crying and saying sorry. Esther said: 'Come on, let's beat her up, 'cause I enjoy it. I just get the hang for it now, so let's get her again'. I heard the group yelling: 'Let her crawl, let her crawl!'.

MONICA: They got closer and overtook me. Chantal pulled my hair so hard that my head turned the other way. Chantal asked me whether that hurt. I said she had hurt me. I heard her friend [Esther] saying: 'Ah, really did that hurt you?'. Right after that she punched me in the face.

According to both the witnesses, attackers and the victim, the group made a lot of noise, shouting 'Beat her up, beat her up!' all the time. Various suggestions to degrade and humiliate were yelled and actually performed. Monica had to kneel down, her hair was burned, and her coat was robbed from her.

Let us first consider the key features of performing badness, which this fragment exemplifies. First, this form of violence is one-sided: the instigators launch their attacks against lonely or otherwise vulnerable or weaker victims. This is sometimes called 'opportunistic' violence in earlier studies to denote situations in which a larger group is deliberately seeking a suitable, vulnerable victim (Homel, Tomsen and Thommeny, 1992; Tomsen, 1997). In the fragment, the two instigators take Monica by surprise. Moreover, they bring a supportive group with them, who stir up the instigators by yelling and shouting. In this respect, performing badness is clearly different from contesting dominance: in the latter form of violence, attaining dominance is the stake of a struggle whereas in performing badness, dominance is already secured from the start. Second, the instigators display meanness, they toy with the victims, humiliate and denigrate them. For instance, in the fragment above, Esther and Chantal hit Monica, let her go and then chased her, caught her and then hit her again. This is a typical feature of performing badness: the instigators hit or kick the victims once, let them go, then the group chases after them, hunt them down to hurt them once more. Other forms of cruelty appear in the above fragment as well. For instance, Esther asked Monica ominously whether she had hurt her, just to punch her again shortly after that. Third, and contrary to contesting dominance, victims often apologize while being beaten up, thus contributing to the emotional dominance of the instigators, as Monica did in the fragment. But apologizing is not a meaningful reaction for the instigators, or at least they do not take saying sorry as an apology, as their attack is not a punishment to undo some prior wrongdoing by the victim. In some cases, saying sorry even results into additional, inexplicable and cruel violence. Similarly, victims often exclaim: 'Act normal!' but the point is that the instigators' whims rule rather than a moral logic. Finally, the instigators seem to enjoy violent action in some cases, as Esther had said that 'she got the hang for it'. In other cases, instigators reported experiencing joy or excitement rather than anger, as they reported they gave the victims 'a good kicking' or they indicated that they 'went for the thrill of it'. The combination of one sided attacks targeted at weaker victims, the cruel meanness and the inexplicable, sometimes joyous humiliation games that attackers play, capture the key features of this form of violence, which revolves around the demonstration of total uncontested dominance, or what Katz (1988) called 'badness' (see also Wilkinson and Fagan [2001: 186] who describe how youth purposively create opportunities for predatory and one-sided violence, which serves to display their tough or bad reputations).

How do the teleo-affective structure, practical intelligibility and signifying chains appear in this form of violence? Starting with the end, the aim of these interactions is again to demonstrate dominance. However, while attaining dominance in contesting dominance is quasi-honorable as it is bound by a 'working agreement' of turn-taking dynamics, attaining dominance in performing badness is not about honour at all. It is a form of dominance that purposively desecrates honour codes, for instance by attacking clearly weaker or vulnerable victims. Thus, attackers work toward a situation that displays that they can do whatever they want, just because they want to do it like that – the why is their will. Another important difference between performing badness and contesting dominance appears when the role of practical intelligibility is considered. In performing badness, attackers create a situation in which victims cannot rely on practical intelligibility. The actions of the attackers must be unpredictable and inexplicable, leaving the victims in doubt what will come next. In Katz's terminology, this element of performing badness is about creating a sense of 'alien-ness'. The attackers must raise a barrier to the others' understanding of the badass's own moral and emotional existence. Even when you try to 'maintain respectful comportment' (Katz, 1988: 99) there is no sure way to predict, let alone avoid, the badass's sudden unleashing of violent chaos.

While the relationship between attackers and victims in performing badness is far from a 'working agreement', it should be noted here that the weakness of the victims is not a given. This is something that must be accomplished by the attackers, and experienced fighters might have developed a sense for targets who give in easily and are likely to submit to their provocations and humiliations. Following Collins (2008), the weakness of the victim is primarily depending on the emotional dynamics in situations of antagonism. While physical appearance and the display and use of weapons may contribute to the shifting of emotional balances, the process revolves around the attainment of emotional dominance itself. As noted above, one of the pathways to attain the emotional dominance that is required to circumvent the barrier of confrontational tension and fear are weak victims. But what makes a victim weak? Weakness appears when victims give in to the rhythm that the instigators want to impose on them and when they demonstrate submissiveness and give up confronting and opposing the other party (Collins, 2008: 39–82).

Returning to practical intelligibility we might ask what it would look like from the viewpoint of the attackers? Again, the data does not allow providing an accurate description of the state of affairs that is experienced by the attackers. There is mention of Monica scolding Chantal's mother, but this could be contrived, since perhaps both instigators were humiliated by an overwhelming power themselves. However, given the desired state of becoming – to express a supreme form of domination – it makes sense to target weak victims, to play cruel humiliation games with them and to do away with all possible empathy. The signifying chain of actions that works toward this goal comprises, among others, the following tasks. First, often one or two participants take the lead in warming up the group for the project. This kind of violence is often arranged and prepared ('let's beat someone up', 'we will give someone a trashing'). Second, vulnerable victims must be found, actively sought for and the group must agree to target them. Third, emotional dominance must be secured from the start – by outnumbering the victim, bringing a large supportive group – rather than attained in aggressive competition. Fourth, participants must act in such a way that the victims are left guessing what will happen next, not knowing what to do or to expect. This requires that attackers are always one step ahead of the victims, perhaps also surprising themselves while acting out their mean impulses.

With regard to the normative emotions, it seems that this kind of violence is not so much related to anger but to feelings of superiority and sometimes even cruel joy. Moreover, attackers must not show mercy or pity. Any identification with the victims must be shut off, in order to display cruelty. In the words of Katz (1988: 80) the performance of badness requires 'toughness': tough persons do not care about the existence of the moral and emotional perspectives of others, they are 'not being morally malleable'.

To conclude the praxeological approach of this form of violence, I consider the use of weapons and the targeted body parts. Above, it was already noted that the use of weapons is much lower in performing badness. This makes sense, because in performing badness, dominance is already secured from the start. Weapons, therefore, are not needed. Furthermore, it was noted above that in performing badness, it was less likely that the head was the only body part that was targeted. This finding corresponds to the idea that performing badness is not about a personal confrontation. Instead, victims are turned into objects of humiliation, whoever they are does not matter much, as long as they can be toyed with. In line with this, it is noteworthy that in 34 out of 48 cases (70.8 per cent), the victims were strangers to the attackers, while this was 47.1 per cent, or 40 out of 85 cases in contesting dominance. This difference is statistically significant (one-sided chi square tests, $p < 0.001$).

Through my praxeological analyses it is demonstrated that violent situations unfold in patterned ways and that they have distinct teleologies and normative emotions to be worked upon. Moreover, the two teleo-affective structures in the cases are shown to be differently related to the use of weapons and the targeted body parts. Nevertheless, the two teleologies and normative-affective structures share a similar transformative capacity. How then does youth street violence change the participants and their worlds? We observed that both forms of violence create or recreate the social hierarchy. With this transformation, the instigators try to attain a dominant status, even if it is ephemeral and situational only. While many studies perceive violence as a reaction to some perceived wrongdoing (Felson, 1982; Felson and Tedeschi, 1993) or as a form of self-defence (Winlow and Hall, 2009) this praxeology shows that the teleology of street violence is about attaining dominance for the sake of dominance.

Conclusion

It is now time to provide an answer to the third research question formulated in the introduction: what can be learnt from analysing violence in praxeological terms? Two points are important in this respect.

First, a practice oriented perspective enables researchers to move away from the prevalent focus on individual perpetrators in both mainstream criminological research and in lay and policy perceptions. One disadvantage of thinking in terms of individual perpetrators is that it hides the variety of forms of violence from view. Moreover, such a perspective neglects the fact that instigators, even in their most impulsive violent actions, follow a teleological and normative-affective structure. Street violence is often portrayed as 'senseless' in public discourse. Blok (2001: 103–114) has explained that the use of such a label runs the risk that violence is perceived as something that cannot be reasonably or sensibly explained or understood. At the same time, he argues that emphasizing the senselessness of violence is a way to keep the phenomenon of violence at an emotional and mental distance, especially in relatively pacified societies where violence invokes strong feelings of abhorrence, disgust and fear. Whatever the reason for calling violence senseless, it is clear from this praxeology that violence has discernible teleologies and therefore cannot be senseless, at least from the perspective of the instigators. Instead of being senseless this chapter shows that street violence consists of structured sets of doings and saying, in which weapons and the targeted body parts are integrated to transform the social hierarchy, at least for a moment.

Second, praxeologies of violence contribute as well to existing approaches to violence that give analytical priority to situations rather than individuals. Both interactionist (Felson and Tedeschi, 1993) and micro-sociological (Collins, 2008) approaches so far have not conceptualized the material arrangements of violence. While this chapter only considered weapons and targeted body parts in a limited way, violent action is clearly intermeshed with materialities in various ways. Consider for instance types of physical space such as schoolyards, clubs, streets, etcetera, each bringing their own affordances (bringing a large supportive group, escape routes etcetera); the use and abuse of various body parts and their meanings (fighting skills, special techniques such as a flying kick high at the back of an opponent, or the symbolic cutting or even burning of hair as a trophy among girls); and also the prepared and ad-hoc creation of weapons of various kinds (ranging from guns to crown caps tied in shoe laces for more painful kicking). Future praxeologies could lay bare the importance of materiality in violence in much more elaborated and detailed ways. Next to emphasizing materialities, our praxeology suggests giving the cultural dimension more analytical weight. Although existing interactonist and micro-sociological approaches have pointed to the importance of the situation to understand violence, they do not give much attention to the role of the culture. For interactionists, the meanings of violence are a property of rationally acting individuals, as they claim that violence is instrumental, mostly a reaction to perceived intentional attacks (Felson and Tedeschi, 1993). In micro-sociological theory, the emotional dynamics are the prime focus of analysis, rather than what is being said or thought. However, the praxeological account offered in this chapter shows the importance of culture, in the form of a teleological structure with its practical intelligibility and signifying chains, in bringing about a shared sense of violent actions as a set of coherent and goal oriented doings and sayings. While it remains awkward to consider such awful and abhorrent actions as a practice, this chapter demonstrates that a praxeology of violence opens up new questions with regard to violence.

Notes

1 This chapter is an adapted and rewritten version of an article that appeared earlier in *Sociological Forum* (Weenink, 2015).
2 For more on confrontational tension and fear and the pathways to circumvent it see Collins (2008: 39–82; 2013).
3 In sum the number of contesting dominance cases is 86, however, in four cases it was not clear exactly which body part was targeted.

References

Athens, L., 1980/1997. *Violent Criminal Acts and Actors Revisited.* First part published earlier as Athens, Lonnie 1980. *Violent Criminal Acts and Actors: A Symbolic Interactionist Study.* London: Routledge and Kegan Paul. ed. Urbana and Chicago: University of Illinois Press.

Athens, L., 2005. 'Violent Encounters: Violent Engagement, Skirmishes and Tiffs'. *Journal of Contemporary Ethnography*, 34, 631–678.

Blok, A., 2001. *Honour and Violence.* Cambridge: Polity Press.

Collins, R., 2008. *Violence: A Micro-Sociological Theory.* Princeton: Princeton University Press.

Collins, R., 2013. 'Entering and Leaving the Tunnel of Violence: Micro-Sociological Dynamics Emotional Entrainment in Violent Interactions'. *Current Sociology*, 61, 132–151.

Copes, H., Hochstetler, A. and Forsyth, C.J., 2013. 'Peaceful Warriors: Codes for Violence among Adult Male Bar Fighters'. *Criminology*, 51, 761–794.

Felson, R.B., 1982. 'Impression Management and the Escalation of Aggression and Violence'. *Social Psychology Quarterly*, 45, 245–254.

Felson, R.B. and Tedeschi, J.T., eds, 1993. *Aggression and Violence. Social Interactionist Perspectives.* Washington: American Psychological Association.

Goffman, E., 1967/2005. *Interaction Ritual. Essays in Face-to-Face Behavior.* Chicago: Aldine Publishing Company.

Hochschild, A.R., 1979. 'Emotion Work, Feeling Rules, and Social Structure'. *American Journal of Sociology*, 85, 551–575.

Hochschild, A.R., 1983. *The Managed Heart: The Commercialization of Human Feeling.* Berkeley: The University of California Press.

Homel, R., Tomsen, S. and Thommeny, J., 1992. 'Public Drinking and Violence: Not just an Alcohol Problem'. *The Journal of Drug Issues*, 22, 679–697.

Jackson-Jacobs, C., 2013. 'Constructing Physical Fights: An Interactionist Analysis of Violence Among Affluent, Suburban Youth'. *Qualitative Sociology*, 36, 23–52.

Katz, J., 1988. *Seductions of Crime. Moral and Sensual Attractions in Doing Evil.* New York: Basic Books.

Katz, J., 1999. *How Emotions Work.* Chicago: Chicago University Press.

Luckenbill, D.F., 1977. 'Criminal Homicide as Situated Transaction'. *Social Problems*, 25, 176–186.

Nicolini, D., 2012. *Practice Theory, Work & Organization. An Introduction.* Oxford: Oxford University Press.

Polk, K., 1994. 'Masculinity, Honour and Confrontational Homicide'. In: T. Newburn and E.A. Stanko, eds. *Just Boys Doing Business?* London and New York: Routledge, 166–188.

Polk, K., 1999. 'Males and Honor Contest Violence'. *Homicide Studies*, 3, 6–29.

Reckwitz, A., 2002. 'Toward a Theory of Social Practices. A Development of Culturalist Theorizing'. *European Journal of Social Theory*, 5, 243–263.

Schatzki, T., 1996. *Social Practices. A Wittgensteinian Approach to Human Activity and the Social.* Cambridge: Cambridge University Press.

Schatzki, T., 2002. *The Site of the Social. A Philosophical Account of the Constitution of Social Life and Change.* Philadelphia: Penn State University Press.

Schatzki, T., 2010. *The Timespace of Human Activity. On Performance, Society, and History as Indeterminate Teleological Events.* Plymouth: Lexington Books.

Spierenburg, P., 1998. *Men and Violence. Gender, Honor and Rituals in Modern Europe and America.* Columbus: Ohio State University Press.

Spierenburg, P., 2009. 'Violence. Reflections about a Word'. In: Sophy Body-Gendrot and Pieter Spierenburg, eds. *Violence in Europe.* New York: Springer, 13–25.

Tomsen, S., 1997. 'A "Top Night": Social Protest, Masculinity and the Culture of Drinking Violence'. *British Journal of Criminology*, 37, 90–102.

Weenink, D., 2014. 'Frenzied Attacks. A Micro-Sociological Analysis of the Emotional Dynamics of Extreme Youth Violence'. *British Journal of Sociology*, 3, 411–433.

Weenink, D., 2015. 'Contesting Dominance and Performing Badness: A Micro-Sociological Analysis of the Forms, Situational Asymmetry, and Severity of Street Violence'. *Sociological Forum*, 30, 83–102.

Wilkinson, D.L. and Fagan, J., 2001. 'A Theory of Violent Events'. In: R.F. Meier, L.W. Kennedy and V. Sacco, eds. *The Process and Structure of Crime.* New Brunswick, NJ: Transaction., 169–195.

Winlow, S. and Hall, S., 2009. 'Retaliate First: Memory, Humiliation and Male Violence'. *Crime, Media Culture*, 5, 285–304.

Chapter 7

How to make sense of suffering in complex care practices?

Frans Vosman, Jan den Bakker and Don Weenink

Introduction

This chapter focuses on the tension between complexity of caring practices and the normative dimension of providing good care. The question we raise in this chapter is whether practice theory provides conceptual space for the good of the patient, being a vulnerable person, longing for cure and support in dire times, receiving care under conditions of complexity? Our answer is that this is possible, by considering the epistemological and moral position of a patient as someone dealing with illness and social vulnerability as well ('precarity'). The very character of being a patient is that he or she is suffering. Suffering, however, is not specific to patients. As the French philosopher Paul Ricoeur puts it, suffering and more broadly being the subject of forces displays what is common to all humans. People are 'passible': they constantly undergo processes, they are subject to time and material circumstances, such as heat, light and air pressure (Ricoeur, 1986: 125). People also constantly undergo acts of other people (pep talk, admonishments, putting a needle in one's back for diagnostic reasons, caressing fingers). And people undergo diseases. Of course some diseases are self-inflicted. But even then, when the disease is raging or slumbering in the body, people undergo it: they feel the contractions, the throbbing pain, the itching. People are also actors but with the constant reality of being 'passible'. Thus Ricoeur balances his idea of human agency with his observation that people are sentient beings undergoing situations, time and space; they are both subjects and objects and often at the same time. The neologism *passibilité* points at something different than passivity. When passivity means remaining without action, *passibility* does indicate movements: inner movements, even if people are not always consciously aware of them. Undergoing evokes inner movements: repulsion, attraction, contraction etcetera. In ethics this interplay of action and undergoing realities is a major shift: what if human acts are not just reigned by intention, decision, will, by principles, by duty, by rational accounts of consequences but by mere passibility as well? We thus propose that it is not evident that a patient is an actor in care practices similar to the acting roles of nurses, physicians, care managers; patients should not be seen as co-players in this field.

In this chapter, we will take up the issue of whether the passibility and vulnerability of patients can be weaved in a practices oriented conceptualization of complex care.

While our aim is to offer a conceptual contribution to practice theory, our considerations are based on five years of qualitative empirical research (2009–2014) of the first two authors in a general hospital in the Netherlands. As care ethicists, we were (and are) interested in how good care can come about and how it can turn, in an instant, into bad care (see Tronto 1993 and Held 2006 on the philosophical ethics of care and caring).

We have shadowed patients waiting for hours in the emergency room; we have witnessed astonishingly good care and unnecessary incriminating acting by one and the same physician on the very same day; we observed the use of high tech and physicians at particular moments relying on more classical experience based diagnostics; we shadowed and interviewed nurses on their rounds distributing medicine while using a computerized safety system, pointing to just one example of the prominent role of materiality in care practices. Complexity became a more and more predominant issue during our observations. Standing explanations from organization theory, interesting as they are, were not satisfying, as suffering of patients or even 'harm added by care' (Van Heijst, 2011) were absent in them. If an organization is an arrangement of things, people, ideas or activities (Hatch, 2011) the lack of any telos, and the absence of any conceptualization of the substance of the work, and the experiences that it brings about, render that definition problematic. Such a formal definition of an organization is theoretically weak: that what is done and what is experienced seems irrelevant (cf. Pellegrino, 2001). As Lyotard has analysed there is no such thing as a 'nil institution', an organization defined as devoid from content. Thus, the presence of patients *constitute* the carework in a hospital, they are not just add-ons to an already existing, morally neutral organization.

As we were sceptical of theories concentrating on complexity that leave out the substance of care and the normative, we were looking for a theory that could serve us better as a heuristic tool for our research. We needed a theory that could help to dig up matters of concern to those working and being ill in the hospital organization and which is also capable of capturing issues of complexity and normativity. How could caring, suffering and the high complexity of the late modern hospital be adequately theorized? We side with Annemarie Mol (2003) as she emphasizes 'that what is enacted' in an organization. However, we do not concentrate, as she does, on the enactment of the body multiple or perhaps disease multiple in various care practices in which health care is leading. Rather, we wanted to understand the very nature of being a patient: the one who is suffering, undergoing both the disease and the care practice. We are interested in the complaints and concerns of patients as they come for assistance and help to doctors, nurses, physiotherapists, nutrition experts, and we are interested in the actions of the care professionals as they take place in the highly complex setting of the hospital too. Any theory that is of heuristic value to our research would have to contain these interests. We adopted a practice approach to understand what the complexity of the organization and the work processes are about, while staying loyal to the fact that people enter a hospital because they are ill, suffer, recover, are in pain or die as well as to the fact that health care workers have professional concerns of their own. The understanding of complex care practices cannot come about if these realities are neglected.

In what follows, we first will discuss what complexity in hospital settings is about. Second, we ask how the moral good of the patient can be understood under conditions of such complexity. After that, we discuss how and to what extent practice theory allows taking the nature of being a patient seriously in complex care practices.

Complexity in the hospital

Complexity in an organization appears when 'things relate but don't add up' as Annemarie Mol and John Law put it (Mol and Law, 2002: 1). With regard to hospitals there is ever increasing complexity but also a constant effort to reduce complexity: the activity of complexity reduction, mostly not grounded on an idea of how the hospital should be, but as relentless labour to keep basic work processes going. And there is good reason to that. Complexity is enhanced by trends that are helpful (e.g. the introduction of new technologies that offer better chances for less harmful intervention) but burdensome as well: it burdens the work of care givers and often it draws attention away from the patients and their suffering. As we are interested in hospital care practice in its present form, permeated by complexity and the question of how good care is conceivable under such conditions, we will have to get a more detailed picture of that complexity.

There is a range of factors that bring about complexity in hospital care. Ongoing specialization is one. In his critical approach of three review studies on upcoming themes in medicine, Cooke (2013), a physician himself, calls these factors 'mega-trends'. 'Across medicine, specialties are becoming subspecialized, and sub-specialties are developing sub-subspecialties'. One of the leading theorists on complexity, philosopher Edgar Morin (2011), argues that what he calls the hyper-specialization in the medical and nursing professions, is one of the hardest form of complexity to cope with: communication between the representatives of the sub-disciplines is becoming increasingly difficult the more the medical domains are splitting up (Morin, 2011). Specificity wins from generality.

The upswing of technology in care is a second factor of increasing complexity. Even if the official goals of medicine are about quality of care enhancement, this pursuit is in fact accompanied by enhancing technology. Technology here points at the broad range of technology usage, ranging from computerized communication, registration, and management systems used in the hospital as well as to high tech medicine, like in neurosurgical robots, nano-technological diagnostic and therapeutic devices but also telemedicine for patients with cardiac vascular conditions. The technological development within domains of medicine and nursing has been considerable and is a driver in complexity: systems have to work together, they take time and tend to absorb the attention of caregivers. This technology is not just about handy devices, it also affects patients. To cite Cooke on this: 'Critical moments of human experience – from conception to death – are now technologically mediated or forestalled.' He points at the difficulty but also the urgency to 'understand the effect on patients and their loved ones of the "technologizing" of these fundamental elements of human existence'. In that sense the practice of medicine in hospital becomes more complex as physicians have to take control over the effects of technology, also in their relationship with patients.

There is another source of complexity growth next to the internal factors of specialization and technology: societal pressure. As there is high pressure on hospital governance to ensure patient safety, control systems have been brought into place, like for instance drug delivery systems. The same goes for demands to increase transparency of hospital outcomes, resulting in reports to be delivered to society and the intervention of controlling and monitoring organizations (governmental agencies and insurance companies). It also goes for the constant political tendency towards austerity measures. The systems installed in hospitals aim at producing desired effects (e.g. no mistakes with drug deliveries, immediate clarity about how any hospital deals with her outcomes, clarity about costs), which involves time consuming labour of physicians, nurses, managers and staff. Even if figures may vary slightly, both physicians and nurses in a hospital setting tend to spend about 30 per cent of their working hours on documentation and registration, mostly via computerized systems (Füchtbauer *et al.*, 2013). While these systems were intended to reduce complexity, they unintendedly increase complexity as well. Complexity here means: while tackling issues of uncertainty, uncertainty grows; while trying to deal with the concatenation of processes the entanglement of them grows (see De Haan and Rotmans, 2011, on Dutch health care systems).

It appears that the problems and misunderstandings that are brought about by complexity, notably in the form of hyper-specialization, are often seen as communication problems. Jeffs *et al.* (2013) have shown that the urge for more communication is reflex like, for example, when doctors notice that serious problems and misunderstandings arise at the moment when patients are taken from intensive care to the ward. Jeffs *et al.* notice in their qualitative study that physicians act as if they are 'working in silos'. Zwarenstein *et al.* (2013) note that the appeal 'Let's communicate and work in teams' seems to be rhetorical and seems to represent a hope for the future, rather than an attainable goal. We have encountered similar, mantra-like talk during our fieldwork. The talk about 'more communication' as a solution for complexity occurred at many instances without ever raising the question why this talk, going on for many years, did not lead to any satisfying results. The talk seems reductionist, as if more communication can match the forces that create an ever increasing number of specialized practices that make up social life in the hospital. Similarly, Ament *et al.* (2014)

provide a set of measures to increase communication and collaboration (administrative reminders, involving a coordinator, booster meetings, working agreements), but they curiously leave aside the very substance of hospital care: the treatment of very sick patients. This brings us back to our original concern: the provision of good care in complex care practices.

Good care under conditions of complexity

Drawing on his extensive ethnographic research on nursing in hospitals, Chambliss (1996) points at ethical problems that are created by the organization. He explicitly wants to refrain from so called 'classical' ethical issues, often phrased as dilemmas, which revolve around the work of nurses and physicians. Instead, Chambliss focuses the attention on ethical issues that are created by the way work is structured in the hospital. More specifically, Chambliss argues that they result from the struggle of the hospital with complexity. These new ethical issues are hard to understand when using classical ethical distinctions like intention or choice. They are not simply or predominantly a matter of choices by actors, nor are they a matter of attaching a moral value to an act. Rather, they are about the moral substance of the interacting itself. As actors participate in complexity ridden bundles of caring practices where buildings, technology and administrative monitoring are pervasive, it is necessary to find out how this complexity affects the moral dimension of care. The moral dimension is not restricted to the realm of purposive action by the participants, like physicians, nurses and managers. Indeed, the moral dimension is in the practice itself. This implies a recasting of what moral care is about. We do stick to the idea that the good concerns the well-being of the patient, which is dependent on the health care work and the healing process. However, under conditions of complexity we have to take into account how the different elements of practices bring about morally good care. Thus, for instance, when technology shapes the work of care givers and takes a hold on the existential experiences of patients, we cannot reduce morality to what the physician did or did not do. Before we elaborate further on how the goodness of care can be brought about in complex care practices, we will first outline how the hospital can be conceptualized from a practice oriented approach.

A practice theoretical view on hospital complexity

Practice theory is about how people act in arrangements of people and things. We can identify an organization as such an arrangement 'as they happen' (Schatzki, 2006). Theories of practices are in the plural, drawing on sources as different as Heidegger, Wittgenstein, Marx and Bourdieu. But they share a common interest in how people, materiality and bodyliness interact to bring something about. Theodore Schatzki (1996: 289) typifies a practice as: 'a temporary unfolding and spatially dispersed sets (or nexuses) of doings and sayings'.

Schatzki installs a tension between the agency of participants on the one hand and the doing of a practice that 'befalls' participants on the other hand (Schatzki, 2010: 170). Participants are *in* a practice and in that sense the practice is upon them, comprises them; they are not sovereign leaders of a practice. Manidis and Scheeres (2013) have shown how this is a fruitful view on how physicians and nurses act institutionally. It is exactly this distribution of (moral) responsibility over both participants and the practice itself which provides an entry to conceptualize the ethics of good caring practices. Similarly, the work of German sociologist Robert Schmidt is helpful to conceive of care as a practice, leaving the idea of morality concentrated in human actorship behind. This postponement of normativity allows arriving at a more apt ethical understanding of care work (like the work done by nurses, physicians and managers), as we are not bothered by what Schmidt – with Bourdieu – calls a 'scholastic ethical misapprehension' (Schmidt, 2012: 35–37). The scholastic position means that actors are seen as dominating action, the normative wish that free will of man reigns over action and is projected on the reality of action, which Schmidt calls 'misleading' (Schmidt, 2012: 37). The praxeological view is that acts and their actors are part of a practice. One cannot follow up acts and actors as long as we see them as sovereign to a practice, which evidently they are not, imbued as they are in a practice, reacting, instead of being free floating minds. We can thus leave (scholastic) ethics behind in order to establish a kind of ethics that fits to complexity, after reframing action within practice. In this respect, Caldwell (2012) speaks of a *paradox*: in order to reclaim agency in an organization, to impose responsibilities on agents in a field, notions like individual intensionality should be replaced by their acting as meshed in a practice. Thus following a practice approach does not mean to dump normativity, but rather (1) making a detour of analysis what a practice is about; (2) of reframing action within practice; and (3) then at another position than previously thought and conceptually imposed, recast moral concerns.

In practice theory, the idea of sovereign actors is replaced by the idea of participants being co-actors, intervening in the environment with other participants and with materiality: the technology and physical space that shape their acting. Schmidt (2012) indicates that nobody acts in isolation, we always ground our doings on what others did before us. In a general hospital, 365 days a year and 24 hours a day, this is quite evident. We can add: shift after shift takes over and passes on. According to Schmidt there is no 'zero zone': there is no such thing as 'the' blueprint hospital care practice, a zero zone before the actual practice takes place. Doctors, nurses enter a practice that was already there. They are just participating in labour that was going on already and will go on after them. It is important to note that this analytical, non-normative view does not remove initiative, nor some kind of freedom, nor responsibilities from participants. Rather, the 'subject' enacts a game that has been played already before the enactment. There is no *auctor originalis* outside the practice, all on the field have the game within themselves. Schmidt resists the separation between ideas and action, as the practice itself, the interplay on the field, determines what is done (Schmidt,

2012: 38–40). Practices are thus a cluster of bodily and mental activities. But the mental activity is quite bodily and it is social: it should not be granted a separate realm, nor should it be individualized as all action, both mental and bodily, originate from practices (Schmidt, 2012: 55). Andreas Reckwitz (2002: 251) argues that 'Practices are routinized bodily activities; as interconnected complexes of behavioral acts they are movements of the body.... A practice can be understood as the regular, skillful "performance" of (human) bodies'. People do not use their bodies to perform an act, 'routinized actions are themselves bodily performances'. Schmidt also draws attention to the idea that artefacts, like a medical instrument, a computerized system, the very hospital building (with the order it imposes on activities: e.g. dying patients are put in a separate room, thus channelling the care work) are subjects of practices too (Schmidt, 2012: 65).

Let us provide an example: in a newly constructed ward two patients, each with a private room, instead of with four or two in one room have to share one bathroom. This architecture influences not only the patients but the nurses as well: on the neurology ward elderly patients report loneliness, and nurses indicate that they only go inside the patients room to perform a specific action, there is no such thing as a casual talk. These nurses' encompassing gaze (as they walk around on the ward, they are acting purposively and at the same time they see a lot) no longer fits the practice due to the physical setting, as Hanneke van der Meide *et al.* (2015) have shown with regard to elderly patients and nurses at the neurology ward.

Schmidt (2012: 38–44) develops the idea of the interconnectedness of complexes of acts: a practice can be seen as a game and a field of play. He uses this idea of a game, e.g. football, as a heuristic (non-definitional) device: in order to make the phenomena under inquiry understandable as 'praktische Vollzugswirklichkeiten', i.e. as practical realities as they happen. In this way, Schmidt enables us to first see what happens, how phenomena present themselves in a Gestalt. Before we discuss these analytical claims in more detail, we will first present some observations from our empirical research. We have shadowed a physician, a young neurologist, during several shifts as he was doing his daily work on the neurology ward.

Scene 1.
8.45 a.m., in a small room in the corner of the ward, with windows on two sides, the physician together with a nurse performs a lumbar puncture with a slender young man of about 32 years. There is a lot of daylight. As we are on the fourth floor, we look into the sky, the trees surrounding this wing show their leaves as they flutter in the summer breeze. This patient was taken from the four bed room to this angle of the ward. As the physician entered, the young man was lying on a bed, a nurse was with him who had given him information and instruction on what was going to come. At a small table nearby all the equipment lies spread out. The patient faces the windows and the table with equipment. The physician invites the patient to

lie down and relax, with his back to him, whereas the nurse is facing the patient. The doctor tries to make the puncture. The procedure fails. The patient gets even more tense than he already was, the lines in his face getting tight. The doctor tells him to relax, tries again, another failure. The doctor then asks the young man to sit up on the bed, with his face towards the nurse, and asks to arch his back. As the doctor prepares for the third attempt the nurse silently holds the left shoulder of the patient, puts her other hand at the right temple, she caresses his head with her thumb, almost unobtrusively. The puncture succeeds, within seconds the fluid is out and the physician cleans the back of the patient and leaves the small room, up to his next activity, leaving the patient and the nurse behind, I hear her talking in a subdued voice to the young man, still somewhat in shock. He has not said a single word, but his body has done the talking.

Scene 2.
12.15 a.m. the same physician performs another lumbar puncture. This time it is at the ward, in a four bed room, with indeed four patients, three women and a young man in and around their beds. The young man, in his mid thirties, lies in his bed as the physician tells him that he will make a puncture. The patient puts his headphones away. A nurse, another person than this morning, assists, pulling the curtain around the bed. This patient is a knowledgeable patient, he has been on the ward several times and the lumbar puncture is not his first. As the doctor fiddles around with needle, the lab tube and a shallow metal bowl, a nurse from another ward comes in, and says something to one of the other patients. In the meantime hot food is delivered by the team responsible for that: tablets are brought for all four patients, the lady patients are asked what they would like to drink. The odour of a detergent mingles with the smell of the hot food. The nurse stands at the foot of the bed. The doctor tries his best to perform a puncture, as the patient lies on the bed with his back towards the doctor and his face towards the curtain. After two failures the young man shrieks in the local dialect 'doctor, doctor, stop, I don't want this anymore, if things are like this than I do not want to have the medical exam'. The doctor convinces him to give it a last try. The patient gives in, but one can see that he is upset and angry. The third try fails as well, the doctor gives up and says, 'we'll see this afternoon' and leaves the room.

What is it that we see? We are not referring to the why question (causes and effects), like the competence of the physician: during the many shifts we have seen the neurologist at work performing the punctures frequently and with success. Thus there are many why's (circumstances, cooperation, time pressure, etcetera). When we talked afterwards about our observation to the care professionals of this ward they immediately started looking for causes and for possible quick changes, or they debased the story: 'you know, this is what happens'. The what question is another question than the why question. What do we see? On an organizational level one can see the density of the second scene compared with the first one: many people, more sounds, more turbulence on the field and activities separated from each other, not taking notice of what activity takes place next to you. If we try to answer the ethnographic question what is done and how, and how the phenomena show themselves while using the practice theory approach, we can see doctors, nurses, patients acting together, reacting or not (at least in a visible, noticeable way) to each other. We can also see, thanks to the comparison of both scenes, what is lacking on the field; so to say the shadow of acts not committed and of positions not taken. Indeed, the nurse in the second scene does not face the patient and does not take a position in eye sight of the patient. If we go one step further we see the co-acting in a diagnostic practice. This does not necessarily imply bringing a practice to some accomplishment. In scene one it seems that the tiniest little gesture of the nurse, striking the patients face, without a word, is part of the practice: she just knows what to do. In the second scene it is striking that even if the same technical procedure is followed there is no co-acting: physician and nurse are not attuned to each other. They do not play the game of getting the intervention done, whilst minimalizing the harm for the patient. One may say that in the second scene all are on the field but the play is no co-enactment. Materiality acts here in a clear way: the small, light room compared with the four bed room does its work.

Schmidt (2012: 30–33) stresses the heuristic character of his idea of practices as games on a field. Schmidt uses the expression 'Sehhilfe' (ibid.: 76). Rather than a definition, the notion of a game as a heuristic tool stands for the ability to see the *what and how* of actions and of events in situ. Observing care practices as a game on a field opens up what is happening in a situated here and now: the positions on the field, who is there, the interactions or the non-existence of interaction, the materiality and how it acts back, how bodyliness works, how the physical presence of the players functions in the game, how their senses (looking, touching and in the hospital often: smelling) are at work. Furthermore, Schmidt (2012: 103ff.) adds the idea of antagonistic play on the field. The co-acting, of a nurse with a physician, can be maladjusted or antagonistic. When a senior nurse guides a young neurologist, who has just started his work on the ward, she gently directs his actions: 'it is advisable to ask for the consultancy of the opthalmogist before 10 a.m., no, do not wait, do it right away, otherwise he'll come only tomorrow'. But in another case she surreptitiously infringes his orders to arrange a meeting with the family of the patient tomorrow afternoon and organizes the meeting for the very same day. 'He [the neurologist] finds it hard to understand that things are deteriorating so quickly; this family has to know asap'. And she takes the heat that very afternoon when the family is there and he says angrily that he has 'other things to do' until he blends in. Patients can be opponents to caregivers as well, even while they are in the hospital for good cause. Nurses have a striking expression for that: these patients are 'not adequate', they do not blend in into what patients are expected to do, say, or how they should cope, take drugs and prepare themselves for a next step. Feldman and Orlikowski (2011) in their analysis of the emergence of practice theories, point to the attention paid to power and inequality. Asymmetry in particular, however, i.e. asymmetric positions in the field, seems to be an important clue for practice theory. Asymmetry may arise when some participants have more opportunities to use materialities and their bodies in the practice and to determine what is being transformed in the practice than other participants. In the case of care practices, nurses and physicians and patients co-act, and materiality acts upon them, but these participants do not have equal opportunities to enact the practice. However, can this heuristic approach, with the idea of a game and of the asymmetrical co-acting on the field, harbour the good of the patient? Can it take into account what the patient has undergone?

Passibility in care practices

Now, on the level of content, with regard to passibility, Schmidt opens up to that dimension, first, as he reflects on the social visibility of what shows itself in the game on the field, and second, as he reflects on what unites all on the field, i.e. bodily knowledge of the game.

In their own way, patients undergo the care practices they participate in: the way they move, speak or remain silent, the very fact that they accept undergoing these practices as such. But they undergo illness at the same time: their disease is a process that just takes place. We recall Ricoeur's ([1960] 1986) *passibilité*. Patients are actors but they are sentient and passible beings as well. Undergoing does not imply reflection, it does imply being subjected to what comes to us and it brings about inner movements, experiences and emotions. The patient of scene 1 does not have to reflect on the light flooding into the room, nor does the patient of scene 2 have to reflect on the noise level or on the smells in the room. Yet they undergo what is done and said. The body knows this, in an experiential way: 'we have been here before, and therefore…'. Passibility is also about painful undergoing, about suffering and dying, phenomena people don't do but undergo. The heuristic approach of a practice should thus not only expose the doings and sayings but the undergoings as well. This seems to be crucial to understand hospital care practices. A lot of these practices are intrusive, be it diagnostical or therapeutical. In the hospital, patients enter a world that molds them, not only via medical practices but also by the web of practices that comprise the organizational molding of everyday life in the hospital. Patients suffer and some will die. In this regard patients are in a really different position than nurses and physicians on the field. Surely, all are vulnerable, patients ánd doctors, but complaints of a serious nature made patients into specific kinds of participants in medical caring practices: they participate in the mode of enduring both the disease and the care process. The heuristics of these care practices have to be able to notice where in the field the undergoing of treatment emerges, where they announce themselves. Using the expression 'announce' does not mean to give a voice to what the patient is undergoing, what he (or she) is 'experiencing'. Mostly the undergoing of treatment announces itself in a silent way, in inner speech, or in the murmuring between patients: 'I get irritated because of the loud snores of that old rattler at the window'; 'I always get upset when that doctor comes in, he is so icy'. 'The pain in my bowels is excruciating, throbbing'. Rarely does it come out loud. The enduring does not become an autonomous kind of participation by voicing these experiences: the passible continues to be there, whether outspoken or silent. Even if official hospital knowledge translates much of the possibility of the patients in words of action (e.g. patients making their complaints known, making a decision and the other way around, reacting on possibility via action of care-givers: informing patients, autonomy, choices, shared decision making), these phenomena are precisely non-active. Any theory, that immediately starts trans-lating possibility into action, moves away from realities that come upon a patient. If we pursue the practice approach of care in order to open up complexity and cope with it, possibility deserves a proper conceptual place, precisely because we are dealing with caring for and being cared for. Otherwise we lose the very essence of the experience of being a patient.

Conclusion: praxeology and possibility

Let us return to our opening question whether practice theory can open up to what we are seeing in complex hospital care practices, notably signs of pain, illness and suffering and of the undergoing of treatment in general. First, Schmidt's (2012: 231ff.) account of how to conduct praxeological research entails that researchers should take an interest in how bodies present themselves, how they make themselves visible for observation. This is not just a matter of a researcher looking at a phenomenon, instead the inquiry is about the practical bringing about of social visibility. Seeing and acknowledging what is seen (by the participants in a practice, a researcher included) are part of the practice itself. When observing a patient lying down for diagnostics, we are in a position to observe a scene that is basically open to other participants in the practice. Drawing on Hannah Arendt's (1958: 63) basic understanding of what is 'public', namely that what can be seen, what is perceivable by all, Schmidt states that there is a plurality of positions: all are basically in a position to share the atten-tion for what shows itself. What seems to be intimate (getting a puncture) is at the same time social visibility. Looking at the puncture is not just observation in an encounter. According to Schmidt observing means taking part in joined atten-tion to what shows itself in a practice. But then what about the not blatantly visible possibility, these inner movements, the inner speech and experiences that befall people? While possibility is often not manifestly open to the immediate gaze, its latency can be turned into a focus of attention. This is because possibil-ity is part of the 'Verweisungszusammenhang' (Schmidt, 2012: 236–237; 244), the network of cross-references of all that makes the practice a practice, includ-ing the unspoken and the unseen. Thus there is an opening for silent passibility.

Second, patients in their bodyliness are participants of care practices. We must add that this vision is more radical than the policy views that attribute a larger role to patients, such as in 'sharing in decision making', or turning patients into 'co-practitioners'. Such statements are often perfunctory: they are about the organizational hassle physicians and nurses have to go through, a job where they can use the help of patients. While appealing to patients and their own will is potentially favourable and may be useful to get care givers out of their self-referential organizational problems, this kind of 'cooperation' is something different than acknowledging that patients are participants in care practices. From a praxeological perspective, the practice is, so to say, *in* the patient: they carry the practice in a bodily way. They are not the objects of a practice, as one might think. Without them there is no game and no field. Yet patients are constantly evicted from the practice. As a manager of the hospital remarked in a quasi-cynical way in a board meeting, 'it is such a pity that we cannot carry on, on our own, and we have to deal with patients' (i.e. without patients we could do things much more efficiently). She was thus critically pointing at the marginalization of patients from the practice of care in the hospital. Patients in their suffering are often seen as object of 'our', i.e. caretakers practices. However, all participants of the practice can acknowledge the suffering and more broadly speaking the possibility of ill people. Such acknowledgement is not a matter of empathy, but a matter of consciousness about positions, including a participant in the practice who is ill, and the possibility to change one's position and take the perspective of the patient. Once again we postpone an immediate normative nor a psychological interpretation (empathy) and advocate realistic heuristics: what shows itself? Taking the perspective of the participant-patient means switching to that particular position, taking that perspective and realizing that apart from complaints (about illness) and of concerns (of what the disease means to the patient) possibility is at work. Participation is not just about autonomy and decisions, it is about being on the field as a sufferer.

We have two leads now with regard to suffering. The first is the social visibility of a practice, i.e. the visibility of the 'what and how' for the participants in the game. Performing as well as getting a puncture is taking part in one single care practice. The patient with his or her suffering is in the practice and can be acknowledged, as all in the practice can be aware of their position in the field and the possibility of changing their position. This is not a matter of psychology, of empathy, or the realm of the inner world. We should not retreat to psychology but remain within the praxeological approach. The position-taking is about awareness about one's position on the field and allowing stepping to another position, stepping behind the patients as co-actors, taking their perspective and getting in touch with possibility as it acts, even if it is in a muffled way. The second lead is that suffering, undergoing pain, disease, being mesmerized by worries is part of the practice of care, as patients in their bodily presence show themselves in the practice. In fact the acknowledgment is an act of identifying what the practice is about; it is about acting on the field, about positions and about what shows itself on the field.

Our proposal is to broaden the sayings and doings of a practice with the undergoing of treatment. This fits into Schmidt's theory, as he emphasizes the occurrences on the field, the positions and the relations between the positions. Our proposal is to replace the subjective-objective dichotomies with the language of acknowledging positions on the field. As we try to include the enormous complexity of hospital care by framing it in a practice theory approach, we could recast the very idea of actorship. Physicians and nurses are not isolated actors. They are partakers in a practice in which materiality (such as technologies) co-act. We can also view patients as partakers of that very same practice. The very fact of suffering and of being sentient passible beings points to a dimension of practice that should be taken into account in practice theory: undergoing treatment next to doings and sayings. We envisage a much broader use of this idea than only in care practices. Indeed, the concept of embodiment, so central in practice theory, can be rethought, including passibility. For instance, if the work done by a 'rational', 'brain centred' engineer is seen as a bodily performance in praxeological terms, this view could also conceptually incorporate the passibility of the engineers' work. Surely our proposition with regard to undergoing treatment is just one step in coping with complexity. With regard to care practices, however, this step helps to uncover what this practice is about.

References

Ament, S., Gillissen, F., Moser, A., Maessen, J., Dirksen, C., Meyenfeldt, M. von and Weijden, T. van der, 2014. 'Identification of Promising Strategies to Sustain Improvements in Hospital Practice: a Qualitative Case Study', *BMC Health Service Research*, 14, 641.

Arendt, H., 1958. *The Human Condition*. Chicago: University of Chicago Press.

Broerse, J.E.W. and Bunders, J.F.G., 2010. *Transitions in Health Systems: Dealing with Persistent Problems*. Amsterdam: VU University Press.

Caldwell, R., 2012. 'Reclaiming Agency, Recovering Change? An Exploration of the Practice Theory of Theodore Schatzki', *Journal for the Theory of Social Behavior*, 42 (3), 283–303.

Chambliss, Daniel F., 1996. *Beyond Caring. Hospitals, Nurses, and the Social Organization of Ethics*. Chicago: The University of Chicago Press.

Cooke, Molly, 2013. 'A More Ambitious Agenda for Medical Education Research'. *Journal of Graduate Medical Education*, 5 (2), 201–202.

Feldman, Martha S. and Orlikowski, Wanda J., 2011. 'Theorizing Practice and Practicing Theory'. *Organization Science*, 22 (5), 1240–1253.

Füchtbauer, L. Maria, Nørgaard, Birgitte and Mogensen, Christian Backer, 2013. 'Emergency Department Physicians Spend Only 25% of Their Working Time on Direct Patient Care'. *Danish Medical Journal*, 60 (1): A4558.

Haan, J. de and Rotmans, J., 2011. 'Patterns in Transitions: Understanding Complex Chains of Change', *Technological Forecasting and Social Change*, 78 (1): 90–102.

Hatch, Mary Jo, 2011. *Organizations: A Very Short Introduction*. Oxford: Oxford University Press.

Heijst, Annelies van, 2011. *Professional Loving Care. An Ethical View of the Healthcare Sector.* Leuven: Peeters.

Held, V., 2006. *The Ethics of Care: Personal, Political, and Global* (second ed.). Oxford New York: Oxford University Press.

Jeffs, L., Lyons, R., Merkley, J. and Bell, C., 2013. 'Clinician's Views on Improving Inter-Organizational Care Transitions', *BMC Health Services Research*, 13: 289.

Klaver, K., Elst, E. van and Baart, A., 2014. 'Demarcation of the Ethics of Care as a Discipline: Discussion Article', *Nursing Ethics*, 21 (7): 755–765.

Manidis, M. and Scheeres, H., 2013. 'Practising Knowing: Emergence(y) Teleologies', *Educational Philosophy & Theory*, 45 (12): 1230–1251.

Meide. H. van der, Leget. C. and Olthuis, G., 2015. 'Feeling an Outsider Left in Uncertainty – A Phenomenological Study on the Experiences of Older Hospital Patients', *Scandinavia Journal of Caring Sciences*, 29 (3): 528–536.

Mol, A. 2003., *The Body Multiple: Ontology in Medical Practice*. Durham (NC): Duke University Press.

Mol, A. and Law, J., 2002. *Complexities. Social Studies of Knowledge Practices*. Durham (NC): Duke University Press.

Morin, Edgar, 2011. *La Voie, Pour l'avenir de l'humanité*. Mesnil-sur-Estre: Librairie Artheme Fayard.

Nicolini, D., 2009. 'Zooming in and out: Studying Practices by Switching Theoretical Lenses and Trailing Connections'. *Organization Studies*, 30 (12): 1391–1418.

Nicolini, D., 2012. *Practice Theory, Work & Organization. An Introduction.* Oxford: Oxford University Press.

Pellegrino, E., 2001. 'The Internal Morality of Clinical Medicine: A Paradigm for the Ethics of the Helping and Healing Professions', *Journal of Medicine and Philosophy*, 26 (6): 559–579.

Ricoeur, P., 1986. *Faillible Man*. New York: Fordham University Press (Originally *L'homme faible*, 1960).

Reckwitz, A., 2002. 'Toward a Theory of Social Practices: A Development in Culturalist Theorizing', *European Journal of Social Theory*, 5: 243–263.

Schatzki, T.R., 1996. *Social Practices: A Wittgensteinian Approach to Human Activity and the Social*. Cambridge: Cambridge University Press.

Schatzki, T.R., 2006. 'On Organizations as They Happen'. *Organization Studies*, 27 (12): 1863–1873.

Schatzki, T.R., 2010. *The Timespace of Human Activity: on Performance, Society, and History as Indeterminate Teleological Events*. Lanham, MD: Lexington.

Schatzki, T.R., 2012. 'A Primer on Practices'. In: J. Higgs, R. Barnett, S. Billett, M. Hutchings and F. Trede, eds. *Practice-Based Education: Perspectives and Strategies*. Rotterdam: Sense, 13–26.

Schmidt, R., 2012. *Soziologie der Praktiken. Konzeptuelle Studien und empirische Analysen*, Berlin: Suhrkamp.

Tronto, Joan, C., 1993. *Moral Boundaries. A Political Argument for an Ethic of Care*. New York: Routledge, Chapman and Hall.

Zwarenstein, M., Rice, K., Gotlib-Conn, L., Kenaszchuk, C. and Reeves, S., 2013. 'Disengaged: a Qualitative Study of Communication and Collaboration between Physicians and Other Professions on General Internal Medicine Wards', *BMC Health Services Research*, 13: 494.

Chapter 8

Grounding the practice

Material elements in the constitution of tennis practices

Hugo van der Poel and Sven Bakker

Introduction

This chapter addresses the role of material elements in the constitution of practices, using tennis as a case study. At the same time, we aim to show that a praxeological perspective is fruitful in understanding (the evolution of) social phenomena, such as the changing prevalence for and diffusion of particular surface types in tennis, and more generally the circulation of innovations and new materials. Our approach is rooted in Giddens' (1984) structuration theory, but is clad in the more present day formulations of practice theory, as developed by, among others, Theodore Schatzki, Robert Schmidt and Elizabeth Shove. As a useful starting point we take the perspective of Shove *et al.* on the dynamics of social practice, and in particular their assumption that 'practices emerge, persist and disappear as links between their defining elements are made and broken' (2012: 21). The defining elements belong to one of three broad categories: material elements, competences and meanings. Our interest is in the material elements, in how they link to competences and meanings, and in the way in which this linking or combining of elements can be shown to affect the performance of the practice. We will also make clear that this linking of elements is not simply or solely a practice internal affair, but may be affected by outcomes of practices that are external to the practice under study, such as, in this particular case, the practice of playing tennis.

First we will discuss how the grounding of the practice makes a difference in the performance of the practice. Grounding here is meant literally, and refers to the different surfaces tennis is being played upon in the Netherlands. How does an element of the setting of a practice become a material component of a practice-as-performance, and thus an integral part of the practice or activity bundle (Schatzki, 2002)? Second we consider the practice of managing tennis facilities and how outcomes of this practice have an affect on the practice of playing tennis. Our assumption is that the teleo-affective structure (Schatzki, 2002: 80ff.) in the practice of playing tennis only partly aligns with the teleo-affective structure in the practice of managing tennis facilities. There is a difference not only with respect to the ends to be realized in both practices – ends that guide the intentions and intelligence in the performance of the various tasks and projects comprised in these practices – but to the related emotions as well. Thus, tennis players use different criteria and judgments to assess courts when compared with tennis club owners or club treasurers. The Annual General Meeting (AGM) of the tennis clubs will be presented as the most obvious and decisive linking pin or primary nexus (Schatzki, 2002: 18) between the practice of playing tennis and the practice of managing tennis facilities. We assume that decision-making processes regarding surface types lead to various outcomes, depending on the interplay between both practices and on the power relations that exist between the decision-making parties involved. Informed by the first two sections and making use of data about the distribution of court surfaces in the Netherlands, the third section will address issues regarding the innovation and circulation of court surfaces, as elements of tennis practices. Empirical references originate from a survey-research commissioned by the Royal Dutch Lawn Tennis Association (KNLTB) and carried out by the authors in 2013. The topic of the research was the preference of KNLTB members for the various surface types tennis is played upon. The survey was conducted among all 8,659 players with grades 1–4 (the best and most competitive tennis players) with an email address and a random sample of almost 11,000 players with grades 5–8 (the recreational players).[1] The response rates among the players with strength 1–4 and 5–8 were 16.4 per cent and 13.8 per cent respectively. A weighing procedure was used to make the survey representative for both groups.[2] The chapter concludes with conceptual and methodological reflections on the relevance of the 'praxeological toolbox' (Nicolini, 2012) for empirical research.

Bouncing balls: emergence, affordance, choreography

This section addresses the practice of playing tennis and, in particular, how the different surfaces the game of tennis is played upon in the Netherlands influences the constitution and the performance of the practice. In their admittedly simple classification of the elements that constitute practices, Shove, Pantzar and Watson (2012: 23) present material elements next to competences and meanings. Material elements refer to anything material, ranging from objects, tools and infrastructures to life forms such as the human body. Competences are 'shared understandings of good or appropriate performance in terms of which specific enactments are judged'. They refer to knowing how to go on to background or practical knowledge – based on practical consciousness – which revolves around, quite literally in our case, a feel for the game (ibid.: 23; Giddens, 1984). Meaning is the shortcut for emotions, mental activities, motivational knowledge, representing 'the social and symbolic significance of participation at any one moment' (ibid.: 23).

The scheme stresses, first, that in any practice one finds material elements, knowing how to go on and forms of meaning, and second, that practices only emerge when these three elements are being linked. For our investigations, the scheme serves as a – very basic – starting point for analysing the impact of the playing ground on the actual playing of the tennis game. Stipulating that materials, competences and meanings are defining elements of practices implies that the material elements necessarily include life forms. Although an interesting discussion might be whether practices exist in the animal world, we take practices to always include both human bodies and non-human objects or materials. To phrase this otherwise: practices do not exist without (human) bodies, because bodies link the various elements of practices and are 'carriers' of practices (Shove *et al.*, 2012: 8; Reckwitz, 2002). The body itself is visible and material, but, contrary to other materials such as tennis balls, rackets or courts, the body is able to move by itself (one way of making linkages). More importantly, bodies are containers of invisible competences and meanings, and it is only in the doings and sayings of bodies – embodied actors – that these competences and meanings become visible at the moments they are instantiated (Giddens, 1984).

The distinction between bodies and non-human materials is crucial, because the competences which are at stake in practices often – and certainly in our case – concern the handling, the use of or the dealing with material objects by more or less skilled human beings. We will use the concept of affordance as suggested by James Gibson to refer to the 'in between'[3] of the playing body and the material circumstances and to make clear how and why the different surfaces matter in the practice of playing tennis. Affordance:

> is neither an objective property nor a subjective property; or it is both if you like. An affordance cuts across the dichotomy of subjective – objective and helps to understand its inadequacy. It is equally a fact of the environment and a fact of behavior. It is both physical and psychological, yet neither.
> (Gibson, 1979/1986: 129; see also Schmidt, 2012: 65–69)

We understand affordances not as properties of individual actors, groups or materials, but as emergent properties of practices-as-performance (events, time-spatially situated instantiations). Affordances are what the emergent practice-as-performance that one is participating in, offers, provides or furnishes. Affordances are meaningful (only) given the intention that one has or had when entering the situation. What is regarded as meaningful emerges from the interaction of the (moving) actor, having certain characteristics, intentions and competences, with the multidimensional (material, time-spatial, etcetera) context. Thus, what one sees is highly volatile and variable, because basically this is a string of options on how to move on, both literally and metaphorically, in the process of intentional behaviour. In the game, affordances are looked or sought for, and discovered in the unfolding performance of the practice of playing.

Shove *et al.* (2012) seem to use the concept of emergence in a rather self evident way. What they basically argue is that practices emerge when links are established between the elements, while practices fade out and disappear when these links dwindle. Dave Elder-Vass (2010; 2012) does not discuss social practices in much detail, but is clear and instructive on the concept of emergence. When elements combine, so he argues, a new entity emerges. This entity has emergent properties which can be explained by the properties of the elements, but cannot be explained away by them. That is to say, these properties exist only in and through the elements being combined, and not by the elements themselves. In our case this helps to understand that the (assumed differences in) playing characteristics of the various court surfaces only come 'into play' – that is they only become visible in the practice of playing tennis – when being combined with the other elements of the practice. Depending on the level of abstraction aimed for, one might consider these differences in the practice of playing tennis as merely differences in (practice as) performance. However, a close analysis of the Dutch tennis world makes clear that the differences in the playing characteristics of the various ground surfaces have resulted in (slightly) different 'temporally and spatially dispersed nexus[es] of doings and sayings' (Schatzki, 1996: 89), that is, in different practices of playing tennis on gravel, artificial turf or hard court.

The practice of playing tennis involves the fine-tuning of various bodies and objects in motion. If we take the basic task of playing a single, we need material elements such as a court, rackets and balls, actors equipped with tennis competences, and (tennis) rules that provide social, emotional and symbolic significance to the activities and makes them recognizable and meaningful as playing tennis. Besides, for the actual performance to emerge, these elements need to be situated in an intersection of particular physical (wind, sunshine) and time-spatial (time of the day, in or outdoor) conditions. In the performance of the practice, and in the minds of the players, the rackets, balls and court change from 'present-at-hand' unto 'to-hand'. Heidegger uses this distinction to make clear that there are many objects in the world (present-at-hand) that – from the perspective of the practice one studies – happen to exist, but are not a significant part of the consciousness of the actor because the actor does not interact with them. By contrast, with these objects and circumstances 'to-hand', the actor develops an intimate relationship as they become his or her equipment. Anthony King, in discussing this distinction, quotes Heidegger's example of the craftsman's hammer to elucidate this.

> The hammer's uses and properties are not determined by the a priori rational properties of the mind. Rather, the hammer's uses are given by the way that the craftsman related to it:
> 'The less we just stare at the hammer-Thing and the more we seize hold of it and use it, the more primordial does our relation to it become, and the more unveiledly is it encountered as that which it is – equipment.'
> (Heidegger, in King, 2012: 175)

The example of the hammer is then extrapolated to our being in the world.

The world which humans *experience* is not ultimately an objective present-at-hand entity which exists independently of them. The kind of world in which humans live is constituted by the attitude which they take towards it: the kinds of projects and practices in which they are engaged. The world ultimately is a form of equipment, enlivened only through the relationship which humans develop with it.

(King, 2012: 176; emphasis added)

We can substitute the hammer by a tennis racket and the world by a tennis court. The attitude towards this equipment is rooted in the intention to make points, in order for the game to go on and win the match. Playing tennis, and more specifically engaging in the project (Schatzki, 2002) of playing a tennis match, is executing a series of 'tasks' (ibid.) by producing a string of rallies, games and sets which are being recorded and counted in a particular way. The players then, in their playing attitude, have to make sure that the ball stays within the lines when they are on strike, and make sure that any ball they receive from the adversary is returned well. The scoring of points is a variable process, as there are many options to make a point and it can always be done otherwise.

In a rally, the player is keen on affordances to prevent the other from scoring and create options for scoring herself. We argue that these affordances are to be found in *all* the dimensions of the *emerging* context or in all *instantiations* of the game. Affordances offer themselves and vanish again as the game develops. The sun may be high in the sky and in one's back, so that playing a lob will make it difficult for the opponent to detect the ball. The wind may help to keep high balls that otherwise would have gone out. Affordances may also be found on the physical and mental level. The adversary may be slow in coming to the net or easily irritated by drop shots and chips. To be sure, these weaknesses of the opponent only become affordances when aptly discovered and when linked to the ability of the player to (immediately) do something with the opportunity offered here, for instance by being able to produce a drop shot when the adversary is too far behind the baseline.

A large part of noticing and making use of affordances is a matter of practising and learning, leading to experience, competences and (practical) knowledge being built up, adjusted and stored in the various layers of consciousness. Although this involves cognitive elements, much of what is learned and stored can best be understood as bodily routines or grinded movements. Better performances result from rehearsing the movements, through an iterative process of for instance playing a volley, seeing and assessing the volley thus produced, adjusting the way the volley was played if necessary, and then starting to assess the process of performing the volley again. An important part of this process of ingraining the various tennis movements is reducing the amount of time needed to assess an incoming ball or situation and 'deciding' how to (re)act. Discussing an example provided by Daniel Dennett, Elder-Vass links the 'conscious decision' to return the serve of the other player to the non-conscious execution of that decision, whereby the non-conscious 'refers to brain entities and events which we can never be conscious of'. Non-conscious is to be distinguished from unconscious, meaning non-conscious of at one time (only 'present-to-hand'), but conscious of ('to-hand') at some other times.

> Thus, the conscious decision takes place at one time and the execution of that decision is done non-consciously at a later moment. [...] There is a decision *before* the other player serves, but there is no decision *between* the serve and the return, only an implementation of that previous decision. Furthermore, the conscious decision only partially defines the behaviour to be undertaken, leaving other details to be 'filled in' non-consciously.
>
> (Elder-Vass, 2010: 94)

The more advanced player is quicker in assessing situations and incoming balls, considering options for alternative reactions (the affordances) and implementing one of these reactions, due to a deeper ingraining of this behaviour or repertoire of apposite movements in the non-conscious. In fact, what distinguishes the advanced player from the newcomer in the tennis world is that the advanced player uses the racket as equipment, and no longer as a material object that is external to his body. The advanced player has turned her own body, supplemented with a racket, into equipment, or better still: has made the racket into an integral part of her own body. She is like a dancer, performing an ensemble with the bouncing ball.

And it is here, in this choreography of tennis movements, that the variability in surfaces becomes an issue. The accuracy of the bodily movements, such as footing, balance and stability while striking, is dependent on the grip of the court surface and the bouncing behaviour of the ball, which in turn depend on the characteristics of the tennis floor. Thus, when one has learned and is used to play on gravel, one's playing behaviour is practically adjusted to gravel as surface. Consequently, a better gravel player will have developed a more primordial relation with the surface – playing on gravel will feel more natural. Playing on another surface however will lead to a more conscious performance, which comes along with the separation of elements. More time is required to think about adjustments to be made in one's playing behaviour.

These assumptions are corroborated in a survey among tennis players questioning them about their experiences with the various court surfaces. The results of the survey show first of all that the court surface matters to the tennis players.

When asked directly, 80 per cent of all respondents ($n=2.755$) finds the type of surface they play on (very) important and only 4 per cent finds it (very) unimportant. Admittedly, there may be a bias in the response because court surfaces are the topic of the survey, but in addition to this finding we also see that the appreciation of the various characteristics of a surface varies widely, indicating that for the respondents it is clear that playing on one surface differs from playing on another surface. Furthermore, players adjust the highest importance to those characteristics of court surfaces that are part of, or directly linked to the grinding of tennis movements (grip at start of the movement, stability while playing, ball bounce, etcetera), whereas more circumstantial aspects (colour of the surface, visibility of ball imprint) are considered of less importance.

All players on average appreciate gravel and gravel-like surfaces most, but this preference is more pronounced among advanced players when compared with recreational players (see Figure 8.2). Looking for the characteristics that contribute most to the higher score of gravel among advanced players compared with recreational players, it becomes obvious that for advanced players all aspects that directly affect their grinded tennis competences, such as rotation and the bounce behaviour of the ball, the grip on the surface and opportunities for 'controlled' sliding, are more important in comparison with recreational players (Figure 8.1). By contrast, recreational players regard as more important the conditions for the game to happen (the playability of the court under different weather circumstances), the practical outcomes or consequences of certain surfaces being applied (the necessity to sweep and water the court), and the likelihood of injuries to be encountered on a particular surface. Put succinctly: the attitude of recreational players is dominated by their concerns about *whether* they can play a game at all, whereas the attitude of advanced players is rooted in concerns for *how* they can play their game. This befits the finding that the more advanced players have invested most in their 'relationship' with a particular type of court surface, and for that reason tend to lose out on physical capital (Bourdieu, 1976) and playing competences when being forced to play on other surfaces.[4]

Zooming out on the game: practices of managing tennis facilities

In the previous section we have shown how the playing characteristics of the various court surfaces impact on the constitution of the practice of playing tennis. We have focused mainly on the practice-as-performance, zooming in on affordances, on the crucial role of human agency in the interplay of elements, and on the emergent properties of the practice. When in this section we start zooming out on the game, we take a look at the distribution of the various types of tennis courts across the Netherlands. We will show how a distinct distributional pattern can be discerned, indicating specific ways in which surface types link with variations in the tennis game. Before we go into such an institutional analysis of the practice-as-entity in the next section, we first pay attention to the managerial practices of decision-making regarding different surfaces.

No doubt shoes, rackets and balls impact on the constitution of the practice of playing tennis in more or less similar ways as court grounds do. Although it is tempting to dwell on the role of these materials or instruments in some detail – particularly on the linking of elements involved through the bouncing ball – we will focus on types of surfaces only. The reason for this restriction is the fact that

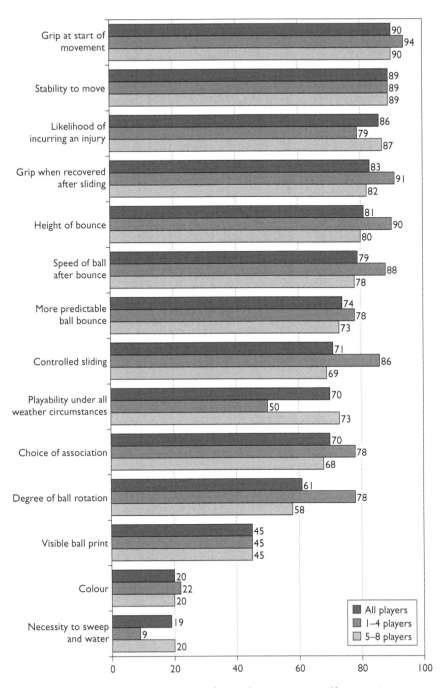

Figure 8.1 Importance of court surface characteristics (1 = not important, 100 = very important) (source: Bakker and van der Poel, 2013: 12).

decision-making regarding balls, shoes and rackets takes place on the individual level, whereas decision-making regarding tennis courts must be regarded a managerial issue. Decision-making regarding court grounds is done by the owners and operators of tennis facilities, as an integral part of the practice of managing these facilities. The dominant 'end' or rationale in this managerial practice is making profits with offering facilities for playing tennis. The profit principle is clear in the case of commercial tennis centres, but plays a role as well in non-profit cases in terms of optimizing return on investment. At the minimum level of profit thinking – the tennis club operating its own facility – the main aim of

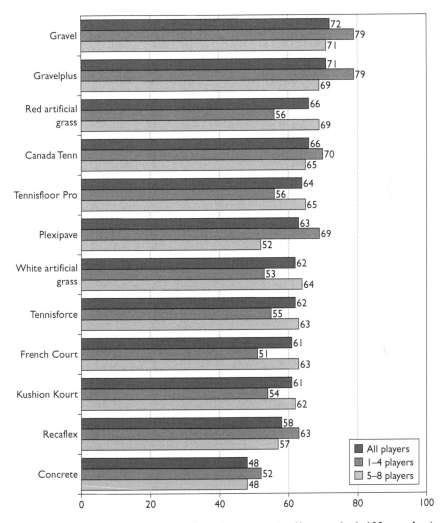

Figure 8.2 Assessment of court surface characteristics (1 = very bad, 100 = perfect) (source: Bakker and van der Poel, 2013: 18).

the managerial practice will be to minimize costs and secure revenues in such a way and at such a level that the long term operation of the facility is safeguarded. Hence there is an operational perspective from which to assess tennis court surfaces: which courts are relatively cheap in capital costs, easy to maintain and at the same time providing a maximum of playing time? Firms constructing and maintaining tennis courts compete with each other to offer the best court surface. Typically, the best court is praised by them as having almost the same playing characteristics as gravel, but without its susceptibility to weather conditions and with lower maintenance costs. So the real advantage is for the management of tennis facilities, while for the tennis players there is the reassurance that the playing characteristics remain almost the same.

Decision-making regarding the court grounds to play upon does not form an integral part of the practice of playing tennis. The outcome of this decision-making process is conditional for the practice of playing tennis, because it leads to the availability of one particular court surface as material element for the constitution of the practice. The court surface is thus an element in – or as Shove *et al.* would have it: in between (Shove *et al.*, 2012: 35–37) – at least two different practices: the practice of playing tennis and the practice of managing tennis facilities. When we focus on the decision-making regarding court surfaces, one of the most important linking pins or primary nexuses (Schatzki, 2002: 18) between the practice of playing tennis and the practice of managing the tennis facility is the Annual General Meeting (AGM) of the tennis clubs, which is a very specific and clear cut sub-practice of the amalgam of practices that together make up the tennis club.

The pivotal role of the AGM is obvious when the club itself owns or at least operates the facility.[5] Also most of the trusts that rent out tennis courts operate at arm's length of a particular club that is the main or sole user of the facility. These trusts are likely to take the recommendations of the AGM of the club very seriously. This can be expected also in case the club hires its courts from a commercial supplier or the municipality.

The AGM is the place to discuss serious issues, such as the type of surface to play on. A preliminary point to make here is that discussion requires more than 'knowing how to go on'. Although the emphasis on practical consciousness in practice theory provides a useful and necessary counterweight to the one-sided emphasis on rational choice making in the dominant social theories, we still need discursive consciousness as well, offering opportunities for reflection, rational choices, explicit and goal oriented learning and dialogues. Shove *et al.* indicate that for their purposes they 'lump multiple forms of understanding and practical knowledgeability together and simply refer to them as competence' (Shove *et al.*, 2012: 23). For our purposes however, it remains useful to consider rationality and discursive consciousness, although closely linked to practical consciousness, as distinct elements of practices.

In the discussion in the AGM about investments in the renovation or building of new tennis courts, the managerial and playing practices are directly linked.

Here it is interesting to see that the advanced players (playing ranks 1–4) can exert any influence at all, given the fact that they are outnumbered – 60 to 1 – by recreational players when looking at the total membership of the KNLTB, and likewise in most of the tennis clubs (van der Poel and Bakker, 2015: 107). This however comes less as a surprise when one realizes that the more advanced players and the members who play competition are also the more involved volunteers in clubs, and the ones showing up at the AGM. An AGM typically attracts only 5 per cent of the membership of a club, and 10 per cent at the most. So at the AGM the minority of the advanced players may become a very substantial minority, if not a majority. In addition we need to acknowledge the authority of the advanced players in serious issues regarding the practice of playing tennis. They know best, simply because they are the best. And the recreational players, acknowledge this. What they know about tennis and what they have come to learn about the game over the years, they have taken over from players they consider to be the better performers. This relationship between advanced and recreational players can be seen as the outcome of a process of socialization, taking the form of 'mimetic apprenticeship' or 'peripheral learning' (Nicolini, 2012: 79ff.). Learning to play tennis is not simply a cognitive process, nor solely a matter of ingraining a particular way of doing, but also a social process, by which 'one absorbs, and is absorbed into, a practice' and becomes progressively involved in the practice 'as one acquires growing competence on what is going on' (Nicolini, 2012: 80). Therefore it is logical that the advanced players, being the masters in tennis, constitute a 'minority with authority' in matters regarding how to play tennis, and on what kind of surface tennis ideally should be played upon.

   Although the main aim or end of 'winning' and the ensuing doings, tasks and projects in the form of playing rallies, scoring points, winning sets and tie-breaks are comparable for all participants in the practice of playing tennis, the adherence to this end and the affection and perfection with which the ensuing tasks and projects are prosecuted, differ among the competitive and recreational players. In terms of Schatzki (1996), the teleo-affective structure of the social practice of playing tennis is organized around winning. Building upon the arguments of Elder-Vass presented in the above, one could argue that this teleo-affective structure of the tennis game will be more embodied in the advanced carriers of the practice in comparison with the recreational players. In the decision-making process regarding the preferred type of court surface, the competitive, advanced players are more likely to resort to the teleo-affective structure of winning the game. It is against this background that they bring up in some detail the playing characteristics of the court surface and its impact on performance. The recreational players on the other hand tend to embrace the operational perspective, referring to the teleo-affective structure of the practice of managing tennis facilities. They stress the importance of all weather surfaces, allowing for year round operation of the tennis park. The differential assessment of surfaces that was shown to exist between advanced and recreational players can be explained by the 'tennis-playing capital', that has been built up by investing lots of time in 'practicing for winning' on a particular, mostly gravel-type of surface.

To bring the argument to a close, we find it plausible that in clubs with a relatively strong contingent of advanced players and with teams participating in the higher level KNLTB competitions, the AGM is more likely to produce a preference for playing on gravel. This in turn leads to serious pressure on actors operating at the managerial levels to provide opportunities for playing on gravel. The competitive and advanced players are relatively young in age and tend to flock into urban areas, where they find opportunities for higher education and suitable work. And indeed, it is in these areas that we find the higher percentages with regard to the availability of gravel courts (van der Poel and Bakker, 2015: 172–173). The exceptions to this rule are the peripheral districts of Zeeland and those in the North of the Netherlands. In these regions, clubs suffer from having low numbers of members per court, and thus low overall income for the club. However, these small community clubs are able to compensate for this loss by organizing the required maintenance work with the help of volunteers. When maintenance is done by volunteers, gravel is the cheapest type of court in operational costs. This can – at least partly – explain the relatively high prevalence of gravel type courts in these more peripheral districts.

Theoretically, this example makes clear, first, how the linking between material elements, competences and meaning within a practice may be affected by the outcomes of other practices. And second, that – regarding relatively permanent and expensive material elements such as court surfaces, potentially having a lasting effect on the practice of playing tennis – a process of decision-making is wanted, in which the actors involved not only draw on their competences and practical consciousness, but also on their discursive consciousness and ability to exchange information and viewpoints and engage in a more or less 'rational' discussion. Such as in the case described here with regard to the pros and cons of the various court surface types.

Intermezzo: space-to-hand

Shove *et al.* (2012: 44) argue that material elements of practices are 'capable of circulating between places and enduring over time'. Although reference is made to infrastructures, the examples given in this respect mostly appear to be consumer durables – items that can be picked up and transported, like sticks for Nordic walking. Less thoughts are given to relatively permanent physical settings, to the built environment or the locales (Giddens, 1984) of social practices. Perhaps rightly so, if one wants to consider these locales not as elements of practices, but as conditions or spatial contexts for practices. Shove *et al.* (2012: 134) advocate in this respect that 'space and time are not elements equivalent to those of materiality, meaning and competence. They do not circulate in their own right, (…)'. So a distinction seems to be made between space and materiality, implying that space is to be considered as the non-material distance or extensiveness in which practices are situated, but not as a physical setting. We find this problematic for two reasons. First, distance, extensiveness or time-space distanciation (Giddens, 1984) presupposes a material world. Distances and the impossibility of two material things being in exactly the same place are functions of materiality. By consequence, the material elements of a practice are always somehow spatially distributed in the practice. Hence, space is not only context to, but also an element of – and 'implied' in the sense of being used in – the practice, because the spatial distribution of material elements is inseparable from the material elements in practices. Looking at tennis practices-as-performance can illustrate this point in a quite obvious way. The whole point of the game is the distribution or movement – the choreography – of material elements, particularly the ball, in or through the space that is instantiated by the game. Or put otherwise, that 'piece of space' that is made 'to-hand', curved out of the spatial context that is 'present-to-hand'. At the same time however, and this is our second objection, we need to distinguish between the movable material objects in the practice, and the relatively unmovable physical setting of the practice. Relatively here means: with regard to or during the practice-as-performance. Infrastructures in general, and tennis court surfaces in particular, are to a certain extent movable, meaning that they can be constructed and broken down. Hence they are not unmovable in an absolute sense. But they are unmovable in the unfolding of tennis-as-performance and in comparison to the mobility of shoes, rackets and balls.

Drawing the distinction between material elements and physical setting elucidates some issues that were raised here before. First, it helps to understand that decision-making regarding relatively permanent and collectively used court surfaces is not the same as decision-making regarding portable and individually used tennis shoes or rackets. Second, it must be clear now that the court surface in tennis is more than just spatial context: it is also a crucial element in the constitution of the practice of playing tennis. Normally courts and court surfaces are space and physical context, thus 'present-at-hand'. However, in the practice-as-performance, in an actual game of playing tennis, the very court one plays upon becomes 'space-to-hand' and an integral part of the equipment or elements that the practice is configured with.

Diffusing grounds: innovation, circulation and power relations

We now turn to issues related to the spatial distribution of the various court surfaces in the Netherlands and the related variants of the practice of playing tennis-as-entities, which result from this. In 2004, in two out of fifteen KNLTB districts (Central and East Brabant) the majority of courts were of some artificial type, and in two adjacent eastern districts (Gelderland and Overijssel) almost half of the courts were artificial. In the other eleven districts natural or mineral courts (such as gravel, Canada Tenn and French Court) dominated the picture, with the exception of the most North-Western district, that at the time also had 43 per cent artificial courts. The picture in 2010 is that everywhere the artificial courts have gained market share, and particularly so in the districts that already had a high market share of artificial courts, and in neighbouring districts, such as West Brabant. So between 2004 and 2010 'new' types of courts spread from the 'core' in Central and East Brabant, first of all to adjacent districts, but gradually also into other districts (Bakker, 2011).

The standard way to interpret this process would be to see this as the outcome of a process of diffusion of innovation (Rogers, 2003). Technological developments are everywhere, and although there is a lot of conservatism in sports, it is undeniable there is technological advancement in sports too. In fact, elite sports are often seen as breeding ground for innovations, as an ideal setting for try-outs, pilots and the testing of new materials, techniques, metal alloys, fibers, drinks and so on. And when proven superior, we see these new materials and techniques diffuse from the elite level unto the level of amateur sports, with the effect that for instance the amateur tennis player in 2015 tends to possess better rackets and shoes in comparison with elite players twenty years ago.

However, as we have seen above, for court surfaces innovation and diffusion do not work quite this trickle-down way, as the more advanced tennis players show a preference for playing on gravel. Contrary to what one would expect and remarkably different from the diffusion of new rackets or shoes, the particular surface type preferred by elite players tends to lose ground (market share), while other types of surfaces do spread successfully.[6] This is the case because the drivers of innovation are not to be found in the playing characteristics of the new types of surfaces. The new court types are better from a managerial perspective, for reasons of longer playability and less maintenance costs. However, for tennis players they do not improve the quality of the game. The actual distribution pattern of the various court surfaces then we understand to show the following dynamics: the core areas of the artificial grass type of courts (East Brabant, Gelderland and Overijssel) are home to a couple of world leading manufacturers of artificial turfs. These manufacturers have succeeded in developing this home market while stressing the managerial advantages of the new court types, arguing their play grounds show almost the same playing characteristics as gravel type of courts. The relative resistance to the spread of this artificial grass type of court surfaces in the Randstad area can be explained by the higher proportion of advanced players and high level competition teams in these areas.

The tolerance for the variety of surfaces, and the market led diffusion of the new court types, is for many parties involved a positive thing, allowing for custom made solutions and innovation. It fits with the history of modern tennis, which developed from an aristocratic pastime to a bourgeois activity (Gillmeister, 1997; van der Poel and Bakker, 2015). Until the 1970s, tennis in the Netherlands was predominantly a local affair, maintained by volunteers and commercial suppliers, doing without support from local municipalities. Thus, tennis developed a relatively strong 'market culture' and a distinct operational practice of managing tennis complexes. In this market culture and the managerial practices that come along with it, there was room for the development of operational arguments about cost effectiveness and operational safety by becoming impervious to seasonal conditions. In the 1970s and 1980s, organized tennis became seven times as big as it was in the 1960s, leaving aside the growth of non-organized forms of playing tennis. This growth took place in the heydays of the welfare state, in which recreation and self-fulfilment were valued higher than competition. Tennis basically became a democratized pastime for a fast growing majority, and a competitive sport for a stable minority.

For a long time, the KNLTB did little more than just organizing competitions for the professional minority interested in playing official matches. The culture of its members and the lack of relevant resources prevented the KNLTB from taking a direct stance towards the clubs in issues that did not belong to the game of playing tennis, as for example in the case of managing tennis facilities. In the relationship between the KNLTB and the local tennis clubs, one can witness a 'dialectic of control' existing (Giddens, 1984). This concept stresses the fact that 'all forms of dependence offer some resources whereby those who are subordinate can influence the activities of their superiors' (ibid.: 16). The KNLTB formally possesses the power to exclude tennis clubs from competition when they, or their courts, do not meet certain standards. However, in reality the KNLTB has to find the balance between nationally defined interests of the sport of playing tennis with the financial and operational interests of the local clubs. If clubs are not allowed to play in the competition, the KNLTB will lose members and run the risk of a failed competition. As long as no other party is willing to pay for their operational deficits, local clubs have a strong argument when claiming that, for operational reasons, they have no option other than to choose a particular type of all-weather court. Only one third of all members of the KNLTB actually plays in a KNLTB competition. The other members are satisfied with playing non-competitive tennis, most of the times in their own clubs (van der Poel and Bakker, 2015: 95). It is against this backdrop that the passive attitude of the KNLTB at the time has to be understood.

In recent times however, the KNLTB has left its passive attitude regarding choice of surfaces behind, and has started to promote gravel. The intention is to prevent the disappearance of gravel courts all together and to preserve a certain contingent of gravel courts, particularly for the purposes of training and high level competition. Interestingly, the advice of the KNLTB to seriously consider the merits of gravel when entering a process of court renovation, mirrors the arguments of the manufacturers of courts surfaces as discussed above. First the KNLTB stresses the playing characteristics of gravel, particularly the fact that it provides the ideal 'grounding' for learning how to play tennis. At the same time however it addresses so-called misunderstandings with respect to managerial issues, and advocates the facts that gravel can be played upon almost year round, that it is low in capital costs, and that it can be low in running costs when volunteers do a substantial part of the maintenance (KNLTB, 2014b).

This section has demonstrated that the diffusion of the various tennis-court surfaces in the Netherlands can be understood as the outcome of power relations both within and between social practices. Within the KNLTB, the board has changed its position with respect to the meanings to be given to the variety of court surfaces, leading to their professed preference for gravel. However, the KNLTB lacks the power to compel managers of tennis facilities to adopt gravel as their preferred court surface. As a result, the national board tries to convince local managers by providing arguments which could underpin the preference for gravel. Within the practices of managing tennis facilities, local managers seek to find a balance between the playing characteristics of the court surfaces on the one hand, and the playability and operational advantages on the other. The balance in any particular case will depend on the relative power of the interests represented within the practice, most notably the more advanced tennis players, the recreational players and the managers of the tennis facilities. We identified the Annual General Meeting as the nexus for these practices, serving as the most important linking pin involved in the decision-making process regarding court surfaces. Such a public form of decision-making is likely to take place when large investments in material elements for the practice of playing tennis are at stake. These investments will have long term effects both on the operation of the tennis club as well as the practice of playing tennis at this club. To be able to understand the dynamics at work, we distinguished between easy movable material elements, such as tennis rackets and balls, and relatively unmovable material elements or physical settings, such as court surfaces. Since physical settings have a shared, collective character, decision-making on these material elements demands collective decision-making and the discursive exchange of information and arguments.

Conclusions

In this chapter we used practice theories to discuss the social practices of playing tennis and of managing a tennis club. In applying the theory to an empirical case, we did not only show the relevance of the theory for understanding reality. We as well sought to contribute to practice theories by confronting a number of both theoretical and methodological issues. We first summarize our contribution to four specific theoretical issues before considering some methodological implications of our practice approach.

First, we discussed the concept of affordance and its relevance for understanding how social practices are performed. The concept provides a theoretical basis for the methodological distinction between practice-as-performance and practice-as-entity or, in Giddens' terms, between the analysis of strategic action (bracketing institutions) and institutional analysis (bracketing human agency or performances). The concept of practice-as-entity refers to the abstracted set of elements and their linkages that we see recurring across time and space. However, these elements and their linkages are not completely fixed, but *afford* to be toyed around with during the performance or instantiation of the practice. Also, we do not see affordances themselves as fixed property of material elements or part of actors' competences, but as an emergent property of practice-as-performance. Affordances are a function of the flux of activities, of the ever changing potentialities of linking the various elements of social practices to each other and to context, in one way or another.

Second we argued that it is inevitable for practice theorists to conceive of space (better still: time-space) not only in terms of context or condition for practices. Because of the presence of material elements in social practices, space should as well be regarded as a constitutive element of practices. How exactly material elements are distributed within practices and how they are moved around in social practices is a distinctive choreography for particular practices and sometimes – as in playing tennis – the essential point of the practice. To fully grasp this role of space in social practices, we argued for the necessity to distinguish between human bodies as being able to move themselves around, objects or things that can be moved around, and relatively unmovable or immobile elements, such as infrastructures, buildings and other physical settings.

Third, we suggested the Heideggerian movement of objects from 'present-to-hand' unto 'to-hand' and vice versa to be very fruitful, both analytically and methodologically. Methodologically, because it helps to limit the elements which should be taken into consideration when studying social practices. Analytically it makes it possible to move beyond conventional thinking in terms of distances, settings, bodies and objects as context or conditions, and to understand these material elements as integral and constitutive parts of social practices.

A fourth conceptual issue raised in the chapter dealt with discursive consciousness, using the example of the Annual General Meeting. Although we agree with practice theorists that most day-to-day activities are done routinely on the basis of background or practical knowledge, we argued that more or less rational decision-making processes do occur and should not be overlooked since they can have far reaching effects on the conditions for day-to-day activities in the future. Our empirical illustration in this respect is the fact that, although most tennis playing is a matter of practical, even ingrained competences, there is only one meeting of the AGM needed to fix one material element of the practice – the court surface – in such a way that it will have a lasting impact on the way tennis will be played over the next fifteen years. Due to the significant and lasting effect of the court surfaces on the practice of tennis-as-performance, the – discursive – exchange of information and arguments in the context of collective decision-making at the AGM is crucial.

As for the methodological implications of our practice approach, the first comment to make is that we would like to stretch the Heideggerian discussion of 'equipment' to its relevance for practice research. Equipment we argued referred to the primordial relation the advanced tennis player develops with the court surface, his racket and so on. In a similar vein it could refer to the relationship the PhD researcher develops with his or her object of social science research. It seems likely that it requires a lot of time working with the praxeological toolbox (Nicolini, 2012), a process of trial and error, in order to develop the necessary methodological experience and skills to use the various concepts in a precise, efficient and effective manner. A 'praxeologist' thus becomes an artisan-researcher. However, most artisans deliver products such as tables, vases and paintings. Products which are immediately understandable and ready for use by anybody. But what if the product is a form of writing like this book? Is it possible to write something that is based on praxeological analysis, that is readable for people that are not introduced to this craft themselves? On the other hand, the more one tries to write for a wider audience, the more questions arise about the reliability of the analysis. Put otherwise, if in the text you leave out the theoretical concepts and references to theoretical discussion (i.e. the tools from the practice theory toolbox), what remains of the possibility of controlling the analysis by re-reading, re-analysing and/or repeating it?

To paraphrase Anthony King (2012: 215), the world of tennis cannot be understood without taking into account the way tennis players understand tennis. We documented the steady decrease of the number of gravel courts in the Netherlands (15 per cent over the last ten years) while also showing that tennis players score gravel surfaces as being highest on playing characteristics and for that reason to be favoured as the most ideal court surface for playing their game. This seemed to be contradictory at first sight. As we have shown, however, only in those cases where the interests of the 'gravel lovers' could be aligned with the interests of management – which is most likely to happen when advanced players control the AGM of a club which owns the courts and has operational responsibility for them – we see gravel courts flowering. In all other cases, the operational perspective is likely to prevail over the game-playing perspective.

The methodological point we like to emphasize here is the fact that our analyses rely on the 'sayings' (responses given in interviews and via questionnaires) of the tennis players and other relevant actors, and much less upon the direct surveying of 'doings'. Gravel and artificial grass do not speak directly to us. What we as researchers know about gravel and artificial grass, about what they 'do' or what difference they 'make' in the constitution of practices, is reported to us by the sayings of players who perform on these surfaces. It is difficult to imagine gaining direct access to the actual doings in a similar way as we have to sayings. We can watch tennis being played on different surfaces, but then we have to rely on what we see. Basically this is substituting the interpretation of the players by our own interpretation, while missing out on the interpretation of the player who is directly involved in the unfolding practice, and on the time-spatial embeddedness of this interpretation of the player. Having said this, it should be clear that the challenge of learning how to use the practice toolkit for praxeologizing social reality in a feasible manner means that researchers should prevent lapsing into a form of methodological actor-centredness, and instead keep their eyes, ears and hands focused on the integral activity bundle we call social practice.

Notes

1 The KNLTB uses a Dynamic Player's Strength System (DSS) by which members are graded from 1 (elite level; 157 members in 2014) to 9 (members starting to play tennis). Two-thirds of all KNLTB members (418,000 out of 610,000) are graded 8 (van der Poel and Bakker, 2015: 106–107).
2 We thank the KNLTB for granting permission to use data from commissioned research and its contribution to the NWO Research Programme Sport Facilities and Sport Participation, and NWO for the support for the research that made this chapter possible.
3 Robert Schmidt in his discussion of affordances argues that it directs analytical attention to 'das Dazwischen' (Schmidt, 2012: 66–67).
4 Although the theory explains why more advanced players value the playing characteristics more than recreational players, it does not explain their preference for gravel. Theoretically, the advanced players can develop an intimate relationship with any type of surface, and thus a preference for the type on which they have learnt to play the game. As yet we have two hypotheses to explain the preference for gravel: (1) It can be a matter of path-dependency: a majority of the present advanced players have learnt the game on gravel. (2) Gravel, due to its playing characteristics, is 'objectively' more suited to learn to play the game. A combination of these factors is also feasible.
5 Some 62 per cent of the Dutch clubs are responsible for daily maintenance of the courts, and 44 per cent for all maintenance tasks (Hoekman *et al.* (eds), 2013: 166).
6 We see something similar happening in the field of soccer. The elite soccer teams in the Netherlands (Ajax, Feijenoord, PSV, etcetera) are the most reluctant to leave their grass turfs. The diffusion of artificial turfs has started on the amateur level and meets resistance on the elite level.

References

Bakker, S., 2011. *The Artificialisation of Tennis Courts* (master thesis). Tilburg: Tilburg University.

Bakker, S. and van der Poel, H., 2013. *Tennisbanen in Nederland. Een onderzoek naar de voorkeuren van de KNLTB-leden voor de verschillende tennisbanenin Nederland. (Tennis Courts in the Netherlands. Research into the Preferences of KNLTB-members for Different Types of Tennis Courts.* (Internal report KNLTB). Utrecht: Mulier Institute.

Bourdieu, P., 1976. *Outline of a Theory of Practice.* Cambridge: Cambridge University Press.

Elder-Vass, D., 2010. *The Causal Power of Social Structures. Emergence, Structure and Agency.* Cambridge: Cambridge University Press.

Elder-Vass, D., 2012. *The Reality of Social Construction.* Cambridge: Cambridge University Press.

Gibson, J.J., 1979/1986. *The Ecological Approach to Visual Perception.* Boston: Houghton Mifflin.

Giddens, A., 1984. *The Constitution of Society. Outline of the Theory of Structuration.* Cambridge: Polity Press.

Gillmeister, H., 1997. *Tennis. A Cultural History.* New York: New York University Press.

Hoekman, R., Hoenderkamp, K. and van der Poel, H., eds, 2013. *Sportaccommodaties in beeld. (Sport Facilities in the Picture.)* Utrecht/Nieuwegein: Mulier Instituut/Arko Sports Media.

King, A., 2012. *The Structure of Social Theory.* London and New York: Routledge.

KNLTB Royal Dutch Lawn Tennis Association), 2014. *Baansoorten in beeld. (Court Surfaces in the Picture.)* www.knltb.nl.

KNLTB (Royal Dutch Lawn Tennis Association), 2014a. G*ravel noodzakelijk voor de tennissport. (Gravel Essential for Tennis.)* Published in *Centre Court* (electronic newsletter), 5 August . www.knltb.nl.

KNLTB (Royal Dutch Lawn Tennis Association), 2014b. *De zes grootste misverstanden over gravel en kunstgrasachtige baansoorten. (The six biggest misconceptions about gravel and artificial grass surfaces).* Published in Centre Court (electronic newsletter), 24 July 24. www.knltb.nl.

Nicolini, D., 2012. *Practice Theory, Work, & Organization. An Introduction.* Oxford: Oxford University Press.

Rogers, E.M., 2003. *Diffusion of Innovations.* New York: Free Press.

Schatzki, T.R., 1996. *Social Practices. A Wittgensteinian Approach to Human Activity and the Social.* Cambridge: Cambridge University Press.

Schatzki, T.R., 2002. *The Site of the Social. A Philosophical Account of the Constitution of Social life and Change.* University Park PA: The Pennsylvania State University Press.

Schmidt, R., 2012. *Soziologie der Praktiken. Konzeptionelle Studien und empirische Analysen.* (Sociology of Practices.) Berlin: Suhrkamp.

Shove, E., Pantzar, M. and Watson, M., 2012. *The Dynamics of Social Practice. Everyday Life and how It Changes.* Los Angeles: Sage.

Van der Poel, H. and Bakker, S., eds, 2015. *Tennis in Nederland. De tenniswereld in al haar aspecten geserveerd.(Tennis in the Netherlands. The World of Tennis Served in all Its Aspects.)* Nieuwegein: Arko Sports Media.

Part III

Zooming out on practices as embedded entities

Chapter 9

Growing urban food as an emerging social practice

*Karin Dobernig, Esther Veen and
Peter Oosterveer*

Introduction

Social practices come and go. They emerge, merge, evolve and disappear amidst a range of other social practices. How these dynamics of change take place, how we can identify emerging social practices and how social practices develop over time are interesting questions, the answers to which can contribute towards a better understanding of what makes up a practice and how different social practices interact. Grasping how social practices emerge, persist and disappear also aids understanding and assessing social change from the perspective of practice theory (Warde, 2005; Shove *et al.*, 2012). In this chapter we aim to address issues related to practice theory and social change by taking a closer look at the practices of growing food in urban environments. Our analysis will be guided by the following questions: what exactly do we mean when referring to 'urban food growing' as a social practice, and how does this specific practice relate to other relevant social practices already existing and unfolding in urban spatial contexts?

In recent years, urban food growing has attracted much interest from science, the public and policy in OECD societies (Kneafsey *et al.*, 2008; Lovell, 2010; Oosterveer and Sonnenfeld, 2012; Sonnino and Spayde, 2014; Steel, 2008). While often framed as an emerging food movement (see for example Mah and Thang, 2013; Renting *et al.*, 2012; Specht *et al.*, 2014), growing food in cities is not a new practice per se. The United States, for example, saw victory gardens during World Wars I and II (Kortright and Wakefield, 2011; Lawson, 2005) and a community gardening movement that took hold in the late 1960s and early 1970s (Lawson, 2005; Saldivar-Tanaka and Krasny, 2004). In Europe, allotment gardens have existed for centuries. As early as in the fourteenth century, Dutch workers grew food to supplement their diets in rented gardens or on land donated by philanthropists (Berendsen, 2001). Today, what we observe is a vast diversity of urban food growing projects, ranging from small-scale window farming to allotment and community gardens to large-scale rooftop farms and hydroponic greenhouses. Some scholars (Cohen *et al.*, 2012) have categorized urban food growing initiatives into community gardens (which are managed by a group of local individuals or volunteers); institutional gardens and farms (which are affiliated to schools, hospitals or churches); community farms (which are managed by a non-profit organization); and commercial farms (which are managed as for-profit businesses).

In both public and academic discourses, the various types of urban food growing tend to be subsumed under the notion of 'urban agriculture' (McClintock, 2014). However, given the diversity of urban food growing initiatives, one might wonder if it is warranted to talk about one social practice? More specifically, we in this chapter address the question whether or not and to what extent one should regard urban food growing as a social practice in terms of what Elizabeth Shove has labelled a 'recognizable entity' (Shove *et al.*, 2012). Although it may be analytically helpful to employ an umbrella concept such as urban agriculture, one then risks losing sight of the multiple logics, dynamics and forms which are present within the field of urban food growing. For example, while in former times, the practice was linked to meanings of self-sufficiency and community empowerment (Lawson, 2005), urban food growing today is increasingly framed as an innovative activity for young and hip urbanites who want to foster new skills and capabilities, gain new experiences and help change the relationship that urban people have with food and the environment. Thus, categorizing all urban food growing initiatives under the heading of urban agriculture would make us treat them as if they were characterized by the same doings and sayings, which might not necessarily be the case.

In this chapter, we use social practice theory to gain a closer and more nuanced view of the heterogeneity of food growing activities unfolding in the urban centres of OECD countries today. We focus on developments in OECD countries because, contrary to developing countries, for many years, growing food in cities was considered a disappearing phenomenon. Over the past decade however, this social practice seems to have become part of a modern urban lifestyle. In the United States, for example, the recent popularity of urban food growing is reflected in the vast number of websites and blogs, the growing number of dedicated print and online publications, the emergence of educational training programmes as well as in the coverage of the topic in United States news media. Also in a large number of cities, for instance Toronto, Malmö and Barcelona, practices of growing food in the city are supported by municipal authorities since they are considered to be key elements of the sustainability profile of the city.

By employing a social practice perspective we go beyond a restricted perspective on food growing per se, aiming to develop a more grounded understanding of the social dynamics that are taking place. This enables us to identify differences between multiple urban food growing initiatives and assess whether urban food growing can and should be defined as a new emerging social practice, as a resurgent practice, or as a combination of both. For this purpose, we apply Shove *et al.*'s (2012) concepts of competences, materials and meanings as integrated elements of social practices to two examples of urban food growing:

an urban community garden in Amsterdam and an entrepreneurial urban farm in New York City. By choosing two cases that appear from the outset to be rather dissimilar, we hope to gain a more in-depth understanding of how the meanings, competences and materials associated with urban food growing may differ. In this way, we contribute to the discussion on practice theory and research by further developing the understanding of what actually constitutes a social practice, by specifying in empirical detail the elements or components which make up a practice, and by showing how different practices interact and how these interrelations co-define what the practice is about. The two cases are likely to show pathways of development which are different because of the interrelationships they establish with other practices over time. By following their pathways of change we are able to better grasp the kind of practice dynamics at work.

In the next section we provide arguments for conceptualizing urban food growing as a social practice. Subsequently, we present the two case studies and then compare them in order to gain a better understanding of their characteristics and dynamics as social practices. Finally, we present our main conclusions and discuss how studying empirical cases is instrumental for deepening the theoretical understanding of how social practices develop and change over time.

Urban food growing as a social practice

Some authors consider producing food within city boundaries as a way of increasing food security in an era where natural resources are becoming scarce and future food supplies are under pressure (Mansfield and Mendes, 2013; Morgan, 2009). Others regard urban food as a more sustainable alternative to contemporary food provisioning. Growing food in the city is presented as a possible response to concerns about mass food that is anonymously produced in contemporary industrialized and globalized societies (McClintock, 2010). These accounts also claim that urban food growing brings food production closer to food consumption and thereby bridges the historic separation between producers and consumers, something which is considered essential to assure safe and sustainable food provisioning (Jarosz, 2008; Mah and Thang, 2013; Mansfield and Mendes, 2013; McClintock, 2010; Morgan, 2009; Sonnino, 2009/2010). Several authors have indicated that the benefits of urban food growing go beyond the production of food only. Grewal and Grewal (2012), for example, summarize the potential benefits of urban food growing as follows: access to healthy and nutritious food, reduced human impact on the environment, strengthened local economies and an increased sense of community. Others report that participating in community gardens helps building social capital, mutual trust and reciprocity (Teig *et al.*, 2009), and may provide wage-earning opportunities for community members (Ferris *et al.*, 2001).

We regard urban food growing as a social practice in the way it is defined by Theodore Schatzki (2002): a particular nexus of doings and sayings. After Schatzki, we also draw on the work of Elizabeth Shove *et al.* (2012) when conceptualizing social practices of urban food growing as shared bundles of activities that integrate materials (technologies, physical entities and the body itself), competences (skills and know-how) and meanings (symbolic meanings, ideas and aspirations), and which evolve over time as changes occur in the ingredients of the practices. Practices come into existence, persist and disappear when links between these three elements are established, sustained or broken (Shove *et al.*, 2012). When used in this way, the framework of social practices helps us to conceptualize stability and change in the reproduction of practices across time and space.

By using a practice perspective, we go beyond the separate studies of management, organization and planning of urban food growing on the one hand, and surveying people's motivations on the other hand. Instead, we recognize that urban food growing is a social, material and cultural activity involving issues of identity, lifestyle, community and fun, in combination with the material production of food and income. We are particularly interested in finding out whether different urban food growing initiatives can be seen as variations of a single social practice, or instead should be treated as distinct social practices. By exploring similarities and differences between (categories of) social practices, we contribute to practice theories in a conceptual way.

In our analysis of practices and social change, we recognize that practices can be seen as 'emerging' in different ways and for various reasons. For instance, when innovative technologies are being introduced, the new materiality might require novel competences and generate new meanings. Hydroponics, for example, involves growing food in mineral nutrient solutions instead of soil and thus demands specific knowledge and skills from the people working with this technology. A practice may also be seen as emergent when an existing practice becomes more popular through changing relationships with other practices. Hence, allotment gardens may attract new groups of people for whom this activity has a different meaning in comparison with the established groups of practitioners, for instance because they see it as a way to contribute to sustainability, linking it to other sustainability practices aimed at increasing their self-sufficiency. Finally, a practice may emerge through combinations of existing practices creating new meanings, sometimes followed by new competences and materials as well. Urban residents may, for instance, combine the practices of food growing and socializing, creating a meeting place out of a garden, simultaneously improving competences regarding cultivation.

Using as our cases community gardening in Amsterdam and entrepreneurial rooftop farming in New York City, we first analyse their specific combinations of materials, competences and meanings in a way as suggested by Shove *et al.* (2012). We then focus on the dynamics of change implied in these particular two cases of urban food growing practices. Dynamics of change which result from their components – we pay particular attention to the constitutive role of the material elements of the practice – and from their interactions with other social practices.

Community gardening in Amsterdam: the case of Trompenburg

The major cities in the Netherlands are relatively small (even Amsterdam has less than one million inhabitants), and planning regulations strictly limit urban sprawl, so the countryside is never far away. Dutch cities do not have 'ghettos', and food deserts are virtually non-existent (Van der Schans, 2010). Medium-sized supermarkets are present in most parts of the city, and they all sell fresh fruit and vegetables. Although this suggests that food is not as far from its consumers as it is in some areas in the United States, urban food growing has taken off in the Netherlands as well. Urban food growing initiatives build on a long tradition in the Netherlands. Allotment gardens (Groening, 2005) emerged in combination with urbanization – particularly since the end of the nineteenth and the beginning of the twentieth centuries (Barthel et al., 2010). Allotments are typically located at the edge of the city, are sized about 300 to 400 m², have a toolshed or small cabin on the plot, and are rented by individual citizens from the municipal authorities. They are used for food production as well as recreation, although over time the second purpose has taken precedence over the first.

In recent years, other urban food growing initiatives have been taking hold, with community gardens popping up everywhere, often stimulated or facilitated by city governments. For example, Cupidohof in Almere was initiated by a group of local residents, aiming to create a meeting place in the neighbourhood. Children maintain small plots in this community garden, which they cultivate under the supervision of one of the residents. 'Tuin aan de Maas' in the city of Rotterdam is another example of a local, bottom-up initiative. A group of local residents started using this plot of land, which was due for development but deferred under the influence of the post 2008 economic crisis. The garden brings together neighbours who communally practice their hobby, beautify the area and meet fellow citizens. To assess in some more detail the novelty of recent urban food growing initiatives in the Netherlands we present the case of Trompenburg community garden in Amsterdam.

Trompenburg community garden was established in 2009 at the initiative of one of the local residents. It occupies a narrow strip of land next to a playground, unsuited for most other uses because of its small width (2.5 m). The strip is divided into fourteen individual plots and one communal herb garden. Each plot is approximately 2.5 m long (hence a total of 5 m²) (see Figures 9.1a and 9.1b). Gardeners visit their garden once or twice a week on average.

We designed an online questionnaire to determine the gardeners' use of the garden and the nature of their produce, as well as their social connections at the garden. We received twelve filled-in questionnaires and also interviewed five respondents face-to-face. The interviews focused on similar themes as the questionnaire but made it possible to speak about the topics in more detail.

Inspired by his involvement in networks related to growing food in the city, the initiator of Trompenburg community garden started the garden in an effort to

Figure 9.1a Trompenburg community garden.

Figure 9.1b Trompenburg community garden.

combine food growing with building social relations in the neighbourhood. Hence, the initiator was attracted by the 'new' social meaning of urban food growing as it emerged in recent years. Our case study material however revealed that most of the other practitioners engaged in Trompenburg community garden are primarily interested in the actual activity of growing food. This illustrates that although Trompenburg may be seen as a manifestation of the emerging practice of urban food growing, the actual competences (skills and knowledge of growing food); meanings (the enjoyment of eating one's own vegetables); and materials (the produce resulting from gardening) involved in this practice are not all that new. Urban food growing in Trompenburg largely resembles the combination of elements that are to be found as well at the more traditional allotments. The relationship with food does not seem to have changed, nor has the garden turned into a cool place to be. Instead of witnessing the emergence of a new kind of practice, urban food growing in Trompenburg seems to reflect a conventional social practice. A practice that is adapted and gradually transformed rather than re-invented and emerging anew. To further elaborate and specify this observation, we discuss the practice of gardening in Trompenburg for its three Shovian components: the competences employed to maintain it, the most important materials associated with it and the social meanings attached to this particular garden.

Enjoying trial and error

Although urban food growing is often a broader social activity (for example involving culture, leisure and social networking), people involved in Trompenburg are primarily engaged in the practice of growing food. Figure 9.2 shows that respondents' main reason for being involved in the garden relates to their enjoyment of growing food. The main meaning of Trompenburg therefore lies in the fact that it gives gardeners the opportunity to practice their hobby.

Although being engaged in the practice of urban food growing requires a specific set of competences, not all incoming participants are proficient gardeners. This gap is individually solved by trial and error. If a certain cultivation technique does not work, practitioners try something different. This experimenting increases people's skills over time. They get to know which vegetables grow best on this particular plot and what kinds of techniques work well. Hence, people become skilled practitioners by being engaged in the practice of gardening over a longer period of time. Learning and becoming a skilled practitioner is in itself a source of pleasure for many gardeners, as illustrated by this quote:

> The best part … seeing how the plants are doing, does it work, and should I do it differently, and if it doesn't work this year, then I try another spot and it works, trying out these kinds of things.
>
> (TB2)

Practitioners also learn from each other. They share experiences and give each other advice. Most interviewees clearly stated that they look at plots of fellow citizens:

> I look at the others and I think, my, they still have endives, I didn't even consider that this vegetable grows so late in the season.

> (TB3)

Hence, it is recognized by gardeners that they need particular skills and competences to engage in the practice of urban food growing. Gaining these competences over time, under the influence of learning-by-doing processes, is

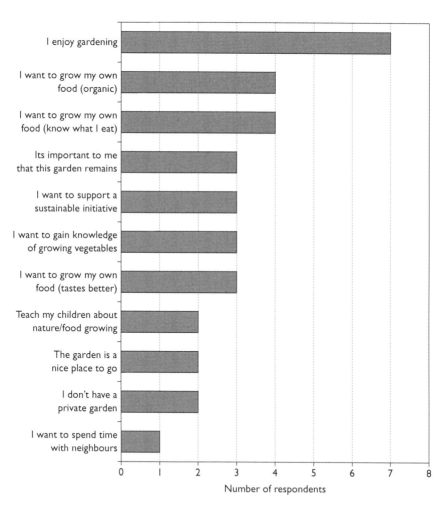

Figure 9.2 What were your main reasons for joining this garden? (*n* = 12, up to three answers possible. Statements which were not ticked were removed).

something that most of them enjoy. The required skills are not limited to the practice of gardening. Practitioners also need to be able to process the produce which they harvest and therefore seek to develop skills in the related practices of storing and cooking self-grown foodstuff.

Eating the harvest

The practice of urban food growing comprises different activities, such as sowing and weeding, and also harvesting. The harvested produce is therefore a result of the food growing practice. Being engaged in the practice of urban food growing means being involved in the acquisition of vegetables (Veen *et al.*, 2014). Trompenburg's plots are only small, however, so the urban-grown vegetables play a limited role in people's diets. Most respondents cook two to three times a month with home-grown food, and the produce constitutes less than half of the vegetables they eat (see Figures 9.3 and 9.4). Thus, while engagement in the practice of urban food growing leads to eating the harvest, the actual role of this garden in people's diets is modest.

Although the quantity of vegetables people harvest is relatively small, the importance attached to eating one's own grown vegetables is high. Our questionnaire shows that gardeners attribute specific qualities to their vegetables, which are important reasons for growing them. Respondents state that they enjoy the vegetables because they are local and organic, and that they appreciate the idea of eating freshly harvested produce because such vegetables taste better than those bought from the shop. Clearly, the meaning of the harvest encompasses more than what could be expected from only judging the volume of the produce.

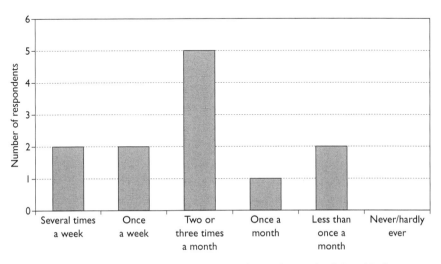

Figure 9.3 How often do you eat vegetables from the garden? (*n* = 12, 1 answer possible).

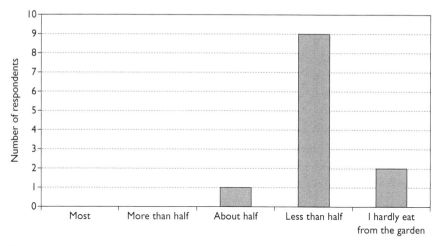

Figure 9.4 What proportion of the vegetables you and your family eat comes from the garden? (*n* = 12, 1 answer possible).

Eating one's own harvest symbolizes eating 'pure' and 'real' food, in contrast to the perceived uniformity of food purchased in the supermarket. Hence, the meaning of the practice of urban food growing is to be found as well in the home-grown nature of its produce (vegetables). Gaining access to these vegetables requires specific competences – cultivating an urban plot yourself – which then also infuse the material entities yielded with specific meanings. This shows the strong integration of the three elements in a way as suggested by Shove *et al.*

Getting to know your neighbours

It was shown in Figure 9.2 that most Trompenburg gardeners did not have social motivations for becoming involved in the garden. However, by engaging in the practice of urban food growing, practitioners meet others who do the same. They have conversations whilst gardening

> Sarah sometimes comes along when I'm working, or Jill, I see her and then we chat and then we continue working and we greet each other.
>
> (TB3)

Such small chats increase the pleasure of engaging in the practice, even though they are only considered 'nice extras', as expressed by this interviewee:

> Well no, they are not important, but it is fun. I enjoy it when somebody else is there too.
>
> (TB3)

Hence, although interactions with others at the garden plots could be considered relatively shallow, the garden does indeed have a social meaning. This is also reflected in the answers to our questionnaire, in which respondents were asked to tick up to three items of a range of statements. Figure 9.5 shows that respondents like the social atmosphere at the garden, and that only a small number of them agree with the statement that knowing people at the garden is not important. Figure 9.5 also supports our finding that the garden does not fulfil an important social role.

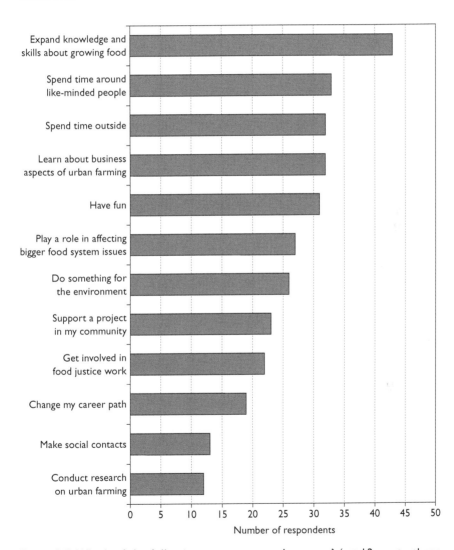

Figure 9.5 Which of the following statements apply to you? (*n* = 12, up to three answers possible).

So, while the appreciation of urban food growing in Trompenburg is primarily connected to the process of cultivation, the learning by doing, and the cooking and eating of the self-grown vegetables, doing this social practice together with others makes it a nicer experience. As summarized by one of our respondents:

> It's hard to weigh what's important. See, if there wouldn't be a garden, then I wouldn't have these contacts. (...) So the garden is first of all ... gardening is the first motivation. I chose to do it, I thought it was a nice idea because it's in the neighbourhood.

(TB4)

This finding shows that the meaning that Trompenburg gardeners attach to the 'new' practice of urban food growing resembles what allotment gardening usually means for its practitioners. In both cases practitioners primarily enjoy the cultivation and the resulting harvest. Social benefits such as chatting to others while gardening are perceived as added benefits, rather than as a reason for becoming involved in the practice in the first place (Veen *et al.*, under review).

To summarize the Amsterdam case of urban food growing in Trompenburg, we argue that this local neighbourhood activity attracts citizens who see the garden as an opportunity to easily engage in growing vegetables and to enjoy the products of their own labour. While the founders of the urban food growing movement are motivated by wider social goals, they are less prominent for the practitioners participating in our research. Social interaction is appreciated, but growing urban food at Trompenburg is not regarded a new practice in terms of being part of this wider social movement of bringing food into the city. The urban food growing practice of Trompenburg can at its best be viewed as a merger of two already existing practices, namely (allotment) gardening and neighbourhood building, without generating some of the new meanings, competences and skills as advertised by some of the founders of the movement on urban agriculture or transition towns (Pinkerton and Hopkins, 2009).

Entrepreneurial rooftop farming in New York City: the case of Brooklyn Grange

New York City presents a node of urban food growing practices unfolding in a cultural and political context that stands in contrast to most European countries, including the Netherlands. Although the city is characterized by high population density and immense property values, its economic and cultural robustness as well as vibrant food culture provide an attractive context for urban food growing initiatives. New York City's industrial and manufacturing areas are especially suitable for rooftop agriculture due to the existing infrastructure, access to capital, and public interest and support (Ackerman, 2011). At the policy-level, urban agriculture is integrated into the city government's plans to transform New

York City's food infrastructure and promote more sustainable food consumption patterns among its citizens (Brannen, 2010; Stringer, 2010).

Brooklyn Grange considers itself the leading rooftop farming and intensive green roofing business in the United States. It currently operates the world's largest rooftop soil farm on two roofs located in Long Island City, Queens (0.4 ha) and in the Brooklyn Navy Yard (0.6 ha). In addition to vegetables and herbs, the farm keeps egg-laying hens and has launched a commercial apiary where bees are bred and cultivated. Moreover, Brooklyn Grange provides green roof consulting and installation services to clients, and rents out the farm for dinner parties, wedding ceremonies and yoga classes. The farm also has an educational non-profit arm which hosts thousands of New York City's school kids each season for educational tours and workshops. Furthermore, the farm collaborates with the Refugee and Immigrant Fund in offering job training to immigrants and refugees.

Brooklyn Grange was established in the spring of 2010 by three motivated food entrepreneurs, who transformed the vacant rooftop of an industrial building in Queens into a functioning commercial venture. For the opening of their location in the Brooklyn Navy Yard in the summer of 2012, the farm received a grant issued by the New York City Department of Environmental Protection to support green infrastructure projects. The business is financed through private equity, loans, and money generated through grassroots fundraising events and crowd funding platforms. It reports steady growth every season after having broken even in its first year of operation. The farm currently employs eleven staff members and also runs a trainee programme in which hundreds of people have already participated. Their mission is to 'create a fiscally sustainable model for urban agriculture and to produce healthy, delicious vegetables for the local community while doing the ecosystem a few favours as well'. Since its establishment, Brooklyn Grange has received considerable media attention, both across the United States and abroad.

To gain deeper insights into the social practices unfolding at an entrepreneurial urban farm such as Brooklyn Grange, data have been gathered through participant observations at the farm from April until November 2013, semi-structured interviews with employed staff members and volunteers ($n=13$), an online survey with volunteers who took part in the urban farm's trainee programme during the 2013 season ($n=45$) as well as a review of documents and social media content. In the analysis, we outline the material elements that constitute the practice of entrepreneurial rooftop farming (that is bodies, soil, vegetables and roof) and their integrated connections to competences and symbolic meanings.

Knowing where your food comes from

The routine farming practices of planting, weeding, watering and harvesting which are unfolding at the rooftop farm hardly entail any advanced technology or machinery. Instead, the bodies of the practice carriers (in particular their hands) represent the key material which is required for the practice to be enacted on a daily basis. Notions of 'I enjoy doing physical work' (BG1) indicate the appeal this way of 'doing work' has for the people at the farm.

The bodies of the participants are also linked to another key material element of the practice – the soil as the medium which essentially all natural food comes from. The soil has high symbolic quality as it connects to meanings of 'knowing where food comes from', which is seen as an essential prerequisite in order to induce change in the current food system:

> So, I think it's silly or naive to think that urban farming is the savior of these issues of the food system. But I think it is part of the solution, especially with education. To have people in the city be exposed to food that comes from the ground and not from the supermarket.
>
> (BG2)

Being demarcated by the materials of soil and hands, the practice of rooftop urban farming is about reconnecting to food, nature and the community (e.g. McClintock, 2010; Dobernig and Mincyte, under review). It is also a process of 'collective remembering', as the practice participants are bringing to their minds the awareness of a competence from past generations. In their analysis of the practice of driving, Shove *et al.* (2012) coined the notion of 'collective forgetting', whereby certain capabilities (such as reading a map) are described as vanishing irreversibly as their linkages with other elements of the practice break. However, competences may also lie 'dormant, persisting in the memory for years without being activated' (Shove *et al.*, 2012: 34). Indeed, we find that growing (urban) food is talked about as a skill that has been forgotten because of the convenience-oriented industrial food system. A skill however that is now being resurrected:

> I mean, our parents' generation, our grand-parents' generation, everybody knew how to grow food. Maybe they chose not to but they all knew how. And then in our generation, none of us knew and now all of a sudden we are getting back interested in it again.
>
> (BG3)

Indeed, in some circles, it is becoming important to know how to produce food for one's own consumption. In the United States at least, cooking, canning, baking, bee-keeping and composting are also trendy things to do nowadays. Also in other contexts, seemingly defunct – or even pre-modern – skills and competences such as knitting, soap making or other artisanal activities are experiencing a sort of renaissance. Hence, urban food growing has found its place in a wider constellation of practices and skills that have been revitalized in certain subgroups of the population and linked to new meanings, while the meaning of growing food as a daily duty and an essential means of survival, known from the past, seems to have changed forever.

Going above the city

In contrast to Trompenburg Community Garden, the farmers at Brooklyn Grange do not consume the vegetables they harvest. Instead, the 50,000 or more lbs (around twenty-three tons) of organically cultivated produce that are grown annually at the farm are sold to local restaurants and retailers, to the public via several weekly farm stands, and through a forty-member Community Supported Agriculture programme which runs from mid-May to October. However, rather than being solely production goods, the vegetables and flowers which are planted, grown and harvested on the farm present key constituents of the practice and are loaded with symbolic meanings:

> But just to understand some of how food is grown. It's kind of a miracle to see plants growing. That definitely is a beautiful thing to me too.
>
> (BG4)

Indeed, in the daily routines of the urban food growers, and even more so in the routines of the trainees, seemingly mundane products such as carrots, kale and tomatoes become artistic artefacts. In the discursive space provided by social networks and the blogosphere, one also finds a vast number of images displaying vegetables of all sorts.

The diversity and materiality of the vegetables grown at the farm have become symbols of beauty, celebrated by the individuals carrying the practices. Moreover, for those enacting the practice, growing food up on a roof is also a symbol of escaping from city life, as the following statement illustrates:

> When you get up there, it's hard work. Definitely hard work. But there's moments like when we were picking the carrots the other day, it's very meditative, it's very peaceful. You're going above the city and you don't have to be down, you know, in all the muck and everything like that.
>
> (BG5)

'I am an urban farmer'

In the case of entrepreneurial rooftop farming, the meaning of the key material element (i.e. the roof) is newly negotiated by linking it to the competence of growing food. The roof is often talked about as the forgotten part of a building or a neglected space within an urban environment. As Shove *et al.* (2012) point out, rather than the physical relocation of the material elements of the practice, the issue is access (in our case a roof) as well as the reframing of the material's usability. Hence, the meanings of a vacant lot or roof are altered when they are connected to other material elements such as flowers, vegetables, dinner parties, as well as to competences such as growing food or running a business.

Indeed, as Brooklyn Grange demonstrates, urban rooftop farming is about much more than simply growing food for sale. Its economic success has been accomplished through diversification in its products and services: ranging from sunset yoga classes, over farm dinners, to weddings and corporate events. Thus, urban food growing has been effectively linked to meanings of mental and physical health, pleasure and self-determination by embedding the practice in contexts related to these meanings. The success of the practice can thus partly be attributed to the opening up of the farm space (which is essentially a production space) for collective consumption practices and experiences, as well as linking a production practice to meanings normally related to consumption practices.

The material elements of the practice – comprising the roof, the cultivated produce, soil and working hands – also serve as means to distinguish the practice from other food growing practices which exist in the city such as hydroponics or community gardening:

> I say I am an urban farmer and I work at a rooftop farm in Brooklyn and it's a really cool thing to be able to say not just you are an urban farmer but you work at a rooftop farm. [...] So, it's better than saying 'I am a farmer', it's better than saying even 'I am an urban farmer' that would peak people's interest but the second you throw in the fact that you are farming on a roof, EVERYBODY wants to hear more.
>
> (BG3)

Thus, it is the difference in the material elements of the practice that its carriers employ to position themselves in the small yet diversified community of food growing practices in New York City. The material elements become part of the practice carriers' identity projects (Dobernig and Stagl, under review) and are employed to demarcate specific variations within the practice of urban food growing.

The case of Brooklyn Grange illustrates how a novel integration of materials (most prominently the roof and grown produce), competences (business knowledge and farming skills) and meanings (of health and pleasure) has attracted carriers of the practice from all walks of life. These new linkages are spread and reinforced through social media users, national and international documentary film-makers, authors of newspaper articles, and most obviously through the vast number of trainees who are enacting and thereby renewing the practice on a daily basis by working on the farm:

> I just feel the people who are doing urban farming, they are awesome people and they are well-educated and they're really cool and they are interesting and fun but there is just like this grounded quality to everybody. I feel like everybody is really real and easy to talk to, and to me it's the easiest group of people I found that I click with, socially.
>
> (BG5)

As Shove *et al.* (2012) point out, in order to remain effective the connections between the different practice elements have to be constantly renewed. In the case of Brooklyn Grange, the trainees mirror the competences concentrated in the farm's founders and employed staff members who are all college-educated and bring in knowledge, skills and experience not only in farming but also in business, marketing, law and engineering. What is clear is that urban rooftop farming constitutes a collective experience, encompassing materials, competences and meanings that go far beyond the traditional conceptualization of urban food growing as food production. Looking at Brooklyn Grange through the lens of practice theory reveals: (1) how a seemingly old and mundane practice (urban food growing) has become re-positioned through a novel combination of materials, competences and meanings; and (2) how subtle differences in materials (roof versus vacant lot) serve as a means for distinguishing different peculiarities in the greater realm of urban food growing practices.

As will be clear from our descriptions of the cases, the social practices of urban food growing in Trompenburg community garden and in New York rooftop farming differ in some crucial respects. In the next section we compare both cases to generate new insights in the key characteristics of the practice of urban food growing.

Community gardening and entrepreneurial urban farming – illustrations of the same emerging social practice?

Community gardening in Amsterdam and entrepreneurial rooftop farming in New York represent two examples of urban food growing. Although they do not capture the diversity of initiatives in this domain, the cases allow us to reflect on the question as to whether they are illustrations of one single or of multiple social practices. We discuss this question through a comparison of their internal dynamics as well as of their relations with other social practices.

Whether or not these two examples form one social practice is not only interesting from an urban agriculture point of view – as argued, we should be careful not to subsume all kind of activities under one heading if this is not warranted – it is also useful for the theory of social practices itself, as one of the issues in the literature is how to delimit a practice (Shove and Spurling, 2013). Comparing two examples of (the internal components related dynamics of) the practice of urban food growing may reveal the doings and sayings representing different social practices. Similarly, studying two examples of embedding – of the relationship between urban food growing and other social practices – may show different ways in which a practice is affected by other practices, and illustrate how this practice is combined with other practices into people's individual lifestyles. We expect that insights into the degree to which the two case studies differ regarding these two points may help us understand whether a particular component or activity should be seen as part of similar or different practices. This issue is important because the moment we talk about social practice X or Y, we are demarcating it from other practices, while also the embedding of the single practice in a nexus or network of other practices co-determines what the practice is about.

Comparing the components of urban food growing practices: materials, competences and meanings

In terms of materials, in Trompenburg as well as Brooklyn Grange, food is grown on soil, both initiatives are located in urban centres, and cultivation is mainly done through manual labour. The absence of technically more elaborate farming methods makes growing food in both places comparable with traditional farming practices and distinguishes it from modern intensive, high-tech agriculture. In fact, the participants of the practice consider the absence of advanced technologies an essential characteristic of their way of growing food because it strengthens their connection with the cultivated food (and the soil) and expresses a critical stance towards mainstream food production. Hence, the bodily activities involved in 'doing the food growing' are essential elements in both cases. Where mechanization of agricultural production reduced the physical, bodily activities of farmers, urban food growing practices rediscover and celebrate this physical dimension. Human bodies, soil and crops are central elements of the 'material identity' of the practices. However, the cases differ in terms of scale, the technical dimensions, the socio-spatial environment in which the growing activities are embedded, and the degree to which they are caught in socio-technical networks.

At Brooklyn Grange, the roof is an additional key material element as it indicates how (and where) the food is grown. It also presents an important aspect of the identities of both the farm and the practitioners. In terms of the 'locales' or physical-spatial contexts of the practices, there is as well an important similarity between the locations of Trompenburg and Brooklyn Grange since both are located in unexpected food growing places. While a roof is of course a relatively new growing space, Trompenburg's location on a narrow strip of land is surprising in much a similar way.

With respect to the competences involved in both practices, the two cases show some remarkable differences. While Trompenburg community garden requires practitioners to be skilled in growing food only, their counterparts at Brooklyn Grange exhibit additional competences in business management, marketing, social media and event management. These skills make urban food growing at Brooklyn Grange a more diversified and demanding practice when compared with Trompenburg. Second, and because of the higher level skills involved, the process of acquiring the necessary competences-to-the practice is more formally organized in New York City through an extensive and structured trainee programme. The well-organized introductory programme is necessary for new recruits in order to become experienced participants and carriers of the practice. The kind of skills and competences needed in New York do not easily lend themselves for an individual trial-and-error approach of the kind that prevails in Trompenburg. A survey conducted among trainees of Brooklyn Grange in the 2013 season also revealed that their main reasons for becoming involved in the trainee programme were not only to learn about growing food (95.5 per cent) but as well to get to know about the business aspects of urban farming (73.3 per cent) and to spend time outside (71.1 per cent).

Like competences and materials, meanings are inherently dynamic because they emerge through initiatives by many different people in many different places and build on meanings shaped in the context of already existing practices, such as urban farming in developing world cities and traditional allotment gardening. Trompenburg community garden illustrates how urban food growing can essentially be regarded as a continuation of already existing practices. Their components seem to be largely a carry-over from traditional allotment gardening. The main transformations from allotment practices taking place in Trompenburg are the movement from the outskirts of town to an inner city neighbourhood as well as an increased attention for interactions with and among local residents. Trompenburg in some particular way illustrates the resilience of traditional allotment practices, as several attempts to transform it into a genuine 'urban, social' form did not show great success. Gardeners tried cooperating with the local school, worked with a programme to support homeless people, and considered organizing communal dinners for the elderly. While these initiatives were intended to develop Trompenburg from a food gardening initiative into a more locally embedded social activity, none of them were very successful because gardeners lacked the competences – were not organized enough – to make this transformation of the allotment practice work in an enduring way. The scope or scale of the connection-making activities was too small, and gardeners seemed not to have enough time for them:

> Alex wanted to do something with the school. And we also wanted to cook for the senior club from the playground society, but our harvest is not so large so…. And the people have less time than one hopes when you start such a garden. So it's not very active. But there were initiatives and thoughts.
>
> (TB4)

Hence, the main participants of the practice in Trompenburg held on to the traditional format of growing food in allotments. This combination of elements or components to the practice differs from the combination attached to entrepreneurial rooftop farming at Brooklyn Grange, which vividly demonstrates that the practice of urban food growing can shake off old connotations of growing food, thereby creating a new social practice. This has worked through positioning the narrative of urban rooftop farming with reference to already established discourses and practices in the city, mainly revolving around local food, green cities and sustainability. The practice of urban food growing more generally is also increasingly integrated into other policy agenda issues such as obesity, storm water runoff and youth unemployment. Practitioners at Brooklyn Grange understand growing urban food as a new way not only of re-establishing connections between food production and consumption, but also of fostering social food entrepreneurship and transforming life in the city. The rooftops, the involvement of many young people, the story-line, and the combination of consumption, leisure and production against the background of a vegetable farm are all innovative and distinguish it from the social practice of community gardening in Trompenburg.

Practices attract the new recruits they require for their continued existence in different ways. At Brooklyn Grange, a well-organized trainee programme is set up to spread the initiative, recruit new members and train them in the necessary skills. Overall, more practitioners are involved here than in Trompenburg's community garden and they invest more hours per week. The result is a more established and professionalized social practice which is well embedded in a broader set of urban sustainability practices. In Trompenburg, recruitment is more informal because only when a plot is vacant can new members be attracted, and this is facilitated by the visibility of the garden in the local neighbourhood. Gardeners thus respond to a latent desire to grow their own food ('and it caught my eye and I thought, that's nice, I'll do that' TB2). Although these new recruits often do not have the necessary skills, there is no formal training arrangement and it is left to the individuals themselves to find their way to develop the necessary competences.

How growing urban food practices connect with other practices

Growing urban food does not take place in isolation. In both our cases, the practice of growing urban food has several links with other social practices, food-related or not. In Trompenburg, none of the gardeners is engaged in other food growing activities and several of them have no previous skills in this respect either. As people grow their own vegetables, the practice potentially competes with the practice of shopping for food. However, the harvested volume is small and replaces only a minor proportion of the need for buying vegetables from shops. This means that the practice of urban food growing in Trompenburg community garden slightly changed the practice of food acquisition, but did not replace it. In terms of food production and acquisition, the participants in the Trompenburg practice just squeezed an additional practice into their daily lives and lifestyles. The practice of growing food did, however, affect other related food practices like storing and cooking fresh food.

The Trompenburg social practice did develop new relations when compared with traditional allotment practices in the sense of being embedded in local, social and neighbourhood level networks and relations. The interviews show that the garden elicits conversations with neighbours, that children stop by to water the plants and that passers-by ask questions or give their opinions.

> The only thing that I noticed in the last years, is that when you were working in your garden, you got contacts because people started talking to you. Ooooh, that is nice, or, you're making it look good, or, what have you planted?
>
> (TB3)

While this social networking is only loose, the garden and its users are highly visible and proximate to the neighborhood. Urban food growing in Trompenburg entails creating social bonds across the neighbourhood, without the bindings being organized and planned in any particular way. In this respect, there is a remarkable difference with the New York case.

As Brooklyn Grange is able to attract trendy, local restaurants and celebrity chefs as customers, urban rooftop farming has become integrated into the 'foodies' culture' of New York City. The distinction between food production and consumption as two separate practices thus becomes increasingly blurred, and new participants in the practice can mentally build upon already established narratives and carry over their symbolic meanings and prestige to the practice of growing food on a rooftop:

> Well, first of all, I think the food, the sort of local food movement is really sexy right now. Like, people are like really into it, you know. And I think this idea of there being this urban farm in Lower Manhattan is like really exciting. [...] That's why I have been sucked in for five years, it's totally sexy. The day-to-day may not be but the idea of it, the concept, is so.
>
> (BG5)

By propagating this meaning and overall identity of the practice, Brooklyn Grange particularly attracts young and well-educated people, types of carriers that are less prevalent in the Trompenburg area.

To recapitulate, the Trompenburg and Brooklyn Grange cases differ in many respects. Although they are both exemplars of contemporary urban food growing, Trompenburg is less formalized, more restricted in its activities and relationships, and of a smaller scale when compared with the well embedded and professional rooftop farming operation of Brooklyn Grange. With these characteristics in mind, we in the next section seek to answer the question of whether we are dealing with two different social practices or a singular one, and how similarities and differences can be discussed in a more conceptual way.

Discussion and conclusion

We studied urban food growing from the point of view of practice theory in order to gain a better understanding of what is going on in empirical reality on the one hand, and to contribute to the further development of practice theories on the other. Important research questions were first how situated practices of urban food growing are to be identified, delineated, defined, characterized and categorized and second, whether and to what extent we are dealing here with 'new' or newly emerging social practices.

For defining and characterizing the practice of urban food growing, we made use of the Shove *et al.* (2012) inspired understanding of social practices as resulting from the combination of three basic elements or components: materials, meanings, competences. By describing and analysing in some depth two individual cases – Trompenburg in Amsterdam and Brooklyn Grange in New York – for their three basic components, we were able to show that this comparative, descriptive analysis can generate only incomplete answers. Of course similarities and differences between situated practices can be highlighted in ways that enhance our understanding of what the practices are (not) about. We showed, for instance, how the materials of 'soil and hands' in both cases were important ingredients in bringing about the shared goal of urban farmers to reconnect food, nature and community in specific, anti-industrial ways. These communalities, however, do not in themselves produce practices which are similar in kind, since crucial differences were also shown to exist, for example, in the nature of the competences needed for participation in both kinds of urban food growing practices. The question of how to empirically characterize (components of) practices of similar kinds is further complicated by the fact that different groups of actors provide different answers. The founders of the urban food growing movement were shown to deviate in this respect from the actual practitioners or carriers of the situated practices in Amsterdam. Finally, also (we as) researchers who are 'praxeologizing' (Schmidt, 2012) urban food growing tend to come up with particular descriptions and interpretations for example of the ways in which 'meanings' are being generated and attributed to (elements of) practices.

Because synchronic description of components cannot generate sufficient answers, the next step in the characterization of practices was to look into the practice and its components in a diachronic way. Here we applied historical analyses, looking for similarities and differences between contemporary practices and similar practices from the past. This methodology allowed for recognizing different trajectories of urban food growing practices in Amsterdam and New York, with Amsterdam being much less of a new or newly emerging practice when compared with Brooklyn Grange. Trompenburg we described as a merger of two already existing practices, namely (allotment) gardening and neighbourhood building, without generating some of the new meanings, competences and skills as advertised by some of the founders of the urban food and transition town movements.

To arrive at more telling answers on the question of how to define and categorize social practices of urban food growing, we applied as a third step the methodology of analysing the linkages with other social practices in urban spaces. This third methodology of analysing the embedding of urban food growing

Chapter 10

Connecting practices

Conservation tourism partnerships in Kenya[1]

Machiel Lamers and René van der Duim

Introduction

Since the early 1990s, in Eastern and Southern Africa partnerships have been established between local communities, private entrepreneurs and nature conservation organizations to enable the development of conservation tourism for generating livelihood and conserving nature (e.g. Ahebwa *et al.*, 2013; Ashley and Jones, 2001; Lamers *et al.*, 2013, 2014; Van der Duim *et al.*, 2015). So far, academics and practitioners have viewed such conservation tourism partnerships (CTPs) with rational actor perspectives, focusing on the extent to which these partnerships generate socioeconomic incentives for local people to change unsustainable land uses (Sumba *et al.*, 2007), with instrumental perspectives assessing the effectiveness of the partnerships for nature conservation and livelihood creation (Ahebwa *et al.*, 2013; Lamers *et al.*, 2014; Van der Duim *et al.*, 2015), and with critical political economy perspectives on the desirability of neoliberal institutional arrangements in nature conservation (Brockington *et al.*, 2008; Sachedina *et al.*, 2010). In this chapter we will provide an alternative perspective by focusing on how such partnerships are connecting practices of livelihood creation, tourism and conservation, with the aim of realizing change in the constituting set of practices. This process of integrating practices will be comparatively analysed in two distinct cases in Laikipia Country, Kenya. The questions which practices underlie such partnerships and how they are changed by these partnerships have remained undisclosed.

This chapter therefore contributes to the practice theory agenda by providing a 'zoomed out' (Nicolini, 2012) analysis of how practices are connected and how bundles of practices compare with the policy aims of enhancing livelihood creation and nature conservation through tourism. We will conceptualize CTPs as deliberate attempts to create distinct nexuses of practices and material arrangements (Schatzki, 2002, 2005) to tackle societal challenges. We will investigate how CTPs originated from existing practices, and how they are sustained and perpetuated, that is how individuals carry them forward (Schatzki, 2005). Second, we will demonstrate how different attempts to create CTPs in different local contexts are shaped in their own distinct ways, perpetuated through successive moments of performance, while also changing over time. We will argue that, and examine how, conservation tourism partnerships emerged out of the co-location and connections between three existing practices. We show how conservation practices of NGOs, livelihood practices (pastoralism) of local communities and business venturing practices of tourism entrepreneurs result in a hybrid nexus of practices, facilitated by particular 'bridging' or 'connecting' practices. By referring to two different CTPs in Kenya we show how conservation tourism only exists and endures because of countless recurrent and situated practices, producing particular interdependencies that are characteristic for CTPs. The value of practice theory for informing policy making and implementation has only recently received some attention (Shove *et al.*, 2012). Also the application of practice approaches to tourism contexts, particularly in developing countries, is very recent. The analysis of nature-based tourist experiences (Rantala, 2010; Rantala *et al.*, 2011) and the exploration of sustainable modes of tourist transport (Verbeek *et al.*, 2011) are two examples, but both in European contexts (for an exception see Lamers and Pashkevich, 2015).

In the next section we will elaborate the conceptual framework used in this chapter, followed by the methodological approach. The empirical part of this chapter focuses on the CTPs developed and implemented by the African Wildlife Foundation across the African continent, with a specific focus on two cases of CTPs in Kenya, the Koija Starbeds lodge and the Santuary at Ol Lentille (see also Van der Duim *et al.*, 2015; Lamers *et al.*, 2014). Having introduced the conceptual framework and the empirical cases, we combine both in order to discuss the four contributions outlined above. We close the chapter by drawing some main conclusions.

Conceptual framework

This chapter builds upon theoretical work of recent authors in the field of practice theory, like Theodore Schatzki (2002, 2005) and Elizabeth Shove *et al.* (2012). According to Schatzki (2002), social practices like making a living, conserving nature, running a business or holidaying, are bundles of activities consisting of doings and sayings and material entities (or material arrangements) hanging together. Schatzki beliefs that the relationship between practices and material arrangements is intimate and can be said to form practice-arrangement bundles (Schatzki, 2012: 15–17). In Schatzki's words:

> just about every practice (…) deals with material entities (including human bodies) that people manipulate or react to. And most practices would not exist without materialities of the sorts they deal with, just as most material arrangements that practices deal with would not exist in the absence of these practices.
>
> (Schatzki, 2012: 16)

The material arrangement includes things, technologies, objects, infrastructures, tools, hardware, animals and human bodies. Practices are spatially and temporally dispersed sets of doings and sayings organized by practical and general understanding, rules and teleoaffective structures (Schatzki, 2002). Practical understanding is the knowhow to execute doings and sayings. General understanding is the shared idea of what a practice entails and what the meaning of the practice is, including the mental image of what the practice is about. Rules, according to Schatzki consist of:

> explicit formulations, principles, precepts, and instructions, that enjoin, direct, or remonstrate people to perform specific actions. To say that rules link doings and sayings is to say that people, in carrying out these doings and sayings, take account of and adhere to the same rules.
>
> (Schatzki, 2002: 79)

Third, practices are organized by what Schatzki calls teleoaffective structures. A teleoaffective structure is the property of a practice linking its doings and sayings to a range of acceptable ends, purposes, beliefs, projects and tasks that ought to be accomplished, including the manner in which these projects and tasks should be executed. In this context one has to note that human bodies are more than merely material objects: they are also the carriers of practical intelligibility, general understanding and teleoaffective structure. According to Schatzki, the bundling of practices and material arrangement entails that they mutually affect and precondition one another (Schatzki, 2012, 2015).

At the same time, bundles of practices and material arrangements link to practices and material arrangements in other bundles (Schatzki, forthcoming).

Practice theory invites us to 'appreciate how the local activity is affected by other practices; how other practices are affected or constrained or enabled by the practice under consideration; and what are the material consequences of such relationships' (Nicolini, 2012: 229). In this respect Shove *et al.* (2012) argue that in certain situations co-location results in new hybrid forms, representing novel practices. Some of these synchronous associations are short lived, but others set new trains of path dependency in motion. Connections between practices can take the form of loosely associated bundles, but also more tightly bound complexes. Bundles of practices are 'loose-knit patterns based on co-location and co-existence, complexes represent stickier and more integrated arrangements including co-dependent forms of sequence and synchronization' (Shove *et al.*, 2012: 84). Bundles of practices require consistent and regular reproduction if they are to carry on in time and if they are to become stickier and more mutually dependent (Shove *et al.*, 2012). Schatzki (2005: 476) argues that an organization, such as a CTP:

> construed as a practice-arrangement bundle (1) is a product of actions performed in extant practices, (2) is a mesh that embraces existing, to varying

degrees altered, practices (possibly supplemented with new ones) and a mix of new and old material arrangements, and (3) continues in existence via a perpetuation of its practices and a maintenance of its arrangements that accommodates evolution and focused changes in the mesh.

In identifying how practices mutually affect one another it is important to focus on the activities and material arrangements that constitute these practices, on the way that these activities and material arrangements precondition and affect one another, and on how interdependency between practices develops over time.

In this context, Figure 10.1 represents three distinct and key steps in the process of practices becoming a specific bundle of practices. The steps represent the identification and understanding of the main constituting practices (step 1), their becoming interlinked through the introduction of connecting practices (step 2), and the analysis of the kind of social change brought about by the new practice-arrangement bundle (step 3).

By introducing and applying this three step approach, we contribute to the practice theory literature in a number of ways. First, we develop a more systematic way of analysing the bundling of practices by differentiating and focusing on constituting practices and connecting practices. We particularly focus on which doings and sayings, rules and materials play an important role in linking existing practices and the consequences this connection has for these existing practices. We will examine how the bundling of livelihood, conservation and tourism practices, mediated by connecting practices of managing the partnership, changes each of the original, constituting practices. Second, we highlight the role of agency in the process of bringing about and changing this particular nexus of practices. We will do this by referring to Manuel Castells concept of network-making power; the power to programme specific networks according to the interests and values, and the power to switch different networks forming strategic alliances (Castells, 2009). According to Castells, programming is the ability to

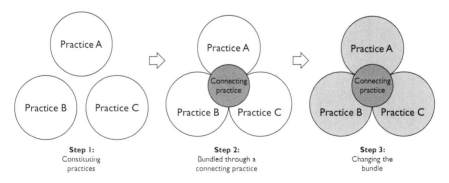

Figure 10.1 Three steps in the process of practices becoming a practice-arrangement bundle.

constitute networks, and to program networks in terms of the goals, values, norms and rules assigned to them. Switching is the ability to connect and ensure the cooperation of different networks by sharing common goals and combining resources. Third, we highlight the merits of a practice approach in developing and evaluating policies for social change (Shove *et al.*, 2012). This means we are not primarily interested in the individual (rational) choices of actors involved or the effectiveness of these arrangements. We rather foreground the connections and relationships between existing practices and the various ways in which linkages between these social practices can be generated, renewed and reproduced 'through intersecting circuits of reproduction that have dynamic qualities of their own' (Shove *et al.*, 2012: 102).

Methodological approach

This chapter focuses on two CTPs, established in the last two decades by the African Wildlife Foundation (AWF), an international non-governmental organization focusing on nature conservation across Africa. In the late 1990s, AWF launched its conservation enterprise campaign (Van Wijk *et al.*, 2015), aimed at changing the detrimental land-use practices of Maasai livestock keepers, such as keeping continuously increasing numbers of cattle and over-grazing. In the next paragraphs, we briefly introduce two CTPs that were established as a result of this campaign by AWF (see also Figure 10.2).

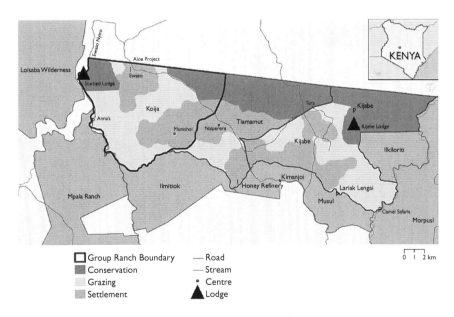

Figure 10.2 Map of the study area (adapted from Sumba *et al.* 2007).

The Koija Starbeds lodge

The Koija Starbeds lodge is a partnership between the Maasai community of the Koija group ranch, a communal land ownership entity (7,500 hectares), Oryx Ltd., a private company that leases and manages the neighbouring Loisaba Wilderness ranch (25,000 hectares) for livestock production and tourism, and AWF. The Koija group ranch consists of around 200 households and 1,200 people. The Koija Maasai had a troublesome relation with the neighbouring ranch because they regularly trespassed on Loisaba's land to graze their cattle in times of drought. The private investor, a Kenyan of white settler origin, realized that a constructive relationship with the neighbouring group ranch would mitigate the effects of future incidents. In 1999, AWF acted as a broker in the conception of a partnership deal with the Koija community. AWF mobilized the Koija community and convinced them to replicate the Kiboko Starbeds concept (one of Oryx's lodges) on the Koija group ranch to enable the community to secure benefits from wildlife by actively participating in conservation. The Koija group ranch set aside a conservation area of a little more than 200 hectares to attract and accommodate wildlife in which the Koija Starbeds lodge would be built. The construction costs of the lodge were granted to the community through international donor funds secured by AWF (Lamers *et al.*, 2013; Sumba *et al.*, 2007). The Koija Starbeds lodge opened for business in 2001 and comprises of three rustic bandas on a raised wooden platform that is partially covered by a thatched roof. The bandas contain a 'Starbed' that can be wheeled out onto the open deck for a night under the stars (at the cost of approximately 500 US$ per night for a non-resident). The Koija Starbeds is managed by Oryx as a satellite enterprise of the Loisaba Wilderness ranch, in terms of its transport infrastructure, marketing links and human resources. The immovable assets of the lodge are owned by the community, while the movable assets are owned by Oryx Ltd.

The Sanctuary at Ol-Lentille

The Sanctuary at Ol Lentille started as a partnership between the Kijabe group ranch (6,000 hectares) and Regenesis Ltd., a foreign entrepreneur, and AWF. Kijabe consists of around 800 people living on the group ranch territory and another 2,000 people living on group ranches elsewhere (Nanyuki and Nairobi). Negotiations with the Kijabe group ranch began in the same period as those in Koija, resulting in an agreement to set aside a third of its area (2,000 hectares) as a conservation area. In 2003, AWF initially aimed to build the lodge with a regional private contractor, funded by Dutch and United States' donor funds. After the initial private investor backed out in 2005, Regenesis Ltd. became involved and signed a 25 year management agreement with Kijabe to manage the enterprise and the conservation area. During the construction, the neighbouring Nkiroriti group ranch, consisting mainly of Samburu livestock keepers, claimed that part of this conservation area belonged to them. Investigations proved inconclusive. Nevertheless, a Memorandum of Understanding was signed to transfer 20 per cent of the group ranch income and employment to Nkloriti, provided that another 600 hectares of their land would be added to the conservation area. Another international grant enabled further constructions and the transfer of the immovable assets to Kijabe. Regenesis Ltd. invested additional private funds to complete the construction and furnish the lodge. The Sanctuary is a high-end tourism enterprise (around US$750 per night for a non-resident) comprising of four exclusive houses, each with their own team of staff (chamber maid, butler, guide). The lodge opened for business in early 2007. Besides Kijabe and Nkloriti, the private investor has been working with other neighbouring group ranches that have added tracts of land to the Sanctuary in return for financial compensation or the establishment of a satellite enterprise (Lamers *et al.*, 2014), which has resulted in a spectacular expansion to around 10,000 hectares in 2015.

The empirical material for this chapter is drawn from several studies undertaken or supervised by the authors, resulting in an extensive base of primary data collected in the form of interviews and observations during multiple fieldwork trips and stakeholder workshops (covering 12 weeks in total) between 2010 and 2014, as well as secondary data sources, such as reports and academic literature (see also Lamers *et al.*, 2013, 2014 and 2015; Nthiga, 2014; Van der Duim *et al.*, 2015). A number of 58 individual semi-structured interviews were conducted with representatives of the three partnerships: at the AWF headquarters in Nairobi, at the group ranches on which the CTPs are located, with the private investors, as well as with state-agencies, tour operators, donors, and managers of other community and private enterprises in the vicinity, involved in conservation tourism. Respondents were selected based on their experience and knowledge of the constituting as well as connection practices. Some informants, such as private investors, AWF officers and community leaders, were interviewed on more than one occasion. In addition, six focus group interviews were held with members of the Koija, Kijabe and Nkloriti group ranches. Interviews were held in English and in some cases assisted by a Maasai interpreter. The interview transcriptions were coded in ATLAS-ti, based on actions of each of the three partners linked to the CTPs, such as marketing, lodging, patrolling, sanctioning, deciding, paying and building. The anonymity of the respondents was safeguarded.

Conservation tourism partnerships as practice-arrangement bundles

Conservation tourism partnerships emerge out of connections between three existing practices: conservation practices of NGOs, livelihood practices (pastoralism) of local communities and business venturing practices of tourism entrepreneurs. Of course each of these three practices should be seen as bundles of various practices and material arrangements in their own right. Through the co-location of these three bundles of practices, it was attempted to create a new hybrid nexus of practices. In creating this novel bundle of practices at the tourism-conservation-development nexus, material arrangements (e.g. the lodge, conservation area, board of members), specific organizational forms and general and practical understandings turn out to be of key importance. Comprehending CTPs through the lens of practice theory not only requires analysing this new practice-arrangement bundle, but also analysing the changes in the various constituting practices (livelihood, conservation and tourism business practices) that result from their being connected.

In this section we first depict the three kinds of practices underlying or constituting the practice-arrangement bundle. We then go on to discuss how, by whom and to what extent they gradually were connected to become CTP-practice-arrangement bundles, sometimes evolving into what Shove *et al.* (2012) would characterize as a complex of practices. Such a complex in the end comes to represent a more integrated nexus of CTP practices and material arrangements (Schatzki, 2002). In this complex, (sets of) social practices take on a different content and shape when compared with their original, non-connected form, as we will show in two proximate cases.

The constituting practices of CTPs

Practice A: livelihood practices

The two CTPs studied in this chapter are both situated in group ranches of Maasai pastoralists, whose practice of extensive cattle herding is the primary economic activity. These group ranches are located in Laikipia, which covers the savannah habitat between Mount Kenya in the south and the low-lying arid lands of Samburu and Isiolo to the north (see Figure 10.2). Extensive pastoralist cattle herding is associated with a range of interrelated problems. The growing population in Kenya's arid lands (i.e. Maasai, Samburu, Turkana) tend to maximize their cattle herds (quantity above quality), while the land available for herding diminishes, due to droughts, over-grazing and private landownership. This leads to a classic tragedy of the commons, whereby there is not enough pasture for everybody. Herdsmen therefore venture further to the land of private landowners and other pastoralist communities, leading to competition and armed conflicts. The increasing droughts are further exacerbating these problems (Sumba *et al.*, 2007). Obviously cows play a key role in the material arrangement of the livelihood practices of Maasai pastoralists, along with a general understanding and teleoaffective structure that maximizing heads of cattle is the way forward to secure a living.

Since the late 1990s, wildlife conservation and tourism have gained greater prominence in land-use practices of large private landowners and group ranches in Laikipia, by expanding habitat and extending wildlife derived economic activities (Gadd, 2005; Lamers *et al.*, 2013). However, according to Homewood *et al.* (2012: 378): 'Maasai households resident in the rangelands remain above all keepers and managers of livestock, and most households both rich and poor derive a very substantial part of their subsistence from their herd'. Despite significant levels of non-herding diversification, such as making and selling beadwork to tourists and cultivating crops along the river, cattle still represents the breath of life for many Maasai communities and other groups in Kenya's arid lands. When given the chance, they choose herding above all other livelihoods. This is illustrated by the fact that community members continue to invest the income they derive from selling beadwork to tourists in additional cows and goats, even though it is in the interests of conservation and tourism practices (see below) to reduce heads of cattle on the land.

> Yes in our place people invest a lot in livestock. [...] They might not actually tell you the exact amount they earn [from tourism], but we can measure the income from the kind of livestock that they have increased, [for example] annually one has increased 10 goats or 3 cows. [...] So [tourism] is a kind of alternative way of livelihood other than just depending on livestock.
>
> (Focus group Koija group ranch)

Practice B: tourism business practices

Tour operators in Kenya all aim to offer safari experiences for groups of tourists in order to make a profit, providing packages of travel, lodging and activities, like game drives or walks, balloon rides and visits to Maasai villages (cultural manyattas). In that sense their daily practices are relatively straightforward and similar, apart from the service and experience levels they offer to different market segments. The tourism facilities and experiences developed in the Maaisai group ranches also have to be sold and marketed according to regular practices in the businesses. This means that the private investors have to develop and maintain networks of specialized travel agencies, travel designers and tour operators who serve high end niche market clients. Travel agents and travel journalists come and visit the establishments that will have to meet expected experience and service levels in order to be sold, regardless of the unique partnership constructions.

> Business is a lot driven by agents; they come on familiarization trips. They go and visit the Starbeds and if they see that everything is beautiful and well kept, that there is grass and wildlife, then we get more clients. If they go there and find some goats sleeping under the platform, forget it.
>
> (Interview private investor Koija Starbeds)

To realize critical levels of occupancy the private investors of the Koija Starbeds lodge and the Santuary at Ol Lentille have to actively engage with the communities in the group ranches and the conservation NGOs. Their business venturing makes use of the same land and wildlife as their partner conservationists and pastoralists, and wildlife and communities are key assets in developing a viable business. Therefore, according to AWF (2011: 16) 'selecting the right investor and management partner is the single most important decision determining the success or failure of most enterprises'. CTPs have not always been successful; recent incidents suggest that failing to govern the partnership challenges may well result in their collapse (Ahebwa et al., 2013; Lamers et al., 2013). Therefore AWF (2011: 16) warns: 'there are good partners and "not so good" ones. A sound due diligence[2] process should reveal which is which.' Private entrepreneurs and other parties involved all agree that it takes a special kind of private investor, one that is not only a skilled entrepreneur, with a global business network to connect the enterprise to the niche market of exclusive ecotourism, but one that also has the patience to listen and talk to pastoralist communities.

> On the private side, you are often dealing with an individual. There is clearly a head; he or she is either the CEO, the owner or the manager. There is a clear primary decision maker and visa card holder. [...] on the other side you are dealing with the many. [...] where there seems to be less strive depends hugely on the attitude of the one and the one's ability to engage with the many.

> (Interview director conservation organization)

Practice C: conservation practices

AWF started out as an organization that deployed a range of different strategies and practices to contribute to wildlife conservation in state protected areas (national parks, reserves) across the African continent, including training a corps of wildlife management professionals overseas, conducting scientific research and monitoring programmes, and engaging communities in conservation activities in buffer zones (Van Wijk et al., 2015). Since the late 1990s, AWF staff also targeted individual and communal landowners in wildlife-rich areas outside state protected areas to undertake measures that would protect wildlife, such as assessing conservation values and threats (AWF, 2011), setting conservation targets, zoning different land uses (including wildlife areas and no-grazing areas, see Figure 10.2), performing impact assessments and species monitoring, and scaling up conservation efforts by creating networks of conservation areas (Henson et al., 2009; Sumba et al., 2007). In other words, the creation of a conservation area is an attempt to change the existing socio-material arrangement by introducing new sets of rules (zoning scheme), new goals (conservation targets), a common understanding of the effectiveness of these measures (monitoring), and connecting these practices into a bundling of practices which is commonly known as conservation. These existing conservation practices, initially developed by state conservation agencies in setting up National Parks and other forms of state protected areas, were copied by conservation areas developed and managed by private and communal landowners, and connected to practices aimed at sensitizing communities, creating conservation enterprises and consequently attracting donor and private finances. For AWF this implied hiring staff with unusual qualifications, such as practical understanding in business development, for a conservation organization with a set of skills and perspectives unmatched in conservation organizations working in Africa (see Van Wijk *et al.*, 2015).

> I was hired to [...] scan for opportunities for nature-based enterprises, find communities partners, find private sector partners, get them into a deal, and put forward the necessary documentation to get those kind of projects funded. [I] build entrepreneurial capacity within the local community organizations, [in order] for them to be able to look around their environment, look at the resources that they have and find ways in which they could economically benefit from those resources.
>
> (Interview business developer AWF)

The conservation practices of AWF have changed significantly from science and monitoring, to community engagement and business development, and increasingly comprises manifold coupled bundles of activities and material arrangements.

Connecting practices

Both CTPs were initiated and established in the last two decades by the AWF, in collaboration with other actors, in which the three (sets of) constituting practices described above were becoming connected into a new 'practice-arrangement bundle'. In our two case studies AWF approached local communities to create conservation areas and become part of CTPs. As conservation practices alone were not enough for the creation of communal conservation areas, AWF started to offer advisory services to 'improve the commercial performance and sustainability of wildlife-related enterprises across Eastern and Southern Africa' (AWF, 1998: 1). These services – including business planning, due diligence, screening and selection of private partners, fundraising, legal contracting and community mobilization (Elliott and Sumba, 2010) – were all geared to develop CTPs. By developing CTPs in biodiversity-rich areas, AWF aimed to incentivize communal landowners outside national parks to protect wildlife and to generate alternative livelihood options, in this case ecotourism (Van Wijk *et al.*, 2014). In our two case studies, AWF attempted to convince Maasai communities to engage voluntarily in conservation by assisting them in zoning their communal land in settlement, grazing and conservation areas, finding a suitable private business partner, financing the construction of a tourism lodge, brokering a fair partnership agreement, mediating the relation between the community and the entrepreneur and monitoring the impacts. In other words, the construction of the lodge and the partnership arrangement both served to connect the livelihood practices of the Maasai community, the entrepreneurial business practices of business partners and the conservation practices of AWF, in an attempt to realize a more sustainable bundle of land-use practices. In this section we show how each of the two CTPs started to function as a new 'practice-arrangement bundle' in distinct and contextualized ways.

An essential role in connecting the existing practices and sustaining the practice-arrangement bundle is played by the trust boards. The main tasks of the trust boards are to provide a platform for reaffirming common ends, exchanging general and practical understandings, rules setting and monitoring across the three constituting sets of practices. Trustees aim to represent the three partnering actor groups, to devise the rules for, and manage the trust income that is generated through the lodge (see Table 10.1) by allocating capital to maintain the lodge and the conservation area, and to make the community benefit from all this. Trustees are also responsible for communicating decisions and updates to their constituencies, such as in the case of the following group ranch representative in the Koija Conservation Trust (KCT):

> I make sure that I attend all the quarterly KCT meetings and contribute to the discussions on the agenda. I also make sure that all that is passed in the meetings reaches the community. I also meet the group ranch members at least two to three times a year to update them on the progress of the lodge. We tell them about the income and expenditure of the KCT money.
>
> (Interview Koija group ranch leader)

The trusts also function as a platform where financial resources generated are allocated and distributed between the three sets of practices. For example, distinct shares of the trust's income are spent on the training and employment of scouts from the group ranch community for protecting the conservation areas, on health care projects and bursaries schemes for young group ranch members wishing to continue secondary or tertiary education, or on the maintenance of the tourist facilities.

> We sat as a committee and looked at the best way to give incentives for the entire community to benefit. We agreed that a bursary fund was the best way to provide secondary education; to give each member a chance to benefit. We have a committee which sits every beginning of the year and considers the applications from members.
>
> (Interview Koija group ranch leader)

The employment and income generated for community members in the lodges – by working as conservation scouts or by selling beadwork – are diversifying livelihood practices in the group ranches and stimulating the development of a money-based economy. The bursary schemes are providing opportunities for the next generation of group ranch members to follow secondary education and to further enhance and diversify their livelihood. Further, the trusts are providing platforms for communication and the development of several monitoring practices.

The two CTPs are also faced with a number of challenges. At Koija, a lack of educated or reliable alternatives has made the trustees reluctant to replace community representatives, which resulted in a board of trustees that has largely remained the same for more than a decade. This has made other leaders in the group ranch suspicious. At the Sanctuary, busy agendas of the trustees have made it difficult to meet regularly. In addition, disagreements over the control of the enterprise and personal tensions between the chair, representing the community, and the private investor have culminated in conflict, which has left the trust board without meetings since May 2010. However, a mediation process by AWF resulted in the basis of a revised partnership agreement in January 2013 (Lamers *et al.*, 2014). As a result, over the last decade both CTPs have managed to generate and distribute income, based on rules established at the start of the partnerships. The results were being monitored by the trust boards to a certain extent. Both boards of trustees however are claimed to not having fulfilled their communication role across the three constituting practices in optimal ways.

The CTP's material arrangement predominantly consists of the immovable (owned by the communities) and movable assets (owned by the private entrepreneur), the lands secured for conservation, the money needed to sustain the partnerships, and the individuals representing the different groups. When comparing the two CTPs it becomes clear that there are considerable differences (see Table 10.1). First, although in both cases the immovable assets are owned by the community and managed by the private partner, the Sanctuary is a larger physical structure that consumed much larger sums of finance during construction and decoration than the Starbeds. Second, the Sanctuary comprises a much larger conservation area than the Starbeds. Although the land ownership has not been clear, the conservation area at the Sanctuary continued to grow in terms of land coverage and the pool of beneficiaries through the private investor's connections with neighbouring group ranches. Third, there are some differences in the origin of the private investors and the compilation and role division of the trust boards. Finally, due to the fact that the private investor of the Sanctuary lives and runs the lodge on the land of the Kijabe community, a rights fee has to be paid annually to the group ranch, in contrast to the Starbeds that is run from the neighbouring private ranch.

The practice-arrangement bundle at Koija has remained relatively stable, as well as the connecting practice (e.g. regular meetings of the trust board) and the material arrangement of the CTPs (e.g. the lodge and the conservation area). On the contrary, the Sanctuary continued to grow and is clearly significantly larger than the Starbeds, along with significantly higher interests. This bundle more or less developed into a contagious practice complex in its own right, introducing new practices (e.g. charity work) and recruiting new participants (e.g. new group ranches) in novel ways.

Table 10.1 Main aspects of connecting practices

Items	Koija Starbeds ecolodge	The Sanctuary at Ol Lentille
Brokering of communities and private investors	Koija group ranch (clear membership) Oryx Ltd.: neighbouring private Kenyan rancher of white settler origin	Initially, Kijabe group ranch and Nkloriti group ranch. Later links with other group ranches and communities Regenesis Ltd.: foreign investor operating on the Kijabe group ranch
Building of lodges	Three wooden bandas on a raised platform, partially covered by a thatched roof	Initially, four independent and exclusive stone houses Later also a new satellite camp
Securing funding	Donor grants: US$70,000 No private investor input	Donor grants: US$500,000 Private investor: US$1.5 million Loan: unknown amount
Securing land for conservation:	200 hectares (clear land ownership)	Initially, 2,000 hectares (contested land ownership) Currently, 8,000 hectares
Compiling and meetings of trust board	Regular meetings of: Koija group ranch (2 members) Oryx Ltd. (2 members) AWF (1 member – chair)	Suspended meetings of: Kijabe group ranch (3 members – chair) Regenesis Ltd. (3 members) AWF (1 member)
Sharing community benefits	Guest-night fee: US$85 Entrance fee cultural village: US$35	Guest-night fee: US$80 Entrance fee cultural village: US$35 Rights fee: US$20,000 per year

Changing the bundle

The next question to tackle then is if social changes can be observed in the three constituting sets of practices after the practices becoming integrated into CTP-practice-arrangement bundles. The bundling of practices into CTPs can only be expected to endure and to become more sticky and mature if the underlying practices become more aligned, by enforcing common rules, by generating general and practical understandings related to the bundle, and by developing teleoaffective structures at the level of the CTP bundle. For example, in terms of the latter, CTPs can only be sustained if there are sets of ends that participants accept and pursue, a range of activities and tasks that they should carry out, accompanied by moods and emotions that participants appreciate (Schatzki, 2002). In this respect, substantial differences can still be identified between the different practices in both partnerships after some years of existence as CPT bundles. The private investors and AWF representatives see entrepreneurship and private sector development as the central vehicle for generating value from wildlife and creating incentives for the community to engage in conservation. In contrast, Maasai group ranch members and leaders still seem more inclined to strive for communal ends and are mostly preoccupied with increasing their share and control over community benefits from the enterprise to enhance livelihood development. As such, group ranch leaders in both partnerships generally aim to increase the community benefits accruing from the enterprise, while AWF and the private investors claim that this is only possible when group ranches increase their conservation efforts and when occupancy rates of the lodges improve. It becomes clear that for accomplishing practice-arrangement bundles, such as CTPs, 'its orientation, and normative force, need to be learned' (Nicolini, 2012: 227), which requires recurrent enactments or specific actions that raise practice-based awareness. The next paragraphs will discuss the level of change that can be observed in each of the three constituting practices.

First, changes can be observed in the livelihood practices in both cases. It is claimed that for such projects to succeed it is necessary for Maasai herders to shift their general understanding of wildlife as '*ngombe za serikali*' (government cattle) to 'second cattle' (Western, 1997: 146 and 285), making wildlife as something of value for them and give them a say in how wildlife fits into their livelihoods. According to the Starbeds entrepreneur it remains a challenge to get 'the community understand that the Starbeds is more important than grazing cattle in that 500 acres [conservation area]. We see that in the dry times they still invade it with their cattle and goats and sheep' (Interview private investor Koija Starbeds). As we have explained previously this has consequences for the number of tourists staying at the Starbeds. Another example is that community members would like to engage in crop cultivation along the river, which is another practice that does not align easily with the CTP practice-arrangement bundle as it exacerbates human-wildlife conflicts. AWF and the private investor claim to be disappointed with the fact that in ten years of existence, the Koija group ranch has not managed to increase their relatively small conservation area. Expansion would make small-scale controlled grazing of livestock in the conservation area feasible and further integrate livestock production and wildlife conservation. This practice of 'holistic grazing' integrates both land-use types and is already practised at private ranches, such as Loisaba, but is currently considered a bridge too far as the practice of livestock keeping of many group ranch herdsmen is still organized by the teleoaffective structure of maximizing heads of cattle. On the other hand, many community members have developed new skills and competencies. Both projects have managed to generate substantial income for the building of schools and healthcare centres, the hiring of teachers and healthcare workers, and the availability of bursaries for secondary and higher education. Some of the Maasai and Samburu diversified their livelihood activities by working as a waiter or guide at the lodge, producing and selling beadwork to tourists or partly acting as a game scout to secure and protect wildlife (Lamers *et al.*, 2013, 2014). Further, over the last decade two additional tourism enterprises have been established at Koija by local Maasai and Samburu entrepreneurs. Most of these additional livelihood practices are strengthening the CTP practice-arrangement bundle, as they depend on it.

Second, it also becomes clear that common entrepreneurial practices are confronted with community expectations and need to sometimes adapt to align with the Maasai community context. For both commercial partners involved, other dispositions than just making profit are at stake. This is for example clearly illustrated by the entrepreneur of Ol Lentille who, after having earned its fortune in the chemical industry, is now running a high end lodge. For example, for purchasing meat and eggs from community producers the entrepreneur uses a tender system, in which any producer from the community can make a competitive offer whereby the best offer is chosen. Such a selection system is common practice in business contexts around the world, but was not understood by the Maasai and Samburu group ranch members, who generally understand economic exchange as a way to establish long term relations with the entrepreneur. Next to running the daily operations of the lodge, many activities of the entrepreneurs are geared towards the community, such as raising donations from wealthy guests for a range of social projects in various communities. According to one of the entrepreneurs the result is an unbalanced situation:

> What we set out here was a three legged stool of economic development, community and conservation. What we've got is a very unstable stool, the community leg is much stronger and much longer than either of the other two [...]. What we need to focus on is funding conservation better and raising the occupancy of this place.
>
> (Interview private investor Santuary at Ol Lentille)

Ceaseless discussions between group ranch leaders and the entrepreneurs on the rules for distributing the financial benefits are an important part of the process of connecting practices. Trust board or other meetings are deliberate communicative acts that arouse conscious reflection about doings and sayings. Still, different interpretations exist over these rules and the way they come about. For example, group ranch leaders question the rules of the game and the distribution of resources as they perceive the role of the private investors to be too dominant in the partnership. They claim for more participation in decision-making in the enterprises. Group ranch leaders of both partnerships also demand more transparency regarding the financial operations of the enterprise to assess if they receive a fair share of the benefits. For these group ranch leaders involvement in the trust board only is clearly not satisfactory or enough; the partnership for them also implies a greater involvement in the running of the lodge to obtain a greater practical and common understanding to assess the fairness of the benefit sharing arrangements. Drawing on their entrepreneurial practice, both private investors initially rejected creating more transparency, as they believe to have the right (i.e. the rights fee in the case of the Sanctuary) and need to be able to run the enterprise exclusively. It is also argued that many community members are not sufficiently educated to understand the financial complexity of a transnational niche tourism enterprise. However, at the Starbeds CTP some measures have been taken to enhance the general and practical understanding of the community leaders in the running of the enterprise by allowing them to sit in the trust board meetings and providing an overview of all the costs and benefits involved. This seems to have satisfied the information needs of the group ranch leaders. In other words, group ranch leaders have been allowed to listen in meetings about management and bookkeeping, but not to participate in bookkeeping and management itself.

Third, the CTPs are also faced with a range of governance challenges (see Nthiga, 2014). For example, the increased complexity of financial streams has made it increasingly difficult for participants of various practices involved to practically understand what is going on. Also, the emergence of new practices (like philanthropy and charity) and new participants (other group ranches at the Sanctuary) have made the CTPs subject to political discussion and controversies, whereby the partnership arrangements and the distribution of benefits are increasingly discussed. These governance challenges necessitate consistent and regular reproduction of the partnerships and therefore also call for the long term involvement of an organization, like AWF, able to mediate reflexive practices and audit financial streams. However, it is not clear if and how such organizations are capable of meeting this requirement, as their involvement is typically sponsored by international donors who are predominantly interested in establishing and not in sustaining projects (Lamers *et al.*, 2014, 2015).

Fourth, AWF executed different things at different stages of the development of the CTP. In both cases the brokering of AWF, as part of their conservation enterprise strategy, first consisted of a number of different activities (e.g. assessing the conservation logic and commercial viability, tendering of business partners, contracting, attracting donor funds) to enable the connecting. These brokering activities resulted in a set of rules, translated in a trust and an agreement, which set out the principles and instructions that invite people to perform specific actions, including trying to connect their conservation interests and goals to those of other actors, informing the communities about the dos and don'ts and the distribution of community benefits. As one of the AWF interviewees asserted:

> If the idea came from the community, and you are not the one who really pushed it down to them, the chances of success are higher because the sense of ownership is higher since you are helping them to achieve their own goals. But most communities are not aware that they can do lodges and other things. So sometimes you have to take them to other group ranches who have arranged it themselves for them to get the idea that they have better wildlife, they can have a better deal than those guys. That's functional awareness creation.

> (Interview senior officer AWF)

The excursions organized by AWF for community members to see and experience the practice-arrangement bundles at work in other parts of Kenya were an effective practice-based approach to awareness building that, literally, moves beyond a cognitive approach of merely providing information. However, the development and fostering of shared sets of acceptable ends, purposes, beliefs and tasks demanded perpetual processes of awareness building, sensitizing, negotiations and exposure to best practices, training and capacity building, which not only precedes the actual start of a CTP but also continued after that and – based on their experiences – is now even documented in a 'decision support toolkit' (AWF, 2011).

In short, it becomes clear that despite being located in relative proximity the two practice-arrangement bundles have followed different trajectories, still face many challenges and are in constant flux. For example, the practice-arrangement bundle of the Sanctuary at Ol Lentille has grown substantially in material terms into a practice-arrangement complex that continues to attract participants, whereas the Koija Starbeds has remained modest. On the other hand, whereas in the Koija Conservation Trust general and practical understandings continuously have been on the table for discussion, the trust board of the Sanctuary has faced major difficulty to meaningfully reflect on the aims of the partnership and the distribution of the resources. In both cases substantial changes in the constituting practices have been realized, in terms of livelihood enhancement and diversification, as well as nature conservation, particularly in the case of the Sanctuary. We have thereby shown that in the two CTPs a range of existing practices have been bundled by the introduction of connecting practices with the aim to change the existing constituting practices.

Discussion and conclusion

This chapter aimed to contribute theoretically as well as empirically to practice theory. By examining CTPs as practice-arrangement bundles and specifically looking at what we coined here as connecting practices, we first showed how conservation tourism partnerships emerged out of the co-location and connections of three existing practices, i.e. conservation practices of NGOs, livelihood practices (pastoralism) of local communities and business venturing practices of tourism entrepreneurs. This resulted in a new hybrid nexus of practices, facilitated by new connecting practices, such as the brokering of the partnership, the funding and building of a lodge, the zoning of land, the communication at trust meetings and the sharing of benefits. This new practice-arrangement bundle only exists and endures because of countless recurrent and situated enactments, each producing particular interdependencies between the constituents of which the practice-arrangement bundle is comprised. Our case study also illustrated how different instantiations of this practice-arrangement bundling in different local contexts shapes local variations, perpetuates through successive moments of performance, but also changes over time. Indeed, our account was on incessant rearrangement and reorganization combining humans and non-humans in the continuously transforming orders of conservation tourism partnerships (Schatzki, 2002).

Second, we argued that and showed how the nexus of livelihood, conservation and tourism practices, including the connecting practices of building, managing and sustaining the partnership, changed each of the constituting practices. CTPs emerged as a part of a web of relationships and mutual dependencies between pastoralism, conservation and tourism, on which they depend and to which they contribute. The CTPs seen as a nexus are established by the three constituent practices, while at the same time they re-establish those practices (Nicolini, 2012). Our story illustrated how 'practices and orders form an immense shifting, and transmogrifying mesh in which they overlap, interweave, cohere, conflict, diverge, enable as well as constrain each other' (Schatzki, 2002: 156). For reasons of simplicity, we distinguished three constituent practices of CTPs. However, each of these three practices is to be seen as a bundle of practices in their own right. For example, conservation by organizations like AWF itself is a bundle of practices, a loose-knit pattern of practices, such as environmental education, fundraising, lobbying, conserving, venturing and monitoring biodiversity, which permanence is based on co-location and co-existence. Similarly the livelihood practices of Maasai communities include a range of practices, such as pastoral and extensive livestock ranching, sedentary crop cultivation, poaching and as we have seen increasingly tourism. Clearly by bundling, these bundles of practices, particular ways of sayings and doings of practitioners, like Maasai or AWF staff, became (less) prominent or were combined, for example in the practice of holistic grazing. Moreover, practice-arrangement bundles are tied to similar nets (e.g. Kenyan governmental and non-governmental conservation organizations; incoming tour operators in Nairobi) resulting in an even larger confederation of nets (e.g. the international conservation movement; the tourism industry): 'all these meshes, nets, and confederations form one gigantic metamorphosing web of practices and orders, whose fullest reach is coextensive with socio-historical space-time' (Schatzki, 2005: 473).

Third, our account illustrated the role of agency in changing the nexus of practices in ways desirable for different participating actors. Interventions are sometimes made to steer social practices towards more sustainable outcomes. One way of intervening in social practices is by deliberately connecting distinct practices to change the nature and output of these existing practices by what we have coined in this chapter as connecting practices. We argue that these connecting practices resemble Manuel Castells concept of network-making power, (Castells, 2009). The reflexive practices of conservation NGO representatives, private investors and community representatives to ensure groups of Maasai cattle herders abide with zonation rules and to decide on, and monitor, benefit sharing arrangements are clear examples of programming. Examples of switching are the efforts of the private entrepreneurs to promote the lodge across the planet to exclusive travel designers and agents. However, it is important to point out that various actors not only deploy their networking power to make or break the connection between, and the configuration of, constituting practices, but also that these activities are 'effects'. The agency to programme or switch is embedded in the network(s), consisting of Maasai group ranch members, employees of AWF or the lodges involved and their understandings, but just as well cows, electricity, money, contracts, land or the tourism industry.

Finally, our account illustrated the merits of a practice approach for developing and evaluating policy (see also Shove *et al.*, 2012). As we have shown, the trajectories of bundling of practices in CTPs have been long, intricate and highly diverse, and CTPs still face a number of challenges and require consistent maintenance and repair if they are to be sustained. By examining CTPs in terms of a practice–arrangement bundle and by revealing their fragility, it became clear that developing and maintaining practice-arrangements bundles like CTPs depend on incessant policy support of NGOs like AWF to have an effect. The internal and external dynamics of CTPs calls for continuously reflexive monitoring of emergent CTPs and guiding processes of selection and variation to ensure that practice bundles are sustained and remain effective and democratic. Regular revision of partnership agreements could contribute to this call. We argue that continuity in this guiding process is needed to safeguard stability (see also Lamers *et al.*, 2014). Although many authors assume that public authorities would be best positioned to take on these roles, our study suggests that non-state actors, such as AWF, can also perform and share these tasks if resources can be secured. AWF has played a vital role in building coalitions and constructing partnerships that made the conditions of practice possible, but is now increasingly confronted with internal (e.g. financial, organizational) and external (e.g. political, operational) challenges that make its long-term involvement in these partnerships uncertain (see also Van Wijk *et al.*, 2014).

Our story clearly illustrated that effects of conservation tourism practices like CTPs are inherently unpredictable, will never be steady and will always be subject to constant reproduction. By analysing the performance of two practice-arrangement bundles, we showed how different meanings and materials can be attributed to the same practice, producing different effects and consequences (Nicolini, 2012), such as political controversy or conflict. Indeed, CTPs are 'not about delivering plans and advancing on ready-made goals, but about moving towards always moving targets' (Shove *et al.*, 2012: 162) and will only have effect when taken up in and through practices. Practice theory might provide the conceptual base to follow and understand this 'moving' and its fickle effects and the way state, or in this case non-state actors like AWF, influence the bundling of practices, shaping the careers of practices and those who carry them. This understanding might not only be beneficial for the evaluation of existing CTPs, but also for the creation of new policy arrangements in which practices are bundled.

Notes

1 This chapter uses some material of Lamers *et al.* (2014; 2015).
2 Due diligence is an investigation conducted prior to signing a business contract to make sure there is a business case and to make sure the main risks and uncertainties are accounted for.

References

Adams, W.M., Aveling, R., Brockington, D., Dickson, B., Elliott, J., Hutton, J., Roe, D., Vira, B. and Wolmer, W., 2004. 'Biodiversity Conservation and the Eradication of Poverty'. *Science*, 306, 1146–1149.

Ahebwa, W., Van der Duim, V.R. and Sandbrook, C., 2012. 'Private-Community Partnerships: Investigating a New Approach to Conservation and Development in Uganda'. *Conservation and Society*, 10 (4), 305–317.

Ashley, C. and Jones, B., 2001. 'Joint Ventures between Communities and Tourism Investors: Experience in Southern Africa'. *Journal of Tourism Research*, 3 (5), 407–423.

AWF, 2011. *Conservation Enterprise: A Decision Support Toolkit*. Nairobi/Washington, DC: African Wildlife Foundation.

Brockington, D., Duffy, R. and Igoe, J., 2008. *Nature Unbound: Conservation, Capitalism and the Future of Protected Areas*. London: Earthscan.

Castells, M., 2009. *Communication Power*. Oxford: Oxford University Press.

Elliott, J. and Sumba, D., 2010. *Conservation Enterprise – What Works, Where and for Whom?* London: International Institute for Environment and Development.

Gadd, M.E., 2005. 'Conservation outside of Parks: Attitudes of Local People in Laikipia, Kenya'. *Environmental Conservation*, 32 (1), 50–63.

Hardin, G., 1968. 'The Tragedy of the Commons'. *Science*, 162 (3859): 1243–1248.

Henson, A., Williams, D., Dupain, J., Gichohi, H. and Muruthi, P., 2009. 'The Heartland Conservation Process: Enhancing Biodiversity Conservation and Livelihoods through Landscape-Scale Conservation Planning in Africa'. *Oryx*, 43 (4), 508–519.

Homewood, K., Trench, P.C. and Kristjanson, P., 2012. 'Staying Maasai? Pastoral Livelihoods, Diversification and the Role of Wildlife in Development. In: K. Homewood, P.
Kristjanson and P.C. Trench. *Staying Maasai? Livelihoods, Conservation and Development in East African Rangelands*. Dordrecht: Springer.

KWS, 2012. *Reaching out to Communities – KWS 2.0: Community Enterprise Strategy
2012–2017*. Nairobi: Kenya Wildlife Service.

Lamers, M. and Pashkevich, A., 2015. 'Short-Circuiting Cruise Tourism Practices along
the Russian Barents Sea Coast? The Case of Arkhangelsk'. *Current Issues in Tourism*,
Online First.

Lamers, M., Nthiga, R., Van der Duim, R. and Van Wijk, J., 2013. Tourism-conservation
enterprises as a land-use strategy in Kenya. *Tourism Geographies*, 16 (3), 474–489.

Lamers, M., Nthiga, R.W., Van der Duim, V.R., Van Wijk, J. and Visseren-Hamakers, I.,
2014. 'Governing Conservation Tourism Partnerships in Kenya'. *Annals of Tourism
Research*, 48, 250–265.

Lamers, M., Van der Duim, V.R., Van Wijk, J., Nthiga, R.W. and Waterreus, S., 2015.
'Implementing Tourism-Conservation Enterprises: a Comparison of Three Lodges in
Kenya'. In: R. van der Duim, R., M. Lamers and J. van Wijk, eds. *Institutional
Arrangements for Conservation, Development and Tourism in Eastern and Southern
Africa*. Dordrecht: Springer.

Meguro, T. and Inoue, M., 2011. 'Conservation Goals Betrayed by the Uses of Wildlife
Benefits in Community-Based Conservation: The Case of Kimana Sanctuary in
Southern Kenya'. *Human Dimensions of Wildlife: An International Journal*, 16 (1),
30–44.

Nicolini, D., 2012. *Practice Theory, Work, and Organization: An Introduction*. Oxford:
Oxford University Press.

Nthiga, R., 2014. *Governance of Tourism Conservation Partnerships. Lessons from
Kenya*. PhD thesis. Wageningen: Wageningen University.

Rantala, O., 2010. 'Tourist Practices in the Forest'. *Annals of Tourism Research*, 37 (1),
249–264.

Rantala, O., Valtonen, A and Markuksela, V., 2011. 'Materializing Tourist Weather:
Ethnography on Weather-Wise Wilderness Guiding Practices'. *Journal of Material
Culture*, 16 (3), 285–300.

Reckwitz, A., 2002. 'Toward a Theory of Social Practices: A Development in Culturalist
Theorizing'. *European Journal of Social Theory*, 5 (2), 243–263.

Sachedina, H., Igoe, J. and Brockington, D., 2010. 'The Spectacular Growth of a Conservation NGO and the Paradoxes of Neoliberal Conservation'. *Current Conservation*, 3
(3), 24–27.

Schatzki, T., 2002. *The Site of the Social: a Philosophical Account of the Constitution of
Social Life and Change*. University Park: The Pennsylvania State University Press.

Schatzki, T., 2005. 'Peripheral Vision: The Sites of Organizations'. *Organization Studies*,
26 (3), 465–484.

Schatzki, T., 2012. 'A Primer on Practices: Theory and Research'. In: M. Hutchings and
F. Trede, eds. *Practice-Based Education: Perspectives and Strategies*. Rotterdam:
Sense Publishers.

Schatzki, T., forthcoming. 'Keeping Track of Large Phenomena'. *Geographische
Zeitshrift*, 2016.

Shove, E., Pantzar, M. and Watson, M., 2012. *The Dynamics of Social Practice: Everyday
Life and how It Changes*. London: Sage.

Spaargaren, G., 2011. 'Theories of Practices: Agency, Technology, and Culture'. *Global Environmental Change*, 21 (3), 813–822.

Southgate, C.R., 2006. 'Ecotourism in Kenya: The vulnerability of communities'. *Journal of Ecotourism*, 5 (1–2), 80–96.

Sumba, D., Warinwa, F., Lenaiyasa, P. and Muruthi, P., 2007. *The Koija Starbeds Ecolodge: A Case Study of a Conservation Enterprise in Kenya*. AWF Working Papers. Nairobi: African Wildlife Foundation.

Thouless, C.R. and Sakwa, J., 1995. 'Shocking Elephants: Fences and Crop Raiders in Laikipia District, Kenya'. *Biological Conservation*, 72 (1), 99–107.

USAID, 2004. USAID–CORE Enterprise Development Fund Report. Washington, DC: United States Agency for International Development.

Van der Duim, R., Lamers, M. and Van Wijk, J., eds, 2015. *Institutional Arrangements for Conservation, Development and Tourism in Eastern and Southern Africa*. Dordrecht: Springer.

Van Wijk, J., Van der Duim, V.R., Lamers, M. and Sumba, D., 2015. 'The Emergence of Institutional Innovations in Tourism: The Evolution of the African Wildlife Foundation's Tourism Conservation Enterprises'. *Journal of Sustainable Tourism*, 23 (1), 104–125.

Verbeek, D.H.P., Bargeman, A. and Mommaas, J.T., 2011. 'A Sustainable Tourism Mobility Passage'. *Tourism Review*, 66 (4), 45–53.

Western, D., 1997. *In the Dust of the Kilimanjaro*. Washington: Island Press.

Chapter 11

Forest governance

Connecting global to local practices[1]

Bas Arts, Daniela Kleinschmit and Helga Pülzl

> There are two different ways of envisaging the macro–micro relationship: the
> first one builds a series of Russian Matryoshka dolls – the small is being
> enclosed, the big is enclosing; and the second deploys connections – the small
> is being unconnected, the big one is to be attached.
>
> Latour, 2005: 180

Introduction

The way forests are being governed and managed today has substantially
changed over time (Agrawal *et al.*, 2008). Discourses such as sustainable
forest management, decentralized forest management and participatory forest
management have become very influential in programmes, policies, and projects all over the world, being practised in diverse forms, and with various
intended and unintended impacts on the ground (Pülzl, 2005; Rayner *et al.*,
2010). Since these discourses and practices have initially been fueled and
funded by international organizations, NGOs and donors, it seems as if these
initiatives have been 'forced' upon countries and communities (Humphreys,
2006). Hence, it is tempting to analyse this global-local nexus from an hierarchical perspective, such as regime theory, which sketches an international
institutional structure that sets rules, norms, incentives and sanctions that
others follow at lower levels of the administrative scale. However, such a hierarchical perspective probably overstates the enforceability of international
rules, norms and discourses, and undervalues the room for manoeuvre for
national and local actors. Therefore this chapter takes another stance by advoc-
ating a flat ontology of world politics, as advocated in the quotation above. It
analyses how ideas, norms and rules travel through global networks that bind
bundles of practices at a worldwide scale.

Such a flat perspective however implies that many traditional definitions of governance no longer hold. One example is 'the setting, application and enforcement
of rules' (Kjaer, 2004: 12). Although this definition might apply to some instances
of global governance, such as in the case of legally-binding trade rules of the WTO

that can be enforced through court ruling, this chapter argues that the majority of global governance initiatives work fundamentally differently. Often, binding and enforceable rules lack, or remain only paper regimes, and yet global governance initiatives produce impacts on the ground through other mechanisms than international rules (Bernstein and Cashore, 2012). Therefore, in this chapter, global governance is conceptualized as the worldwide diffusion of certain practices through: (1) ideas and discourses; (2) standards and procedures; and (3) technologies and resources (Dobbin *et al.*, 2007; Shove *et al.*, 2012). The assumption is that practices – such as eating hamburgers or curries – diffuse around the globe anyway, but that governance initiatives can promote the spread of certain practices that aim at addressing specific policy problems. Such a diffusion can take different forms: as speech acts, as policy plans, as institutionalized norms, as technical handbooks or as a supply of resources and materials.

The examples we in this chapter investigate from this perspective all relate to global forest governance. Consequently, the practices this chapter looks at are those that address the issues of deforestation and forest degradation, ranging from administrative practices in offices to management practices on the ground. Examples of the latter are initiatives that might reverse the loss of forests (the use of innovative technologies for agricultural intensification), increase the area of protected forests (the designation of new forest protected areas) and enhance their sustainable management and use (the introduction and application of certification schemes) (McDermott *et al.*, 2007; Rayner *et al.*, 2010). At the same time, we look at global governance practices that advance such preferred forms of forest use, management and protection, like spreading ideas, providing resources, codifying norms and designing global standards. Thus, practices of global governance in our analyses imply both the governing of people and the management of forests. For that reason, practices of forest governance illustrate in detail the role of agencies, objects, technologies and infrastructures in the reproduction and transformation of (bundles of) practices that connect multiple global and local sites (Schatzki, this volume).

The above picture matches well with the view of globalization theorist and *New York Times* columnist Thomas Friedman (2006) who argued that the world has become 'flat', being connected through networks of global cities, computers, social movements, companies, etcetera, which stretch beyond national borders and operate on a global scale. It also mirrors many of the insights of Manuel Castell's (2005) theory of the network society. So when for example discussing the conflicts between forest-poor developed and forest-rich developing countries in the context of global forest governance (Kolk, 1996), we should bear in mind that these unequal power relations exist next to many horizontal links which co-shape the field. Global ideas, norms and standards, for example on sustainable forest management (SFM), travel from the global to the local and have an impact on practices of forest management on the ground (Overdevest and Zeitlin, 2012). In turn, practices and experiences in specific sites may feed into national and international dialogues on forests (Arts, 2004).

This horizontal perspective of 'glocal' networks in which ideas and norms travel to remote places is very different from the conventional and vertical way of looking at global forest governance. In such hierarchical, top down accounts, the concepts of 'international regime' and 'domestic politics' are often key elements (Giessen, 2013; Rittberger, 1993). An international regime refers to rules – principles, norms, regulations and procedures – that govern international issues such as food security, deforestation or climate change. Besides being interested in the design of regimes at the international level, regime scholars also study the effectiveness of particular regimes at the nation state level. They investigate whether or not the regime objectives and commitments are being realized within the countries that are party to it. Often, from a regime perspective, it is argued that global forest governance has largely failed (Dimitrov *et al.*, 2007; Humphreys, 2006). The first reason for this failure is that the scale of deforestation and forest degradation has hardly been reduced at the global level, despite the many international initiatives that have been developed to reduce or halt the processes (FAO, 2010). The second argument is that the forest regime lacks a legally binding international treaty at its core, which could have enforced change upon countries (Dimitrov, 2005).

In what follows, we question this perspective on global forest governance – including the notion of 'failure' – as put forward by international regime theorists. In developing our argument, we build upon theories of governance and theories of social practices. Theories of governance (Pierre and Peters, 2000; Rosenau, 1995) are needed to provide an initial sketch of the field of global forest governance. However, in order to build our alternative horizontal perspective, these theories of governance are to be complemented with the flat ontology that theories of practices generally advocate (Latour, 2005; Schatzki, 2001; this volume; Shove *et al.*, 2012). Such a flat ontology helps us to go beyond hierarchical worldviews inherent in many contemporary policy, institutional and governance theories.

The format of the chapter follows the line of argumentation developed so far. First, global governance and global forest governance are elaborated upon in sections two and three, respectively. Then in section four the use of a flat ontology for analysing global-local interrelations is discussed as an alternative for the hierarchical perspectives used in the mainstream literature. The very notion of 'flatness' – so we argue – opens new perspectives on global forest governance. Third, practice theory is discussed as offering a middle-range theoretical perspective which can be used to give shape to our 'flat approach' of global forest governance. Finally, the conceptual framework as stepwise developed so far will be applied to two empirical cases: National Forest Programmes (NFPs) and Participatory Forest Management (PFM). In both cases, the global-local nexuses and their bundles of practices are reconstructed in some detail, illustrating the ways in which they stretch out from the UN offices in New York, to the FAO offices in Rome, to participatory fora in Austria and to a village in Ethiopia.

Global governance: connecting multiple actors, levels and instruments

Etymologically, the concept of 'governance' can be traced back to the Greek verb *kubernan*, which means 'to pilot' or 'to steer', and thus did it traditionally refer to 'what governments do to realize public ends' (Kjaer, 2004). Recently, the concept has been attributed new meanings. In its broadest interpretation, governance can be defined as:

> The many ways in which public and private actors from the state, market and/or civil society govern public issues, i.e. solve societal problems or create societal opportunities. They do so autonomously or in mutual inter-action, and at single or multiple administrative levels and spatial scales.
>
> (Adapted from: Arts and Visseren, 2012; Kooiman, 1993;
> Lemos and Agrawal, 2006)

This definition refers to governing by, governing with and governing without the state, either in domestic or international politics. Jan Kooiman (1993) has labelled this variety as different modes of governance. He refers to hierarchical governance (state), co-governance (public and private actors) and self-governance (private actors), respectively. Consequently, the so-called 'modes literature' acknowledges the actual and potential role of both public and private actors in providing public goods – such as welfare, health, environment – and in managing or solving public bads – such as poverty, disease, pollution – at various levels and scales.

This broad definition of governance can be distinguished from a stricter, more confined interpretation of governance. The term governance is then discussed in the context of a 'paradigm shift', which is argued to have occurred in the way in which we govern societies and organizations today (Pierre and Peters, 2000). To keep up a clear distinction with the 'modes of governance literature', Arnouts *et al.* (2012) have coined this second body of literature the 'shifts in governance literature'. According to this latter conception, the old paradigm of top-down, state-led, command and control ways of steering has lost its legitimacy (Agrawal *et al.*, 2008; Pierre and Peters, 2000). The 'big' government of the welfare state lost authority and credibility during the economic crisis of the 1980s, while its bureaucracy and old boy networks raised questions about efficiency and demo-cracy (Pierre, 2000). As a consequence, new modes of governance beyond the confines of the nation state emerged as alternatives for managing public affairs (Kjaer, 2004). Examples are network-like arrangements, self-regulation by busi-nesses, public-private partnerships, emission trading schemes and certification (Agrawal *et al.*, 2008; Kickert *et al.*, 1997; Visseren-Hamakers and Glasbergen, 2007). In addition, faith or trust in the formal institutions of the state as being the steering instrument to change human behaviour, for example through binding law and enforceable sanctions, lost ground as well (Jordan *et al.*, 2005; Weale, 1992). As a result, economic and voluntary instruments have been identified as alternatives to legal regulations and physical infrastructures. Particularly market-based instruments have received incredible attention in governance studies and practices over the last fifteen years or so (e.g. emission trading, certification schemes, payment for environmental services; see Stavins, 2001; Wunder, 2005). The shift from government to governance is by now well documented, with both market actors and civil society organizations taking on new responsibilities for the governance of societies and organizations.

In the study of international relations (SIR), the concept of governance is not defined primarily at the national level but instead referred to as 'global governance' (Nye and Donahue, 2000; Held and McGrew, 2002). One crucial difference with the debate on governance in national politics is the fact that the international system lacks a central authority comparable with the authority of the sovereign nation state. As a consequence, the term governance has always been a problematic concept in SIR, 'because we don't really know what to call what is going on' (Finkelstein, 1995: 368). Yet we do see various forms of international order, coordination and law without a sovereign, authoritative central government. Rosenau and Czempiel (1992) have labelled this 'governance without government'. This concept of global governance departs from mainstream, nation state based approaches to SIR, particularly neo-realism, in four important ways (Dingwerth and Pattberg, 2006).

First, besides states, non-state actors are acknowledged as being equally relevant to world politics, although states may hold strategic positions, e.g. access to information or decision making power (Held and McGrew, 2002). The group of non-state actors is substantial, and their numbers are estimated up to about 75,000 (Higgot *et al.*, 2000). They vary from transnational corporations (Shell) to NGOs (Greenpeace), scientific networks (IPCC), terrorist groups (Al-Qaeda, Islamic State) and religious organizations (World Council of Churches). Second, whereas SIR generally focuses on international politics, as opposed to domestic politics, global governance takes a multi-level perspective on the global polity, often referred to as 'multilevel governance' (MLG) (Held and McGrew, 2002; Hooghe and Marks, 2001). One crucial argument of MLG is that the old distinction between international and domestic politics has become blurred, due to Europeanization, globalization and localization (or 'glocalization', see Robertson, 1995). Even local communities are currently heard and addressed at the global level, while they face the consequences of global decision making, such as on free trade, or intellectual property rights, at the same time (Arts, 2004). Third, a variety of mechanisms to steer the behaviour of others, besides force, power and authority (neo-realism), or diplomacy, law and sanctions (neo-institutionalism), is acknowledged by global governance scholars, and in principle no hierarchy exists among them (De Búrca *et al.*, 2013). One can think of (non-binding) codes of conduct, recommendations, standards, charity funds, action programmes, criteria and indicators, and dialogue and conferences. The world is too complex and disaggregated to allow for one overall steering discourse, mechanism and actor, according to James Rosenau. Fourth, as a consequence of all arguments so far, new spheres of authority

(Rosenau, 1995), besides the nation state, have emerged. Non-state actors have gained private authority, examples of which are the monitoring of international standards by private audit organizations, the management of global production chains by firms, the governance of banks by the Basel standards, and the authority of NGOs on human rights, the environment and biodiversity (Cashore *et al.*, 2004; Willets, 1986). Thus, the notion of global governance offers another perspective on world politics in which non-state actors, subnational policy practices, diverse steering instruments and new spheres of private authority all play decisive roles in the governing of transnational public issues, besides the 'usual suspects' of nation states, intergovernmental organizations and international law.

Global forest governance: non-regime or regime complex?

Traditionally, the state has been very dominant in governing forests, not only in Europe, let alone in the Socialist East before 1989, but also in the colonies and in the post-colonial era (Scott, 1998). In order to prevent a Tragedy of the Commons (Hardin, 1968), it was believed that the state should regulate ownership and access to natural resources such as forests, as otherwise private resource users – in their continuous pursuit of personal gain – would jointly erode the resource base. In many cases, however, colonial, post-colonial and also capitalist and socialist states proved to be even worse managers of the forests than ordinary people, by exploiting the resource to the extreme, often in conflict with local needs and the state's own conservation objectives, by issuing concessions to private companies or public enterprises, without any effective monitoring mechanism in place, by accepting – or even informally promoting – practices of corruption in forest value chains and timber markets, and by being absent as a manager, particularly in remote areas, leaving the forests open to whatever (illegal) use (Bunker, 1985; Irland, 2008; Repetto and Gillis, 1988). This situation led to increasing criticism on 'state forestry' from different angles (Scott, 2006). There was opposition by grass-roots movements, which fought for local forest rights; there was pressure from international organizations and donors, who advocated sustainable forest management; and there were protests by NGOs, which claimed the need for forest conservation (Bose *et al.*, 2012; Humphreys, 2006; Peluso, 1992). For all these reasons, many countries around the world have recently reformed public forest policy and law – a process which is generally called 'forest governance'. According to Agrawal *et al.* (2008), the term refers to the (partial) move away from centrally administered top-down regulatory forest policies that characterized much of forestry in the nineteenth and twentieth centuries towards the more decentralized, community-based and market-oriented policy instruments and management approaches that we see today. This change in forest governance parallels the 'paradigm shift' in governance from top-down, state based governments to more local and horizontal forms of governance, including non-state actors, subnational levels and various instruments, as discussed in the previous section.

In international politics, the term 'global forest governance' emerged over time too. At the beginning of the 1980s, the topic of deforestation hit the international political agenda really hard (Kolk, 1996). NGOs like Greenpeace and the Rainforest Alliance had started successful international campaigns and found resonance among larger audiences worldwide. Particularly the images of (seemingly) untouched wildlife-rich forests being destroyed by greedy humans – following the forces of global capitalism – were appealing. Although the rate of deforestation has diminished in the 2000s compared with the 1990s, the topic is till current. According to the Food and Agriculture Organization (FAO, 2010), the world loses about five million hectares net – an area 1.5 times the size of the Netherlands – annually today. This deforestation has been reported to have numerous consequences: local and global climate change, erosion of biological and genetic resources, soil degradation, loss of water regulation, adverse impacts on human livelihoods, etcetera (Humphreys, 2006). A related theme is illegal logging (Concalves et al., 2012). It is said that about 30 per cent of the global trade in tropical timber is based on illegal sources and that in individual tropical countries illegal logging can amount to 50 or even 70 per cent of all harvested timber (Hansen and Treue, 2008). This not only contributes to deforestation and biodiversity loss but also reduces income for forest workers and revenues for governments.

The above problems – deforestation, the loss of forest biodiversity and illegal logging – have provoked various policy responses. Over time, an extensive system of international forest instruments has developed, collectively striving for a reverse of the loss of forests worldwide, for a significant increase in the area of protected forest and for the enhancement of sustainable forest management to attain socio-economic benefits for people while maintaining ecosystem values and services from forests (Beeko and Arts, 2010; Cashore et al., 2004; FAO, 2011; Giessen, 2013; Hoogeveen and Verkooijen, 2010; Humphreys, 2006; Pülzl, 2005; Rayner et al., 2010; Tysiachniouk, 2012; Visseren-Hamakers and Glasbergen, 2007). These instruments for global forest governance include:

- non-legally binding instruments, for example adopted by the UNCED Rio Conference in 1992 ('Authoritative Statement on Forests' and Chapter 11 of Agenda 21) and by the United Nations Forum on Forests (UNFF) in 2007 ('Non-Legally Binding Instrument on All Types of Forests');
- voluntary instruments of international organizations like FAO, UNFF and Forest Europe, such as National Forest Programmes (NFPs) and Criteria and Indicators (C&I) for sustainable forest management.
- agendas and programmes of international organisations and bodies, such as FAO (agro-forestry), UNFF (forest dialogue in the UN), International Tropical Timber Organization (ITTO; timber trade), UN Commission for Sustainable Development (the role of forests in sustainable development), and the World Bank (funding of forest programmes and projects, particularly in developing countries);

- private instruments, such as certification programmes, to promote sustainable forest management and sustainable production and consumption of timber in the international chain and the market (Forest Stewardship Council [FSC], and Program for the Endorsement of Forest Certification, [PEFC]);
- agendas and programmes of public–private partnerships, such as the Round Table of Sustainable Palm Oil (RSPO) and the Collaborative Partnership on Forests (CPF);
- legally binding treaties on forest issues that cover only part of the international forest agenda, such as the International Tropical Timber Agreement (ITTA), which aims for the expansion and diversification of trade in tropical timber;
- legally binding treaties on related topics, such as CITES (to ban or limit trade in endangered species), RAMSAR (protection of wetlands), UNFCCC (climate change), UNCCD (prevention of desertification) and CBD (conservation and sustainable use of biodiversity) that all in their own way relate to forest issues (respectively: endangered tree species, forests in wetlands, carbon stocks, anti-erosion measures and forest biodiversity);
- bilateral agreements, such as the Forest Law Enforcement, Governance and Trade (FLEGT) initiative of the EU and timber-exporting tropical countries, to ban illegally logged timber from the European market via timber-tracking systems, public procurement policies and timber regulations for the private sector.

No scholar will challenge the existence of these instruments, but they differ widely in terms of interpreting their meaning and evaluating their effectiveness (see Table 11.1). Some see them as symbolic, fragmented and ineffective, neither really addressing the underlying causes of deforestation and illegal logging, such as national economic interests, corporate power and environmental crime, nor

Table 11.1 Diverse interpretations of global forest governance

Author(s)	Interpretation	Evaluation
Dimitrov, 2005; Dimitrov et al., 2007	Non-regime	Symbolic norms; no impacts on the ground
Giessen, 2013	Regime complex	Fragmented; marginal effects
Hoogeveen and Verkooijen, 2010	Portfolio of instruments	These matter; make a difference on the ground
Humphreys, 1996; 2006	Regime failure	It does not address underlying causes
Pülzl, 2005	Global narrative	Narrative without regulation
Rayner et al., 2010	Regime complex	It matters; makes a difference on the ground

changing national and local (forest related) policies and practices (Dimitrov, 2005; Humphreys, 2006). Dimitrov *et al.* (2007) even speak of a *non*-regime in the forest case, because legally binding rules that can be enforced upon countries and, through them, upon forest users are absent. This is remarkable, according to them, because the circumstances seem to have been favourable for such a regime (high value of forests, high rates of deforestation and forest degradation, and strong political pressures from NGOs). Instead, governments have only agreed upon a set of symbolic international norms that have no practical effects. Others, though, are more positive about the relevance, coherence and impacts of these international forest instruments, referring to, for example, the effects of sustainable forest management programmes and standards on national and local policies and management practices (Cashore *et al.*, 2004; McDermott *et al.*, 2007; Tysiachniouk, 2012). Rayner *et al.* (2010) speak of a 'forest regime complex' that contains voluntary norms and rules, private standards, as well as binding treaties on forest-related topics, such as climate change (UNFCCC), desertification (UNCCD) and biodiversity (CBD).

To conclude, scholars on global forest governance generally acknowledge that a diversity of public and private norms and instruments has emerged at the global level that works through various administrative levels and spatial scales, thus recognizing the expanded roles of private actors and multi-level governance in the regulation of transnational forest issues. Yet they differ in opinion whether we deal with 'new spheres of authority', as Rosenau and his followers claim, that can (cognitively or morally) enforce changes on the ground towards better forest conservation and management practices, or whether we still deal with the old situation in which political authority is exclusively related to the nation state and its intergovernmental bodies and formal rules. In the latter view, new modes of private or hybrid governance will *always* remain symbolic or ineffective in nature, because these lack such formal authority. However, we do not think that this debate is very fruitful. On the one hand, global forest governance over the last decades has evolved in new directions, something which is more or less acknowledged by all scholars. On the other hand, forest management practices on the ground have substantially changed, as observed by many scholars too. We therefore believe that it makes more sense to analyse the connections between the two and assess how global ideas, norms and instruments perform in local practices, instead of continuing to play the 'blame game' of regime (in)effectiveness. For that reason, we radically depart from regime theory in the next section and present an alternative 'flat' perspective on world politics, based on practice theory, that is in our view much better equipped to conceptualize the global-local nexus in forest governance than any classical – either neo-realist or neo-institutional – model.

Global forest governance: from an hierarchical to a flat ontology

Whatever stance one takes on global forest governance – either an ineffective non-regime or a regime complex that matters — both positions implicitly share the assumption of a hierarchical ontology that offers a 'top-down' representation of the dynamics at play in international politics (see Figure 11.1). When writing about 'ontology', we mean ideas that people hold about the 'fundamental' nature, structure, dimensions or elements of some social phenomenon (Schatzki, this volume). Following most elementary models of institutional theory, which we for example find in the work of both Noble Prize Laureates North (1990) and Ostrom (1990), many regime theorists assume that collectively designed international rules will, under certain conditions, steer the behaviour of individual countries in preferred directions. But for such governance to happen, in order to make the rules effective, the regimes should not only be well designed – addressing the 'right' problem, the various interests, the issue of power and authority, available capacities and knowledge, etcetera – but being enforceable through systems of monitoring, verification and, ultimately, sanctioning as well (Miles *et al.*, 2002; Rittberger, 1993). The latter may work directly and openly, for example through negative evaluation reports, blaming and shaming in the media, official court cases and – in the last instance – punishment, or indirectly and silently by the so-called 'shadow of hierarchy' that make countries change their behaviour 'voluntarily', because they anticipate potential negative consequences when being non-compliant with rules and norms (Héritier and Lehmkuhl, 2008). In such institutional models, ontologies are definitely hierarchical in nature in that institutions 'at the top' shape the behaviour of groups and individuals 'at the bottom', through incentives, rules and sanctions.

Hierarchical ontologies apply both to 'deniers' and 'believers' of an international forest regime. The former argue that legally binding international rules on forests are absent and that the voluntary norms that have replaced them are only symbolic in nature; hence, these are not meant to have any effect (Dimitrov, 2005). In other words, the international system lacks an effective institutional top layer to regulate forest issues, so the target audiences at the bottom can do with forest resources whatever they like, with no political or financial consequences what so ever. The regime complexity

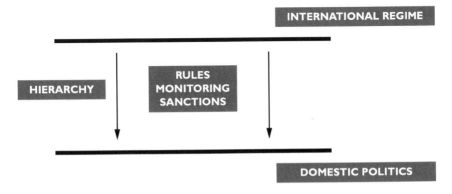

Figure 11.1 Hierarchical ontology in regime theory.

thinkers however disagree, because they believe that voluntary norms, as well as ideas and discourses, can – and do – change the behaviour of target groups. However, such behavioural changes work according to different logics than the one of 'consequentalism' in the case of binding rules and sanctions (the fear of being punished when not complying with rules; March and Olsen, 1989). Two alternative logics are relevant here: the 'logic of appropriateness' (people change their behaviour to conform to new norms in social groups) and 'the logic of communication' (people start to do things otherwise because of new persuasive ideas, arguments and knowledge) (March and Olsen, 1989; Pouliot, 2008; Risse, 2000). Such logics are, according to regime complexity scholars, also operative in global forest governance, since over the years new norms and discourses, for example on sustainable forest management, have been established and subsequently been followed through on the ground (Arts *et al.*, 2010; Bernstein and Cashore, 2012; Rayner *et al.*, 2010). Consequently, hard law is not a necessary precondition for regime effectiveness, because ideas, discourses and norms can also contribute to social change. Yet, in onto-logical terms, these scholars too perceive the world of international regulation as hierarchical in principle, although they replace the binding rules of hard law 'at the top' with the ideas and norms of soft law and international discourses. In both cases, though, human agencies are conceptualized as being shaped and steered by an overarching layer of ideas, norms and rules, irrespective of whether these are legally binding and enforceable or socially and discursively disciplining.

Whether the use of a hierarchical ontology is judged to be adequate and appropriate for understanding global forest governance, or whether it is not, we would in all cases argue that the use of any particular ontology is never a neutral or an innocent thing, since they produce images of certain 'realities' at the expense of others. Just like language or discourses, they are performative (Butler, 1988). They do in our view not represent a pre-given world, as is often claimed or implicitly assumed in science, but they actively produce it, in inter-action with the social and material phenomena the ontology at hand is address-ing (Savransky, 2012). This also implies that it can never be true or false. Ontologies can neither be confirmed nor falsified by science in a universal sense, although empirical research and data can definitely make the use of a specific ontology more plausible and credible than another. So the world of international regulation is not hierarchical by its universal nature or essence, but is analytic-ally made to be represented as such (Wendt, 1992). This implies that it is always possible to think of alternative ontologies which picture the world differently. Note that this position differs from the one defended by Theodore Schatzki in this volume. Whereas Schatzki's ontology entails a transcendental philosophical position that expresses a core belief in the flatness of the social world ('how it essentially is'), our position is close to a constructionist one in which ontological pluralism is put centrally ('how the world is differently produced through diverse cosmologies') (Savransky, 2012).

We in this chapter argue for the need to radically rethink the hierarchical ontology in regime theory as used in the debate on global forest governance. Following up on authors in the school of practice theory in particular, we suggest a flat ontology as an instrument to analyse global forest governance. A flat ontology holds that social phenomena are laid out on *one* level of reality and, hence, opposes hierarchical conceptualizations such as agency-structure, micro-macro, individual-society, actor-in-context, multi-level governance or multi-scalar politics (Latour, 2005; Schatzki, this volume; Shove *et al.*, 2012). Such a flat perspective opens up new ways of understanding global forest governance, beyond the various forms of regime theory and regime (in)effectiveness, but it definitely closes off other ways of looking at it as well. Hence, our ontology is neither claimed to be more comprehensive, in the sense that it offers a more complete picture of the world, nor better, in the sense that it is more valid, than others. It does however produce a radically different view of affairs in global forest governance. A view which is perhaps more interesting in theoretical terms (post-institutional; see Cleaver, 2002) and more plausible as an instrument to make sense of forest governance in empirical terms as well (Arts and Babili, 2013).

The flat alternative we propose here is roughly sketched in Figure 11.2. Ideas, norms and rules are not conceptualized as an overarching layer that shapes human conduct from above, but as elements that travel from forest practice to forest practice all over the globe, through carriers, linkages, and processes of packing and unpacking (Shove *et al.*, 2012). This travelling is always accompanied with processes of translation (instead of implementation) (Latour, 2005; Yanow, 1993). When local actors engage with global ideas, norms and rules, they by definition renegotiate and re-interpret them in order to make sense of such ideas, norms and rules, and to activate them, in their situated practices. Together, these elements and their linkages and carriers bring together loosely connected bundles of practices (Schatzki, 2001), which we would like to label 'glocal networks of forest governance practices'. This terminology, which is also derived from the glocalization literature (see for example Robertson, 1995; Swyngedouw, 2004), wishes to express that forest practices are always localized, from United Nations offices designing forest policy to local communities working in participatory forest management projects, while they as bundles stretch over the globe at the same time.

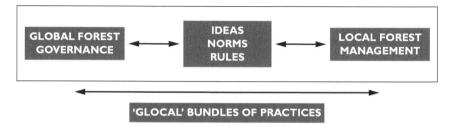

Figure 11.2 A horizontal ontology of 'glocal' forest governance.

Practice theory as flat ontology

The most well-known flat ontology in today's social sciences is Latour's (2005). In his actor-network theory (ANT), the world is considered to be made of actors – including both humans and non-humans, examples of the latter being things, artefacts and animals – and their associations. Some actors only look bigger or more overarching than others because of being more and better connected to the network, not because they stand in a hierarchical relationship vis-à-vis others:

> Yes, Wall Street is connected to many places and in this sense, but in this sense only, it is 'bigger', more powerful, overarching. However, it is not a wider, larger, less local, less interactive, less an inter-subjective place than the shopping center in Moulins, France, or the noisy and smelly market stands in Bouaké, Ivory Coast.
>
> (Latour, 2005: 178)

An alternative to Latour's flat ontology is the one suggested by Schatzki (this volume). He agrees with Latour that there is nothing 'above' the social:

> The site of the social is a mass of linked practices and arrangements spread out across the globe and changing through time. All social phenomena are slices or aspects of this mass.

Hence, micro and macro form, according to Schatzki, a flexible distinction of scale in the single mass of social phenomena. However, the two scholars of flatness also differ. First, as already pointed at in the above, Schatzki's position is a philosophical one ('how the world is'), whereas Latour's position is a methodological one ('how the world is produced') (Callon and Latour, 1983; Latour, 2005; Schatzki, this volume). In other words, whereas Schatzki takes a transcendental position, Latour's ontology offers students concepts and tools to follow actors, actants and associations in practice and – on the basis of that – record their realities. Second, whereas Latour delimits his ontology to actors (humans), actants (non-humans) and associations, Schatzki adds the concepts of 'social practice' and 'material arrangement' to his repertoire. He does so first to maintain the conventional distinction between humans (practices) and non-humans (arrangements), and second to account for 'organized sets of activities' (practices) besides individual acts. In this chapter, we take a bit of both scholars. To start with Latour, and following our own practice based approach (Arts *et al.*, 2013), we prefer the more 'open' methodological position – in order to analyse (or better: perform) global forest governance from an alternative, non-hierarchical perspective – and moreover endorse a post-human approach, to balance humans, nature and technologies in analysing glocal forest networks. Hence, we depart from Schatzki's transcendental position as well as from his first distinction of practice versus arrangement. Yet, like Schatzki, we think that an a priori distinction between individual acts and practices is useful, to express the view that all human conduct is socially and historically situated and that such cannot be reduced to the sum of individual acts in specific sites.[2]

One misunderstanding of practice theory is that it is considered to be strong on the understanding of small localized practices, e.g. family, school, community or company, but weak on large social phenomena, like transnational corporations, countries or even the EU. But, as Schatzki (this volume) asserts, it does have interesting things to say about larger phenomena too, because any large social constellation can be considered a (complex) bundle of more or less related practices. Glocal networks, as we metaphorically described global forest governance in the above, then take the form of complex bundles of practices around the world. But how to keep the ontology of such large complexes and bundles 'flat' while analysing the global-local nexus in forest governance? Here the work of Shove et al. (2012) is of great help. While Schatzki (this volume) and Latour (2005) provide us with philosophical and methodological foundations of a flat ontology, Shove et al. (2012) offer a more tangible, concrete policy oriented perspective. They consider policy practices as being constituted by three related elements: meaning, competence and materiality. Any practice – from snowboarding to daily showering to writing policy plans – implies symbolic understanding and sense-making, competent bodies and performances and technologies and resources to execute the practice. But these three components of 'know-what', 'know-how' and 'hardware' are of course strongly related: without meaning there is no reason to do things; without competence there is neither skilful execution of tasks nor attainment of preferred outcomes; and without hardware the things cannot be done anyway. Practices therefore have, according to Shove et al., a double face; they are at the same time entities (associations of elements) and performances (the execution of practices by agencies through which these are reproduced, or transformed, as entities).

Crucial in Shove et al.'s analysis is that practices and their constitutive elements travel around the world, through processes of 'packing' and 'unpacking', thus diffusing social practices from New York to Amsterdam to Nairobi, as well as to their rural hinterlands. This is the most obvious for hardware: technology or resources can be put in trucks, trains, ships or planes, travel from A to B over the globe, and be unloaded in the new local site. But the same can be said, at least metaphorically speaking, of meanings and competences. They can be classified and coded in site A; transported through carriers and networks (people, telecommunication, internet, etcetera) to B; and be unpacked and re-interpreted in the new site. Such unpacking is always paralleled with translation of generalized meanings and knowledge to new situated practices (see Latour, 2005). So snowboarding in the Alps is not similar to snowboarding in the Rocky mountains, although the differences may be very subtle. And the same applies to sustainable forest management in the Netherlands and in Tanzania, although similar terms, symbols, codes and technologies may be used in both countries. This travelling of elements and practices should however not be misunderstood as automata or imposition. There is nothing certain about a practice in site A to be adopted in site B. It can emerge and persist, but not necessarily so, or it can disappear quickly as well. Such is dependent on many factors: the carriers of the new practice, resonance with local habits, routines and histories, the anchoring process itself, unexpected events, etcetera. Hence, Shove *et al.* (2012) do not speak of 'policy implementation', as so many policy scientists like to do, but of policy translation (compare Yanow, 1993). Whereas the former has an hierarchical and mechanistic connotation, in the sense that higher-level policies are implemented at lower-level ones, the latter's meaning is much more flat and dynamic, connecting policy practices spatially that change while travelling.

Below, we will present two illustrations from global forest governance. First, the worldwide diffusion of National Forest Programmes (NFPs) and its performance in Austria. Second, the advocacy of Participatory Forest Management (PFM) by international organizations, consultants, NGOs and donors, and how its meanings, competences and materialities have travelled to and work out in practice in an Ethiopian village.

National Forest Programme (NFP): how the concept was 'unpacked' in Austria

Vienna, Austria, November 2014: a large room is filled with representatives of forest owners associations, delegates of the Austrian forest industry, the national and regional forest and nature protection authorities, environmental and social NGOs, forest-related ministerial advisors, state forest owner associates, hunting associations, the mountain bike forum, social and natural scientists, and many others. This is the Austrian forest dialogue, set up as part of the recently introduced National Forest Programme (NFP) process. A moderator opens the meeting that aims at formulating a forest vision for the near and more distant future. Invited participants gather around blackboards and discuss texts of suggested future perspectives for seven different fields of action. Besides, presentations about various forest-related topics are given to update participants on international debates and national activities. Key assumption of the forest dialogue in Austria is to give those that have a stake in forest policy, including actors coming from outside the forest sector, the possibility to take part in the discussions about the future of Austrian forestry and to generate a common vision for decision-making. New rulings and guidelines for the participatory process have been established. They aim to ensure a consensus decision-making process, with the possibility of visualizing opposing views in the final NFP, if necessary.

So what has happened? How did this new forest governance practice in Austria come about? Traditionally, forest policy in Austria was determined by close cooperation between the forest owners association on the one hand and national forest authorities on the other (Pregernig, 1998). Interest representation was well settled through this neo-corporatist system, and other forest-interested organizations, such as for example environmental NGOs, had no or very limited access to decision-making. This practice seems – at least from the outside – to have changed, as nowadays, within the national dialogue, forest owners and forest authorities are only two groupings among many others that are being heard. Power relations have seemingly changed, since the set-up of this process has been broadened and democratized (albeit not as radical as some actors had hoped for). Compared with earlier periods in which only a very limited number of actors were involved in forest policy-making, forest governance now has become more transparent and in part more open to viewpoints from non-forest sectors. This change from neo-corporatism to network governance in Austrian forest policy is said to be strongly connected to the international NFP discourse and movement (Pülzl and Rametsteiner, 2002).

So what meanings do these National Forest Programmes have? Generally spoken, NFPs provide, according to the FAO (2010: 149): 'an internationally agreed framework which many countries use for the development and implementation of national forest-related policies and international commitments'. A more generic definition sees NFPs as a 'wide-range of approaches towards forest policy formulation, planning and implementation at the subnational and national levels' (UNCSD/IPF, 1996). A generic aim of NFPs is promoting and ensuring sustainable forest management through participatory policy processes, with the aim of developing a strategic planning document of on average a validity of ten years. Central ideas are the inclusion of private and non-state actors, the involvement of sectors outside forestry, iterative and adaptive planning processes as well as monitoring of implementation (Glück and Humphreys, 2002). Furthermore, the importance of decentralization and multi-level coordination is an essential pillar of NFPs. Enabling mechanisms of participatory deliberation, conflict resolution and policy learning are to be built in such processes as well (Howlett and Rayner, 2006). In contrast to 'normal' national forest policy, NFPs aim of increasing consistency with international policies, thereby building a bridge to global forest policy-making efforts (Glück, 1999, Glück and Voitleitner, 2004).

Responding to NFP definitions available, related guidelines to develop competences of how to establish such programmes have appeared in a rich variety. Political processes within the United Nations (UNCSD/IPF, 1996, UNCSD/IFF, 2000), but also within Europe (Vienna Resolution 1, MCPFE, 2003), donor and funding agencies (Finland, Japan, Switzerland, Germany), and within specific facilities (FAO, PROFOR, UNDP, World Bank), have led to the development of guidelines as well as of handbooks (FAO, 1996, 2006). In the various country contexts, specific rules for NFPs have also emerged. Key actors guiding the NFP process mostly belong to the respective national ministries. In some developing countries, consultants and international organizations, such as the FAO or World Bank, have assisted in developing competences to write strategic documents and to design NFP elements. Some NFP processes – for example in Austria and Germany – involve external personnel in the form of moderators. Rather recently, scenario planning has started to become an important technique for conceptualizing the future, for instance in Finland and Austria. It has also been taken up by the FAO in their effort to strengthen NFP programming (Herder *et al.*, 2014).

Materialities involved in NFP processes can be analytically distinguished into financial means on the one hand and the scope of participation (embodiment) on the other. The former include funding received by less developed and developing countries to start and give guidance to NFP processes. The European Commission, the PROFOR programme (initially established within UNDP in 1997 and then relocated to the World Bank in 2002) and the now called FAO Farm & Forest Facility have financially and technically supported the set-up of NFPs in various countries. When it comes to the scope of participation, this has varied among countries as well as during NFP processes themselves. Expert administrators and professional stakeholders, like for example forest industries and forest owners, have participated in most, if not all, NFPs. Several countries however have enlarged the scope of participation beyond the set of participants mentioned. For example, the Austrian and Finnish NFP processes have even engaged the public at large in different ways, for example through public hearings. The involvement of moderators and facilitators has also created different decision-making settings and results. Small working and discussion groups have been installed to collect participant views in many instances, as well as editorial teams being used to streamline group outcomes.

How have these new NFP practices evolved over time? NFPs first emerged in the mid-1990s. The FAO then renamed their Tropical Forestry Action Plans (TFAPs) as NFPs. TFAPs were initially meant to put a halt to the loss of tropical forests in developing countries, but largely failed (Liss, 1999: 27). In parallel, the tropical deforestation discourse, so dominant in the 1980s, started to decline by the beginning of the 1990s, while others – like the sustainable forest management discourse – gained more prominence (Arts *et al.*, 2010). Ideas about proper forest policy planning – from hierarchical to participatory and deliberative – also changed in those days (Pülzl and Rametsteiner, 2002). These developments forced the FAO to reconsider its TFAPs. It issued new guidelines on the formulation and implementation of NFPs (FAO, 1996) and towards the end of the 1990s a Practitioner's Guide was prepared (Six-Country Initiative, 1999). Other United Nation bodies than the FAO (UNCSD/IPF, 1996, UNCSD/IFF, 2000, UNFF, 2002) supported this change, while referring to NFPs as means to implement sustainable forest management. Globally, bilateral and multilateral donors accepted this new emerging framework for designing national forest policies and for funding development cooperation as well (COM, 2005; Humphreys, 1996).

At the European level, various NFP-related initiatives were soon to follow. The European Commission in its forestry and rural strategies stressed the need to implement an NFP – or an equivalent programme – in each member state in order to assess forest-related funding (COM, 1998). This has put additional pressure on EU members to adopt an NFP. In a rather different arena, European scientists agreed to assess NFPs more closely (Glück *et al.*, 1999) and started a related COST Action[3] that was operative between 1999 and 2003. Within Pan-Europe, the Ministerial Conference on the Protection of Forests in Europe (MCPFE) worked towards a common understanding of NFPs, culminating in an 'MCPFE approach towards NFPs in Europe' (MCPFE, 2003). This also led to the inclusion of a separate NFP indicator in the European criteria and indicators (C&I) for sustainable forest management. In addition, the latest draft negotiation text of the legally binding forest agreement at the pan-European level states that parties, in order to achieve the objectives and to implement the obligations of the Convention, shall develop, implement and update NFPs or equivalents (INC Forests, 2013).

Simultaneously with global and European initiatives, national expectations and demands to change forest governance has fostered the implementation of NFPs. Sweden is an example where the pressure for a new forest programme is boosted by a critical national discussion on its forestry sector and forest policy. Based on such national demands, while resonating international discourses, an assessment of the Swedish Forest Agency (SFA) recently concluded that a NFP could provide added value to the traditional Swedish forest policy framework.

The idea of NFPs travelled over the globe rather quickly, particularly after the year 2000, through carriers and processes of (un)packing as referred to in the above (UN organizations, conferences, donors, handbooks, money, lead countries, NGOs, local participation processes, etcetera). In 2010 up to 75 per cent of all forests in the world were covered by NFPs (FAO, 2010: xxiii). Nearly 100 per cent of the forest area in Europe and Asia currently falls under an NFP, while more than 80 per cent of the forest area in Oceania and Latin America is covered. However, Africa as well as North and Central America show a much smaller coverage. Some countries, such as Austria or Finland, can be classified as lead countries, while others have failed to implement a substantive NFP so far (Italy). Again others have claimed no necessity to design an own NFP, as adequate programmes are said to already exist (Netherlands, Sweden). The former ones (Austrians and Fins) are now invited to share their experiences with those that aim to start similar processes. Furthermore, regional and international bodies and their guidelines and handbooks act as global carriers of how to set up an NFP process. This diffusion process is supported by the funding provided to less developed and developing countries by various donors. However, requirements initially introduced by FAO, CSD/IPF, and MCPFE (and others) do not necessarily match the national or local contexts of the countries where NFPs have to be processed. Howlett and Rayner (2006) argue that the various types of NFPs in many countries are characterized by different mechanisms for coordination, participation, conflict resolution and policy learning. Hence, they argue that regional and international bodies only play rather limited roles in policy convergence. Howlett and Rayner instead highlight the essential role of domestic factors in the implementation and adoption of NFPs.

From the above we can conclude that, although no legally binding requirement to set up NFPs exist, the diffusion of related ideas, guidelines, handbooks, resources and technologies can be observed across the globe. It has led to the establishment of a series of practices that challenge traditional forest policy-making, for example by the need to include more and different actors and sectors than before. The variety of NFP designs and implementation practices supports the conclusion that the notion of NFP has travelled from the global and regional levels to national and local ones, but – while doing so – has been translated to nation- and site-specific modalities.

Participatory Forest Management (PFM) in Agama (Ethiopia): local translation of a global concept

Agama is a small village in the South-Western part of Ethiopia, located in one of the few remaining forested areas in the country, Bonga forest (Ayana *et al.*, 2015; Vandenabbeele, 2012). Historically, the lives of the local people have always been intrinsically related to the forests economically, socially and cultur-ally. The forests hold manifold timber and non-timber resources for livelihoods and income generation, they contribute to agricultural production – like the famous *Coffea Arabica* agro-forestry systems – and they offer spiritual places. Moreover, the forests are important hotspots of biodiversity (*Afromontane* rain-forests and numerous rare monkeys, birds, frogs, trees and plants). Over time, though, parts of the forests have been degenerated and converted into other land-scapes. In the region, up to one third of the forests have been lost since the early 1970s and standing forests have often degenerated due to human use, including coffee production (Vandenabbeele, 2012). This not only threatens biodiversity, but local forest-dependent livelihoods as well.

Traditionally, the political response to local forest loss has been the nation-alization of forest areas and top-down, state-led forest management approaches, on the premise that local people are caught in a tragedy of the commons, which foster overuse of the resource through growing populations, increasing demands and lack of knowledge to rationally manage resources (Hardin, 1986; Scott, 1998). In Ethiopia too, this has been the dominant approach under various political regimes (the Empire under Haile Selassie in the 1970s, the socialist Derg regime in the 1980s and the current semi-democratic state established in the early 1990s; Ayana *et al.*, 2013). However, global discourses on proper forest management shifted while these diverse Ethiopian political regimes succeeded over time (Arnold, 2001; Wiersum, 2009). Since state forestry hardly delivered its promises, particularly in the Tropics, where state intervention was often weak, incompetent and corrupt, other forest management approaches became in vogue (Agrawal, 2001). The global debate on Community-Based Natural Resource Management (CBNRM) has been very influential. Various scholars argued that the tragedy of the commons thesis is theoretically flawed and they also empirically falsified it by showing many examples of successful, local, traditional management systems of scarce resources from all over the world (Ostrom, 1990). This scholarly literature had an enormous impact on global debates on natural resource management, such as in the FAO, World Bank, UNEP, UNDP and more recently, the UN Forum on Forests (UNFF). More and more, international policy makers, diplomats and NGOs started to advocate the CBNRM approach and references to it emerged in all kind of policy documents, such as Agenda 21 and the Non-Legally Binding Instrument on All Types of Forests. At the same time, local communities and indigenous peoples became stronger in propagating their forest rights in international fora, thus fueling the CBNRM debate (Dupuits, 2014). Subsequently, this glocal discourse slowly but surely entered into national policies and local practices. Some countries assumed a leading role in translating this approach to their needs, like Nepal, India and Mexico, while others followed, like Bolivia, Vietnam and – indeed – Ethiopia.

In Ethiopia, PFM – Participatory Forest Management, as the national variant of CBNRM is called – started as an experiment, strongly driven by international NGOs (like Farm Africa) and donors (like GIZ). Only recently has PFM become formally part of national forest policy (Ayana, 2014). Bonga forests was one of the first PFM experiments, hence Agama became part of it at an early stage, about twenty years ago. This, however, had enormous consequences for the people and the forests. Together with the idea of PFM, a new package of norms, competences, resources and technologies had entered the village: for example, the need to establish a village forest committee; the urgency to (better) demarcate and zone the forests; the establishment of forest restoration projects; the need for new rules on forest access, use and management, through permits, sanctions, fees and fines (thus setting limits on timber harvesting, grazing and charcoal production); and the urgency to establish a system of monitoring of compliance. All this became a new reality for the villagers in Agama. Its implementation, though, was not a smooth trajectory (Ayana et al., 2015). For example, the process of re-demarcating the forest under the PFM approach revived old and painful memories of forest demarcation under the socialist Derg regime in the 1980s that forced many locals out of the forests and deprived them of many of their traditional forest rights. In addition, the set-up of the PFM village committee met resistance, because it fuelled old conflicts among the various ethnic communities in the village. Also, the district forest department did not live up to many of its promises under the PFM arrangement, and forest officials hardly changed their arrogant attitude towards the villagers. Farm Africa – as the leading manager of the project – therefore encountered hostility right from the start. Partly to remediate this, partly to decrease social pressure on the forest, this NGO started to invest resources in alternative livelihood projects in Agama, such as a tree nursery and small cattle husbandry, to increase local support for PFM. Over time, though, these projects started to overtake the actual aim of PFM, namely improving local forest management. Since villagers mainly used the new rules as a way to formalize their forest land claims vis-à-vis the state, while management and use were regulated mainly by customary norms and traditional authorities, the PFM project and the forest committee 'never really got into the forests' (Vandenabbeele, 2012). So the project affected village life, but was locally translated in ways that differ from the original aims. As a consequence, it had hardly any impact on forest management practices – and thus hardly affected forest quantity and quality – around Agama.

This short case study is not meant to evaluate the success or failure of this PFM project (and contrary to the problems in Agama, diverse success stories can be referred to, for example from Tanzanian CBNRM; see Arts and Babili, 2013; Blomley *et al.*, 2008). The point here is to show how certain meanings, competences and materialities (CBNRM, PFM guidelines, donor funds and projects) travel from the global to the local and co-shape situated practices on the ground. In the case of Agama, PFM has enabled the formalization of land claims, fuelled ethnic conflicts and established new livelihood projects, while forestry practices have hardly changed. This does not happen through binding law or command-and-control mechanisms, but through scholarly debates, policy discourses, advocacy coalitions, voluntary guidelines, and earmarked funds. Often, this glocal dynamic surpasses the national state. Here as well, PFM has only become a formal part of Ethiopian forest policy about twenty years *after* its inception in donor-driven projects. In addition, we cannot speak of a linear implementation trajectory, like in a top-down, command-and-control fashion of regulation. While being introduced locally, original meanings, competences and materialities become accommodated to situations at hand. In Agama as well, PFM rules became linked to forest land claims more than that they were applied to forest management. It raised additional income not so much through improved forest use, but through livelihood projects in the village; and it fuelled social conflict more than that it restored forest lands. As such, local people 'spoke back'. They did not passively accept the PFM project of Farm Africa and GIZ, neither did they radically revolt against it, but they strategically translated it to their needs. Additional income and securing forest rights were welcomed, but forest use and management remained under customary control. But the project had adverse, unintended consequences for them too, like the increase of social conflict.

Conclusion

Global forest governance is maybe much more about preferred forest policy and management practices 'travelling' around the globe as particular meanings (ideas, discourses), competences (guidelines, handbooks) and materialities (bodies, standards, resources) than about the setting, application, implementation and enforcement of formal laws, rules and regulations, as traditionally conceptualized by policy analysts and regime scholars. From the latter perspective, a global forest regime does not exist, and the soft norms and rules that do, are considered neither relevant nor effective. From the former perspective, however, global forest governance does perform in the sense that it produces intended and unintended impacts on the ground, in social spaces and in forested landscapes, although impacts are always subject to local translations of general meanings, competences and materialities in specific sites. We thus sketch a glocal network society (Castells, 2011) that shows a plurality of (loosely) connected actors, levels and instruments in which their performances are highly contingent and unpredictable. This perspective sharply contrasts with the old social engineering paradigm in modernist policy analysis, including regime theory, that holds an instrumental view on human agency, a hierarchical model of the policy process and an unfounded steering optimism.

Our two illustrations also point at these issues and critiques. Global discourses on NFP and PFM, respectively, have diffused to various sites around the world through diverse carriers (humans, papers, websites, technologies, money, etcetera) where they have become tailor-made – unpacked and translated, as Shove *et al.* (2012) would claim – to local practices by people involved. For example, Austria shows a deep, far-reaching interpretation and elaboration of a soft instrument like NFP, compared with other countries' performances, while Agama's PFM-related practices have – *nolens volens* – tempered donors' and NGOs' high ambitions at the spot. Moreover, these illustrations do not at all exhibit linear and hierarchical implementation trajectories, but contingent and dynamic translation processes in glocal networks.

To conclude, we used flat ontology assumptions, as put forward by Schatzki and Latour in particular, to critique the use of hierarchical models of global governance, which have been very prominent in the field of forest policy analysis. By focusing on the global-local connections among diverse forest governance practices, we were thus able to show the added value of practice theory for analysing 'large' phenomena, such as glocalization dynamics. Hence, doing research with practice theory does not necessarily only imply the analysis of local situated practices. While zooming in and zooming out on situated practices on the one hand and by showing connections between globally dispersed practices on the other, we were able to sketch the dynamics of global forest governance in a way that corresponds with the open, flexible, glocalized network society of our age.

Notes

1 This chapter uses some materials from Arts, Behagel *et al.* (2014); Arts and Babili (2013); Arts and Visseren-Hamakers (2012).

2 This is not to say, though, that Latour claims such, but he leaves the 'thickening' of networks into macro-actors, organizations or scales open to empirical investigation, while Schatzki – and we – theoretically assume the clustering of actors and their associations into practices a priori.

3 COST Actions are EU-funded networking instruments for researchers, engineers and scholars to cooperate and coordinate national research activities on current/innovative topics.

References

Agrawal, A., 2001. 'Common Property Institutions and Sustainable Governance of Resources'. *World Development*, 29 (10), 1649–1672.

Agrawal, A., Chhatre, A. and Hardin, R., 2008. 'Changing Governance of the World's Forests'. *Science*, 320 (5882), 1460–1462.

Arnold, J., 2001. *Forests and People. 25 Years of Community Forestry*. Rome: FAO.

Arnouts, R., Van der Zouwen, M. and Arts, B., 2012. 'Analysing Governance Modes and Shifts in Dutch Nature Policy'. *Forest Policy and Economics*, 16 (March 2012), 43–50.

Arts, B., 2004. 'The Local-Global Nexus: NGOs and the Articulation of Scale'. *Journal of Economic and Social Geography*, 95 (5), 498–511.

Arts, B. and Babili, I., 2013. 'Global Forest Governance: Multiple Practices of Policy Performance. In: B. Arts, J. Behagel, S. van Bommel, J. De Koning and E. Turnhout, eds. *Forest and Nature Governance. A Practice-Based Approach*. Dordrecht: Springer, 111–130.

Arts, B. and Visseren-Hamakers, I., 2012. 'Forest Governance: a State of the Art Review. In: B. Arts, S. van Bommel, M. Ros-Tonen and G. Verschoor, eds. *Forest People Interfaces*. Wageningen Academic Publishers, 241–257.

Arts, B., Appelstrand, M., Kleinschmit, D., Pülzl, H. and Visseren-Hamakers, I. *et al.*, 2010. 'Discourses, Actors and Instruments in International Forest Governance. In: J. Rayner, A. Buck and P. Katila, eds. *Embracing Complexity: Meeting the Challenges of International Forest Governance*. IUFRO World Series 28, 57–74.

Arts, B., Behagel, J., Van Bommel, S., De Koning, J. and Turnhout, E., eds, 2013. *Forest and Nature Governance. A Practice-Based Approach*. Dordrecht: Springer.

Ayana, A., 2014. *Forest Governance Dynamics in Ethiopia: Histories, Arrangements, Practices*. Wageningen: Doctoral Dissertation. Wageningen: Wageningen University.

Ayana, A., Arts, B. and Wiersum, K.F., 2013. 'Historical Development of Forest Policy in Ethiopia: Trends of Institutionalization and Deinstitutionalization'. *Land Use Policy*, 32 (May 2013), 186–196.

Ayana, A., Vandenabbeele, N., Arts, B., 2015. 'Performance of Participatory Forest Management in Ethiopia: Institutional Arrangement versus Local Practice'. *Critical Policy Studies* (accepted for publication).

Beeko, C. and Arts, B., 2010. 'The EU-Ghana VPA: A Comprehensive Policy Analysis'. *The International Forestry Review*, 12 (3), 221–230.

Bernstein, S. and Cashore, B., 2012. 'Complex Global Governance and Domestic Policies: Four Pathways of Influence'. *International Affairs*, 88 (3), 585–604.

Blomley, T., Kerstin, P. *et al.*, 2008. 'Seeing the Wood for the Trees. An Assessment of the Impact of Participatory Forest Management on the Forest Condition in Tanzania'. *Oryx*, 42 (3), 380–391.

Bose, P., Arts, B. and Van Dijk, H., 2012. ' "Forest Governmentality": a Genealogy of Subject Making of Forest-Dependent "Scheduled Tribes" ' in India. *Land Use Policy*, 29 (3), 664–673.

Bunker, S., 1985. *Underdeveloping Amazon: Extraction, Unequal Exchange and the Failure of the Modern State*. Chicago: University of Chicago Press.

Butler, J., 1988. 'Performative Acts and Gender Constitution: an Essay in Phenomenology and Feminist Theory'. *Theatre Journal*, 40 (4), 519–531.

Callon, M., Latour, B., 1983. 'Unscrewing the Big Leviathan'. In: K. Knorr-Cetina and A. Cicourel, eds. *Advances in Social Theory and Methodology*. London: Routledge and Kegan Paul, 277–302.

Castells, M., 2011. *The Rise of the Network Society. The Information Age: Economy, Society and Culture* (2nd edn). Chichester: Wiley-Blackwell.

Cashore, B., Auld, G. and Newson, D., 2004. *Governance through Markets – Forest Certification and the Emergence of Non-State Authority.* New Haven and London: Yale University Press.

Cleaver, F., 2002. 'Reinventing Institutions. Bricolage and the Social Embeddedness of Natural Resource Management'. *European Journal of Development Research*, 14 (2), 11–30.

COM, 2005. Commission staff working document. Annex to the Communication on the implementation of the EU Forestry Strategy. European Commission 84 final.

Concalves, M., Panjer, M. and Greenberg, T. *et al.*, 2012. *Justice for Forests. Improving Criminal Justice Efforts to Combat Illegal Logging.* Washington DC: The World Bank.

De Búrca, G., Keohane, R. and Sabel, C., 2013. *New Modes of Pluralist Global Governance.* New York University Public Law and Legal Theory Working Papers. Paper 386. http://lsr.nellco.org/nyu_plltwp/386.

Dimitrov, R., 2005. 'Hostage to Norms: States, Institutions and Global Forest Politics'. *Global Environmental Politics*, 5 (4), 1–24.

Dimitrov, R., Sprinz, D., DiGuisto, G. and Kelle, A., 2007. 'International Nonregimes. A Research Agenda'. *International Studies Review*, 9 (2), 230–258.

Dingwerth, K. and Pattberg, P., 2006. 'Global Governance as a Perspective on World Politics'. *Global Governance*, 12 (2), 185–203.

Dobbin, F., Simmons, B. and Garret, G., 2007. 'The Global Diffusion of Public Policies: Social Construction, Coercion, Competition or Learning?' *Annual Review of Sociology*, 33 (August), 449–472.

Dressler, W. *et al.*, 2010. 'From Hope to Crisis and Back Again? A Critical History of the Global CBNRM Narrative'. *Environmental Conservation*, 37 (1), 5–15.

Dupuits, E., 2014. 'Transnational Self-Help Networks and Community Forestry: A Theoretical Framework'. *Forest Policy and Economics* (doi.org/10.1016/j.forpol.2014.07.007).

FAO, 1996. 'Basic Principles and Operational Guidelines: Formulation, Execution and Revision of National Forestry Programmes'. Rome.

FAO, 2010. 'Global Forest Resources Assessment 2010'. Rome: FAO.

FAO, 2011. 'Framework for Assessing and Monitoring Forest Governance'. Rome: FAO.

Finkelstein, L., 1995. 'What is Global Governance?' *Global Governance*, 1 (3), 367–372.

Friedman, T., 2006. *The World is Flat. The Globalized World in the 21st Century.* London: Penguin Books.

Giessen, L., 2013. 'Reviewing the Main Characteristics of the International Forest Regime Complex and Partial Explanations for Its Fragmentation'. *International Forestry Review*, 15 (1), 60–70.

Glück, P., 1999. 'National Forest Programs – Significance of a Forest Policy Framework'. In: P. Glück, G. Oesten, H. Schanz and K.R.Volz, eds. *Formulation and Implementation of National Forest Programmes. Volume I: Theoretical Aspects. EFI Proceedings No. 30.* Joensuu, 39–51.

Glück, P. and Humphreys, D., 2002. 'Research into National Forest Programmes in a European Context'. *Forest Policy and Economics*, 4 (4), 253–258.

Glück, P. and Voitleitner, J., 2004. 'NFP Research. Its Retrospect and Outlook'. Proceedings of the Seminar of COST Action E19: *National Forest Programmes in a European Context*, 2003, Vienna. Publication Series of the Institute of Forest Sector Policy and Economics. Vol. 52. Vienna.

Glück, P., Oesten, G., Schanz, H., and Volz, K.R. eds., 1999. *Formulation and Implementation of National Forest Programmes. Volume I: Theoretical Aspects. EFI Proceedings No. 30.* Joensuu, 39–51.

Hansen, C. and True, T., 2008. 'Assessing Illegal Logging in Ghana'. *International Forestry Review*, 10 (4), 573–590.

Hardin, G., 1968. 'The Tragedy of the Commons'. *Science*, 162 (3859), 1243–1248.

Held, D. and McGrew, A., 2002. *Governing Globalization. Power, Authority and Global Governance.* Cambridge: Polity Press.

Herder, M., Khadka, C. and Pelli, P. *et al.*, 2014. *Scenario Development to Strengthen National Forest Policies and Programmes. A Review of Future-Oriented Tools and Approaches that Support Policy-Making.* Forestry Policy and Institutions Working Paper No. 34. Rome, FAO.

Héritier, A. and Lehmkuhl, D., 2008. 'The Shadow of Hierarchy and New Modes of Governance'. *Journal of Public Policy*, 28 (1), 1–17.

Higgott, R., Underhill A. and Bieler, A., eds., 2000, *Non-State Actors and Authority in the Global System.* London: Routledge.

Hoogeveen, H. and Verkooijen, P., 2010. *Transforming Sustainable Development Diplomacy. Lessons Learned from Global Forest Governance.* PhD Dissertation. Wageningen: Wageningen University.

Hooghe, L. and Marks, G., 2001. *Multi-Level Governance and European Integration.* Lanham: Rowman and Littlefield.

Howlett, M. And Raynor, J., 2006. 'Globalization and Governance Capacity: Explaining Divergence in National Forest Programs as Instances of "Next Generation" Regulation in Canada and Europe'. *Governance*, 19 (2), 251–275.

Humphreys, D., 1996. *Forest Politics: The Evolution of International Cooperation.* London: Earthscan.

Humphreys, D., 2006. *Logjam. Deforestation and The Crisis of Global Governance.* London: Earthscan.

INC Forests, 2013. *INC4 Draft Negotiating Text.* Available at: www.forestnegotiations. org/INC/ResINC4/documents [Accessed 26 February 2014].

Irland, L., 2008. 'State Failure, Corruption and Warfare: Challenges for Forest Policy'. *Journal of Sustainable Forestry*, 27 (3), 189–223.

Jordan, A., Wurzel, R. and Zito, A., 2005. 'The Rise of New Policy Instruments in Comparative Perspective: Has Governance Eclipsed Government?' *Political Studies*, 53 (3), 477–496.

Kickert, W., Klijn, E. and Koppejan, J., eds., 1997. *Managing Complex Networks. Strategies for the Public Sector.* London: Sage.

Kjaer, A., 2004. *Governance.* Cambridge: Polity Press.

Kolk, A., 1996. *Forests in International Politics: International Organizations, NGOs and the Brazilian Amazone.* Utrecht: International Books.

Kooiman, J., 1993. *Modern Governance. New Government-Society Interactions.* London: Sage.

Latour, B., 2005. *Re-Assembling the Social. An Introduction to Actor-Network Theory.* Oxford: Oxford University Press.

Lemos, M. and Agrawal, A., 2006. 'Environmental Governance'. *Annual Review of Environment and Resources*, 31 (November), 297–325.

Liss, B., 1999. 'The Role of the Tropical Forests Action Programme and National Forest Programmes in Sustainable Forest Development'. In: Glück, P., Oesten, G., Schanz, H.

and Volz, K.R., eds. *Formulation and Implementation of National Forest Programmes. Volume I: Theoretical Aspects. EFI Proceedings No. 30.* Joensuu, 25–38.

March, J. and Olsen, J., 1989. *Rediscovering Institutions: The Organizational Basis of Politics.* New York: The Free Press.

McDermott, L., O'Carroll, A. and Wood, P., 2007. *International Forest Policy. The Instruments, Agreements and Processes That Shape It.* New York: United Nations Forum on Forests Secretariat.

MCPFE Fourth Ministerial Conference on the Protection of Forests in Europe. 2003. *Vienna Resolution 1. Strengthen synergies for sustainable forest management in Europe through cross-sectoral co-operation and national forest programmes.* 28–30 April 2003, Vienna, Austria. Downloadable at: www.foresteurope.org/docs/MC/MC_ vienna_resolutionV1.pdf.

Miles, E., Underdal, A., Andresen, S. *et al.*, 2002. *Environmental Regime Effectiveness: Confronting Theory with Evidence.* Boston: MIT Press.

North, D., 1990. *Institutions, Institutional Change and Economic Performance.* Cambridge: Cambridge University Press.

Nye, J. and Donahue, J., 2000. *Governance in a Globalizing World.* Washington DC: Brooking Institutions Press.

Ostrom, E., 1990. *Governing the Commons: The Evolution of Institutions for Collective Action.* Cambridge and New York: Cambridge University Press.

Overdevest, C., Zeitlin, J., 2012. 'Assembling an Experimentalist Regime: Transnational Governance Interactions in the Forest Sector'. *Comparative Research in Law & Political Economy. Research Paper No. 16/2012.* http://digitalcommons.osgoode.yorku.ca/clpe/18.

Peluso, N.L., 1992. *Rich Forests, Poor People. Resource Control and Resistance in Java.* Berkeley, Los Angeles and Oxford: University of California Press.

Pierre, J. ed., 2000. *Debating Governance. Authority, Steering and Democracy.* Oxford: Oxford University Press.

Pierre, J. and Peters, G., 2000. *Governance, Politics and the State.* London: Macmillan.

Pouliot, V., 2008. 'The Logic of Practicality: A Theory of Practice of Security Communities'. *International Organization,* 62 (2), 257–288.

Pregernig, M., 1998. 'Forstwirtschaft ist angewandter Naturschutz: Waldbewirtschaftung und Umweltschutz im Meinungsbild der österreichischen Forstleute'. *Centralblatt für das gesamte Forstwesen,* 115, (1), 25–46.

Pülzl, H., 2005, *Die Politik des Waldes: Governance Natürlicher Ressourcen bei den Vereinten Nationen.* Vienna: BOKU, PhD Dissertation.

Pülzl, H. and Rametsteiner, E., 2002. 'Grounding International Modes of Governance into National Forest Programmes'. *Forest Policy and Economics,* 4 (4), 259–268.

Rayner, J., Buck, A. and Katila, P. eds., 2010. 'Embracing Complexity. Meeting the Challenges of International Forest Governance'. *IUFRO World Series* 28.

Repetto, R. and Gillis M., 1988. *Public Policies and the Misuse of Forests.* Washington DC: World Resources Institute.

Risse, T., 2000. Let's argue: communicative action in world politics. *International Organization,* 54 (1), 1–39.

Rittberger, V., ed., 1993. *Regime Theory and International Relations.* Oxford: Clarendon Press.

Robertson, R., 1995. 'Glocalization: Time-Space and Homogeneity-Heterogeneity'. In: M. Featherstone, S. Lash and R. Robertson, eds. *Global Modernities.* London: Sage, 25–45.

Rosenau, J., 1995. 'Governance in the 21st Century'. *Global Governance,* 1 (1), 13–43.

Rosenau, J. and Czempiel, E., eds., 1992. *Governance without Government: Order and Change in World Politics.* Cambridge: Cambridge University Press.

Savranski, M., 2012. 'World in the Making: Social Sciences and the Ontopolitics of Knowledge'. *Postcolonial Studies*, 15 (3), 351–368.

Schatzki, T., 2001. *The Site of the Social. A Philosophical Account of the Constitution of Social Life and Change.* Pennsylvania: The Pennsylvania State University Press.

Scott, J.C., 1998. *Seeing Like a State. How Certain Schemes to Improve the Human Condition Have Failed.* New Haven and London: Yale University Press.

Shove, E., Pantzar, M. and Watson, M., 2012. *The Dynamics of Social Practices. Everyday Life and How It Changes.* London: Sage.

Six-Country Initiative, 1999. *Practitioners' Guide to the Implementation of the IPF Proposals for Action.* Prepared by the Six-Country Initiative in Support of the UN Ad-hoc Intergovernmental Forum on Forests, Eschborn, Germany.

Stavins, R., 2001. *Experience with market-based environmental policy instruments. Discussion paper.* Washington DC: Resources for the future.

Swedish Environmental Protection Agency, 2013. About us. Available at: www.swedishepa. se/About-us/ [accessed 31 March 2014].

Swyngedouw, E., 2004. 'Globalisation or Glocalization? Networks, Territories and Scales'. *Cambridge Review of International Affairs*, 17 (1), 25–48.

Tysiachniouk, M., 2012. *Transnational Governance through Private Authority: the Case of FSC Certification in Russia.* PhD Dissertation. Wageningen: Wageningen University.

UNCSD/IFF, 2000. *Report of the Intergovernmental Forum on Forests on its fourth session.* Eight Session, 31 January–11 February 2000. Commission on Sustainable Development/Intergovernmental Forum on Forests, New York. (E/CN.17/2000/14).

UNCSD/IPF, 1996. Report of the Secretary General. *Ad hoc Intergovernmental Panel on Forests.* Third Session, 9–20 September 1996. Commission on Sustainable Development/Intergovernmental Panel on Forests, New York. (E/CN, 17/IPF/1996/14).

UNFF, 2002. National forest programmes. *Item 4 (h) of the provisional agenda.* Report of the Secretary-General. Second session. 4–15 March 2002. United Nations Forum on Forests New York. (E/CN.18/2002/4).

Visseren-Hamakers, I. and Glasbergen, P., 2007. 'Partnerships in Forest Governance'. *Global Environmental Change*, 17 (3/4), 408–419.

Vandenabbeele, N., 2012. *A Case Study of Local Practices of Participatory Forest Management (PFM) in Kaffa, Ethiopia. Self-Formation between Principle and Practice.* Master Thesis. Wageningen: Wageningen University.

Weale, A., 1992. *The New Politics of Pollution.* Manchester: Manchester University Press.

Wendt, A., 1992. 'Anarchy is What States Make of It: The Social Construction of Power Politics'. *International Organization*, 46 (2), 391–425.

Wiersum, K.F., 2009. *Community Forestry between Local Autonomy and Global Encapsulation: Quo Vadis with Environmental and Climate Change Payments?* Paper presented at the First Community Forestry International Workshop, Pokhara, Nepal, 15–18 September 2009.

Willetts, P., ed., 1986, *The Consciousness of the World: the Influence of Non-Governmental Organisations in the UN System.* London: Hurst & Company.

Wunder, S., 2005. *Payments for Environmental Services: Some Nuts and Bolts.* Bogor: CIFOR Occasional Paper 42.

Yanow, D., 1993. 'The Communication of Policy Meanings: Implementation as Interpretation and Text'. *Policy Sciences*, 26 (1), 41–61.

Chapter 12

Conclusion

The relevance of practice theory for researching social change

Machiel Lamers, Gert Spaargaren and Don Weenink

Introduction

Conceptual elaboration of practice theories and their positioning in the academic field are important because this makes them more visible and prominent in academic research as well as in education.[1] The distinctiveness and attractiveness of practice theory has been linked to its ability to offer a third-way perspective on society, moving beyond individualist/subjectivist and structuralist/objectivist understandings of the social. Not individual agents or social structures, but social practices are put forward as the adequate starting point for organizing both theorizing and carrying out empirical research.

However, practice theories are frequently seen as being relevant for the study of small social phenomena only, such as daily routinized activities and face-to-face interactions. Studies on situated practices (Stones, 2005) praxeologize the realm of the social by diving into, taking a close look, developing a view from within and providing thick descriptions of social practices that most of us are familiar with. It is true that numerous practice-based studies of mundane activities at the micro level have been carried out the last decade, such as washing practices, Nordic walking practices, medical practices, canteen practices, energy practices, sports practices and day trading practices (e.g. Schmidt, 2012; Shove *et al.*, 2012; Kuijer, 2014; Nicolini, 2012; Spaargaren *et al.*, 2013; Naus *et al.*, 2014). However, social life also consists of large social phenomena, such as industries, markets, civil aviation, educational systems, sports leagues and international organizations. Until recently, the characteristics and transformations in these large social phenomena were the domain of other social and economic theories, like neo-institutionalism (Powell and DiMaggio, 1983) and transition theory (Grin *et al.*, 2010; Geels *et al.*, 2015), while hardly any practice-based studies existed of such phenomena. This situation is now changing as practice theorists and practice-based researchers are starting to think big. Nicolini (2012) and Schatzki (forthcoming) have been theorizing how to analyse large scale social phenomena from a practice perspective, while others have engaged in empirical research of complex chains of social practices (Lamers and Pashkevich, 2015), transitions in global food practices (Spaargaren *et al.*, 2012) and the governance of sustainable development practices (Shove *et al.*, 2012; Shove and Spurling, 2013). While this book shows how practice-based research can be put to use to study a wide variety of small scale social phenomena, it also contributes to the ambition of practice theories to investigate larger scale social phenomena.

The objectives of this book were two-fold: first, to demonstrate how practice theories can be used for empirical analyses that aim to understand social repro-duction and social change; and second, to outline the conceptual and methodo-logical challenges connected with the use of practice theories when applied to both small and large social phenomena.

To meet these objectives the contributions to this book were organized in three main ways. First, by combining research on small and large phenomena into one book, we aimed to show that research on social practices can and must engage with practice-arrangement bundles of different sizes. Practice-arrangement bundles refer to interconnected social practices and material arrangements (Schatzki, forthcoming). They can be more or less stretched out in time and space, and their extensiveness can be investigated with the lens alternating from the proximity modus to ever more distant views, and back. Second, since the focus of the book is on conceptualizing and researching the dynamics in contemporary societies, the contributions cover a diverse set of empirical phenomena. The reader is introduced in social phenomena as diverse as street violence, playing tennis, growing food, preventing waste, governing forests, suffering in medical care practices and managing conserva-tion tourism partnerships. By exploring such diverse corners and segments of the plenum, practice theories are tested for their most generic and specific qualities at the same time. Generic in the sense that the book demonstrates that taking social practices as the privileged unit of analysis is instrumental for generating new knowledge about the social across a wide range of social phenomena. Specific in the sense that when practice theories are applied to, for example, the field of violence research, they are shown to be innovative on a number of aspects in that domain, which are however less relevant for the positioning of practice theories in, for example, sports or forest govern-ance. Third, we also invited the authors of this volume to be sensitive about the policy or governance dimension of their research. Reflecting on the socio-political impact of research is important because new knowledge can be used in the ongoing reproduction of social practices by different actors in different ways. Furthermore, being more clear on the insights that practice-based research delivers for policy making and evaluation raises its overall relevance.

This chapter will discuss how and to what extent we have reached the aims of this book. The remainder of this chapter is structured as follows. In the next section we will make up the balance of the book, highlighting the key contribu-tions made by both the individual chapters and the book as a whole. The chapter will conclude with a future agenda for practice theory and practice-based research.

Making up the balance

In this section we discuss the conceptual and methodological insights for praxe-ologizing the social, the merits of a flat ontology for analysing small and large social phenomena, the value of practice theories for understanding social change, notably in large scale phenomena, and the insights that practice-based studies yield for governance.

Concepts and methods for praxeologizing the social

One of the first challenges faced by researchers interested in using practice the-ories is how to identify social practices as the central unit of analysis. Identifying a relevant set of practices for research depends on both theoretical and empirical criteria, as well as on practical and pragmatic considerations, such as having access to the practices as a researcher. When Weenink in his study of street viol-ence aimed to reconstruct what happens within and between groups of young-sters in the minutes preceding the actual acts of street violence, he depended on the official written court reports of these cases by legal authorities (Chapter 6). In contrast, the analyses of practices in hospital care (Chapter 7) and conserva-tion tourism partnerships (Chapter 10) were based on extensive periods of field-work. Also, when writing their chapter on the social practice of playing tennis (Chapter 8), it was of help to the authors that they are not just well-trained soci-ologists but also reasonable tennis players with some experience in the manage-ment of tennis clubs. Empirical criteria for selecting the set of practices are used by Dobernig *et al.* (Chapter 9) when they define their key objects of growing food in urban areas. In Glover's chapter (Chapter 5), the decision to look at domestic practices of divesting household materials against the background of preventing waste also already narrows down the range of potentially relevant practices. Most discussed in this book, however, are the theoretical criteria for deciding what counts as a relevant set or bundle of social practices. In an effort to pinpoint what comprises a social practice, Shove *et al.* (2012) proposed three basic clusters of elements: materials, competences and meanings. This three-component model provides an easy entry when embarking on a study informed by practice theory. It turned out that most authors in this volume discuss and use these Shovian elements to specify the characteristics of a practice, to compare different practices, and to analyse the ways in which practices can change. However, when they engage in empirical research on how and why these ele-ments combine, interconnect and align, the chapters in this volume tend to rely on one or more of Schatzki's (2002; 2010) organizing principles (i.e. practical and general understandings, rules and teleo-affective structures). Especially the concept of teleo-affective structure is used by a number of authors to discuss the goals of the practices, their directionality, and the kind of affects and emotions that play a role in the enactment of the practice. For example, in explaining the integration of practices of youth violence (Chapter 6) the teleo-affective structure is used as a decisive organizational principle. This is expressed in the names Weenink uses for the situated practices that are the objects of his research: 'contesting dominance' and 'performing badness'. When characterizing the engagement of households with divestment practices, Glover (Chapter 5) also emphasizes the importance of the teleo-affective structure and also uses this concept to identify particular ways of handling things at home: 'making do', 'passing on' and 'getting something for it'.

Based on how the authors of this volume tried to make sense of what social practices are about conceptually, we propose that future studies use different conceptualizations of social practices that are available in the social practice literature, while seeking to avoid only snapshot like descriptions of the elements of social practices. Defining practices, we argue, requires at least three steps: providing a description of the relevant components and how they combine; looking at the embeddedness of the social practices in broader sets or bundles of practices and material arrangements; and making an analysis of the trajectory of the practice, i.e. its historical development and its connections with other practices. This strategy was followed by Dobernig *et al.* (Chapter 9) in their contribution on growing food in urban settings. After having conducted a short historical analysis of growing food in urban environments, they then used the three Shovian elements in comparative analyses of 'similar' practices in Amsterdam and New York, ending up with a discussion on how the networks of related practices have been developing over the past decades in both cities. Only by playing all three analytical cards at the same time, the authors were able to arrive at their conclusion regarding the novelty of the practices under investigation. As a conclusion we would argue that studying 'the dynamics of practices' (Shove *et al.*, 2012) is not possible by just mapping the elements and by discussing the ways in which they hang together. Studying stability and change in social practices implies taking a comparative and historical perspective to dive into the trajectory of specific practices and their changing embeddedness in wider practice-arrangement bundles. In the next section we will provide a more detailed discussion on the concepts suggested for studying the embeddedness and connectivity of social practices.

Another point we want to make on theoretical work is that several chapters suggest conceptual innovations regarding the elements to be studied of social practices. In their chapter that is almost completely focused on the role of emotions in the reproduction and change of social practices, Weenink and Spaargaren (Chapter 4) argue that the emotional dimension of practices deserves wider discussion within theories of practices. The authors suggest connecting practice theories with Randall Collins' (2004) Interaction Ritual Theory in particular, since this Gofmanian and Durkheimian view on how practices produce emotions fits very well with the key assumptions of practice theories. Emotions navigate the social in important and circumscribed ways, as Weenink shows in his chapter on street violence (Chapter 6). The relevance of emotions are obvious again in the chapter by Vosman *et al.* (Chapter 7), who investigate the position of patients in practices of giving and receiving care. Concerning the teleo-affectivities of care practices, the authors propose the concept of 'possibility' to describe a specific 'non-doing' or rather 'undergoing' as a kind of agency in the enactment of practices. Finally, when they discuss the ways in which material elements of different kinds are involved in the spatial structuring of the practice of playing tennis, van der Poel and Bakker (Chapter 8) put forward the concept of 'affordances' to capture the interplay of objectivities and subjectivities in the performance of the practice. The concept of affordances is not new in sociology but has not been discussed much among theorists of practices so far (Gibson, 1979/1986; Schmidt, 2012).

Next to making theoretical contributions, the book aimed to show how practice theories can be put to work in empirical research, which involves the elaboration of methodological issues. The chapter by Robert Schmidt in particular discusses epistemological and methodological aspects of using practice theories. Schmidt offers the concept of praxeologizing to refer to the kind of engagement of social scientists with their object of study. Researchers should be aware – so he argues – about the problematic distinction between theory and theorizing on the one hand, and doing research on empirical reality on the other. He argues that Bourdieu's theoretical-cum-empirical approach still serves as a role model for doing social science in a reflexive manner, with researchers being aware of their role as co-constructors of the very kind of reality they help constitute with their (practice) theories.

The empirical chapters rely on a diverse range of methodological tools, albeit of a rather conventional nature. Although some authors express a clear preference for qualitative, ethnographic and ethnomethodological approaches and comparative case studies (Chapters 9, 10, 11), quantitative methods (Chapters 6 and 8) can be found as well. As Schmidt argues in his chapter on praxeologizing (Chapter 3) it seems difficult to imagine practice-based research without qualitative methods being applied. Most authors seem to be at ease with Nicolini's suggestion of taking the best of all available instruments that are around, with the research questions indicating the kind of combinations of methodologies to consider (Nicolini, 2012). His suggestion of using the metaphor of zooming in and zooming out on the plenum of practices was made into a central theme throughout the book, and we think with satisfying results. Schmidt's argument (Chapter 3) that quantitative methods should only figure as subordinated procedures in praxeologizing perhaps needs some nuancing. Our position is that there is a place for both qualitative and quantitative methods when used in the right way at the right moment, whereby the first appears to be indispensable when zooming in and the latter being particularly helpful when zooming out (see also Higginson *et al.*, 2014; Holz, 2014).

The merits of a flat ontology for researching both small and large social phenomena

As indicated above, the emphasis on providing understandings of small phenomena has resulted in practice theories being judged as irrelevant for the understanding and steering of social changes in large phenomena, such as trans-national organizations, carbon markets or the tourism sector. In an effort to make up for this shortcoming, some practice theorists started to reflect on conceptual ways to enrich practice theories with new concepts for studying the plenum with the practice lens in the zoomed-out position (Nicolini, 2012; Schatzki, forthcoming). In the chapter by Schatzki (Chapter 2), a conceptual foundation is provided to study large social phenomena without going against the flat ontology which is essential for practice theories. Schatzki starts his chapter by stating that the differences between small and large phenomena are not qualitative in nature. Thus, from the perspective advanced in this book, the difference between what is called micro or macro is just a matter of scale, a matter of differences in extensiveness across time and space. Macro phenomena are made up of the same material as micro phenomena: there is no social reality other than practices. Macro-sociological phenomena such as states, globalization, capitalism, institutions or social structures more generally, are conceptual short hands to denote degrees of extensiveness. That is to say they are 'dense' or 'thick' in terms of the connections between activities within practices and between practice-arrangement bundles, 'far-flung' or 'large' in terms of their spatiality and 'long-lasting' or 'durable' in terms of their existence over time (see also Schatzki, forthcoming). There is no ontological difference between micro and macro phenomena; the social happens at only one level and not – as in transition theory – at three distinct levels, such as landscape, regime and niche.

We believe that the concept of practice-arrangement bundles is the most general concept to refer to the mass of social practices that fill the plenum. Throughout this book, however, many different concepts are used to refer to such practice-arrangement bundles, such as pairs, chains, nexuses, compounds, complexes, circuits, constellations, networks or configurations of social practices. All give a specific colour to the idea of connections between practices. We think this conceptual diversity has to do with the rather recent emphasis within the family of practice theories on the analysis of large social phenomena. We argue that the concept of practice-arrangement bundles deserves further elaboration when discussing non-singular practices, since this concept highlights the hanging together of the social and material components in social practices. Practice-arrangement bundles are open-ended in the sense that every act of reproduction is also a creative act of the production of something (most of the time slightly or marginally) new or different at the same time. This is to prevent deterministic views on causality and social change, and to give proper weight to the notion of double hermeneutics at work in praxeologizing the social (see Chapter 3).

In several chapters of the book, practice-based approaches are used to understand larger scale phenomena in more or less explicit ways. In Chapter 5, Glover demonstrates how smaller scale household divestment processes are affected by the larger scale social diffusion of information and communication technologies. Practical information on repairing is now readily available from Youtube, and communication between buyers and sellers of household materials is now extended over much larger distances. In Chapter 8, van der Poel and Bakker argue how in decision-making practices on tennis court surfaces the number and types of actors involved is extended considerably, during the tennis clubs' Annual General Meetings, but also because of the market supply of innovative material arrangements by private companies and the experiences of other tennis clubs in the region. The chapters in Part III of the book have an explicit focus on practices as embedded in larger practice-arrangement bundles. First, Dobernig et al. Chapter 9) show how food growing in urban areas can be seen as a larger social phenomena by comparing the emergence of urban food growing practice-arrangement bundles in two global cities, as well as by analysing the ways in which practices of urban food growing are more or less connected to wider bundles of social practices in the plenum. Particularly their research in Brooklyn Grange, New York, demonstrates how rooftop food growing becomes embedded in thicker and more extensive bundles of other practices and material arrange-ments, such as leisure and lifestyle practices (e.g. yoga) and gastronomical, educational and managerial practices. Second, in their chapter on conservation tourism partnerships, Lamers and Van der Duim make an explicit attempt to discuss how connections between bundles of practices and material arrangements are formed. They show how efforts are being made to combine and integrate three formerly separate practice-arrangements bundles: pastoral cattle herding, conserv-ing wildlife and nature-based tourism. Although the three bundles themselves are composed of smaller bundles of practices and arrangements, the integration of these specific bundles into a larger kind of conservation tourism practice arrange-ment bundle is aimed for by different groups of stakeholders. For this integration to occur, Lamers and Van der Duim argue that the organized doings and sayings of a specific group of 'connectors' are crucial. The practices performed by these connectors are labelled as 'connecting practices' by the authors. Connectors bring specific 'local' knowledges from, for example, international NGOs or cattle herders together, and recognize when and how programmes of stakeholders do (not) easily go together to form a larger bundle. When connecting practices manage to survive and prosper, the original practices undergo gradual changes as they become more and more directed to the rules and teleo-affective structures of the larger practice arrangement bundle. This analysis resembles Castells' (2009) understanding of the operation of power through organized groups of program-mers and switchers in networks. Managing connectivity is their main task and the legitimation of their activities. Third, the chapter by Arts, Kleinschmit and Pülzl (Chapter 11) considers the relationships between small and large arrangements for the worldwide sustainable governance of forests. They argue that a practice-based 'flat' analysis results in richer, more creative and dynamic insights in global forestry governance than the vertical and multilevelled perspectives that have dominated this field of research so far. They propose perceiving forest govern-ance in terms of the travelling through the plenum of (new, more sustainable) ideas and discourses, standards and procedures, and technologies and resources. Inspired by the ideas of Shove et al. (2012) and Latour (2005) on how components of practices travel, and how they are translated and adapted to site-specific circumstances and contexts, they offer two forestry governance cases to illustrate the horizontal movement and diffusion of different elements of practices through the plenum. The flat ontology claim is here used to criticize existing theories and policy arrangements and to produce a radically different view of forest governance in an open, flexible, glocalized network society.

Practice theories and social change at large

All large scale social phenomena must bear upon actual doings and sayings that take place in concrete, physical space, if not they are reifications rather than concepts that approach the empirical reality of social phenomena (see also Collins, 1981). Macro-sociological phenomena, such as states, globalization, capitalism, global cities, transnational tourism networks or other social structures, do not act. The movement, the energy, what brings about something else in the plenum of practices as a more or less extensive repetitive pattern across time and space, must be located in social practices (see again Collins, 1981). If we accept that social practices are the entities of social life, then we should see large scale social changes as series of connected changes that happen to the practices of the more extensive practice-arrangement bundles of which they are part. Also, the cause of any large social change should then be found in the multitude of causes of smaller changes in these bundles of practices (Schatzki, forthcoming). However, this does not deny the fact that macroprocesses can influence these mechanisms: they may alter, redirect, restrict, emphasize, extend or delimit the causal nexus of practices. In each of the three chapters presenting analyses of embedded practices we have seen how the authors both base and also translate the extension of the practice-arrangement bundles back to changes in situated performed practices.

We argue that as practice theories are moving into the terrain of studying the dynamics of large phenomena, a discussion with transition theory, or other theories on social change and transformation, becomes unavoidable and indispensable. Some practice theorists, such as Shove and Walker (2007) and Spaargaren (Spaargaren *et al.*, 2012), recognize the relevance of transition studies as developed in Europe over the past decades. Concepts like co-evolution, socio-technical innovations, non-linear processes of change, multi-actor processes, analyses of pathways of change and the governance of transitions seem to be of shared interest to both practice theorists and transition theorists. While the issue of a flat ontology seems to stand in the way of combining both kinds of theories in empirical research (see Chapter 2), both approaches can learn from each other when it comes to analysing particular aspects of social change. As transition theories are strong on mapping historical pathways of change in large phenomena, and practice theories are strong on showing the open, undetermined character of the reproduction and innovation of both small and large practice-arrangement bundles, both approaches could profit from a rapprochement and constructive dialogue on how to understand and govern transitions in social life.

In the context of our discussion on practice theories and (the management of) social change, it is important to take a closer look at what practice theories have to offer when it comes to analysing and characterizing patterns of change in smaller and larger practice-arrangement bundles. In practice theory, questions about causality tend to be taken as retrospective how questions. Causal explanation then involves the description of change extending over time. Both Nicolini (2012) and Schatzki (forthcoming) suggest tracking large scale changes in the 'zoomed-out' or 'overview' modes respectively. Overviewing involves a combination of sketching or tracking down the chain of movements in series of practices that have brought about the patterning in time and space on the one hand, and showing how the causal nexus worked in particular significant practices or in, and between, practice-arrangement bundles on the other hand. The chapters presented in Part III of this volume are telling illustrations of this approach. For example, in Chapter 10 (this volume) Lamers and Van der Duim show how reflexive and discursive practices (i.e. the trust board where partnership issues are discussed and decided), as well as material arrangements (i.e. the zonation of the land and the eco-lodge), are used to connect a range of practice-arrangement bundles and trace the changes in each of these constituting practices over time. Similarly, Arts *et al.*, (Chapter 11) demonstrate how contemporary forestry governance approaches, like Participatory Forestry Management, can be tracked as they circulate across the world and arrive in different contextual settings where they are unpacked and implemented. In other words, in association with other land-use practices these conservation tourism partnerships or forestry management approaches are interwoven and solidified, leading to their persistence, accumulation and aggregation, or to their separation or dissolution. To get a further sense of how an analysis of change in large scale phenomena by tracking the multitude of smaller scale changes that comprise them could be understood, Schatzki (forthcoming) provides a series of concepts that capture the variety of changes that happen in extensive phenomena, such as those presented in this book. With concepts like association, aggregation, disassociation, dissolution, absorption, diffusion, circulation, solidification, persistence, bifurcation, differentiation, interweaving, convergence, divergence and separation, he allows researchers to describe the variety of happenings in complex action chains that bring about the formation, persistence and dissolution of large phenomena. With Schatzki we argue that when tracking the causal processes that undergird large scale phenomena, it is particularly helpful to focus the attention on governance and monitoring activities, coordinating devices and discourses, and material infrastructures that provide the backbone of the causal nexus.

Practice-based insights for policy and governance

Reflecting on the socio-political impact of research is important because new knowledge can be used in the ongoing reproduction of social practices by different actors in different ways. This general fact of life gains particular relevance when dealing with social practices that lead to impacts or relations that are societally deemed as undesirable, such as environmental degradation, poverty, social marginalization and cost overrun, or more desirable, such as sustainable development and fair play. Each of the empirical chapters presented in this volume is situated in a particular and different socio-political setting, formed by different constellations of governance actors. Each of the empirical chapters contributes in their own way to better understanding undesirable social practices (e.g. youth violence, suffering, deforestation) in order to advise more effective policies, or highlights how more desirable social practices emerge and can be fostered by policy, such as alternative material divestment, local food production and consumption and conservation tourism partnerships. Practice-based research is valuable for its unpacking and 'opening up' of social phenomena like household divestment, playing tennis, undergoing a medical treatment in a hospital, or experiencing nature. Praxeologies show how these practices are performed by different groups of participants in different ways, while analysing how they emerge, diffuse, change and dissolve. Moreover, the chapter by Lamers and Van der Duim (Chapter 10) shows that new social practices can also be deliberately introduced by change agents in particular governance arrangements, by connecting undesirable practices with more desirable ones in order to derive more desirable output.

In all the practices mentioned, power relations between attackers and victims, managers and employees, doctors and nurses, tourism entrepreneurs and local pastoralists are shown to be a relevant axis along which the reproduction of these practices are organized. However, the knowledge generated by practice-based researchers could in principle be (mis)used by those in power to further increase their control of the settings under investigation. Andrew Sayer argues that this risk is enhanced by a focus on small social phenomena without taking into account the bigger picture of the embedding of social practices (Sayer, 2013). Of course the very same knowledge can also be used by subordinated actors in their efforts to diminish existing inequalities while empowering certain groups of participants. Social science researchers do not write the scripts for the future reproduction of the practices under study and they do not control the impact of their knowledge. They do however share responsibilities for the future state of social affairs and for the possible impacts and consequences of their research. Reflecting on these impacts and consequences, by actively using the practice zoom lens, should be part and parcel of praxeologizing to make practice-based research more policy relevant.

Finally, by adopting a practice-based perspective several of the chapters in this volume challenge the dominant paradigms that inform and legitimize policies of both state and non-state actors. Schmidt suggests following Bourdieu's 'negative' way of praxeologizing the social, whereby existing modes of governance are shown to rest on core assumptions that can be criticized on scientific grounds. For instance Weenink (Chapter 6) argues that there is no such thing as senseless violence and that more attention for the interactions between youngsters before and during violent encounters generates more valuable insights for policy rather than relying on categorical explanations of, for instance, degree of urbanization, class or ethnicity. Arts *et al.* (Chapter 11) show that standing debates on sustainable forest management can profit from doing away with hierarchical, top-down schemes of governance while opening up for thinking about local to global interfaces in terms of a practice theory's flat ontology. Also, Lamers and Van der Duim (Chapter 10) argue that a practice-based perspective on the governance arrangements of conservation tourism partnerships can generate in-depth insights for policy-making and evaluation that remain hidden from view if they had been analysed with the rational actor perspectives that had informed the various groups that formed these partnerships in the first place. Reflecting on the policy and governance aspects of practice research is an important first step for improving the recep-tiveness of companies, politicians and NGOs for practice-based approaches and research designs for both small and large social phenomena.

A future agenda: practice theory and large scale social change

In this final chapter we have made up the balance of this book. We conclude that practice theory and practice-based research holds added value for understanding and steering social change. Whatever the speed or extensiveness of social changes, the challenge for practice-based research is to demonstrate that every-thing happens in the plenum of social practices. We close this chapter by identi-fying directions in which practice theory could venture to further enhance its relevance for understanding the dynamics of large scale social phenomena. We have already argued for a continuation of the discussion between social practice theorists and theorists of societal transitions in this regard. In addition, we see two important but relatively unexplored domains that open up opportunities for further empirical and conceptual development of practice theories.

First, Anthony King (2010) has argued that the practice theories that were developed by Bourdieu and Giddens in the 1970s, in their fixation on the agency–structure conundrum, have failed to spot one of the most important trends in the social sciences today: the conceptualization of a globalizing network society. To quote King at length:

> A new consensus is apparent in sociology globally which no longer under-stands social reality in terms of structure and agency but in terms of networks. Instead of the closed systems so favoured by functionalist sociology in the middle of the twentieth century, many sociologists are now more interested in the open and indeterminate social webs which transcend national borders, pre-cipitating particular kinds of activity at specific locations.
>
> (King, 2010: 256)

Practice theories have not been connecting to this increasingly influential view of the social as a networked and networking phenomenon explicitly – even though their core assumptions fit very well to it. Since analyses of the dynamics of contemporary large-to-small practice-arrangement bundles take place in the present historical phase of the globalizing network society, we argue that practice theories could benefit from sociological theories which use network concepts to depict the horizontal, open and fluid character of the social. More specifically, we would be in favour of a theoretical confrontation and dialogue with the work of Manuel Castells, John Urry and Saskia Sassen, amongst others (Castells, 1996, 2009; Urry, 2000, 2003; Sassen, 2006). In practice theory terms, these social theorists describe the social as a globally networked constellation of practice-arrangement bundles. We think it would be useful to discuss this issue more often, by different members of the practice family, in different ways.

The second domain is related to the analysis of social changes that occur at a faster pace in the plenum of social practices. More specifically, we think of the travelling of objects or ideas that are strongly emotionally charged with group feelings. Such symbols of group membership are always tied to a particular group, as they emerged from local group dynamics (see Chapter 4). However, it is their intense emotional loading that allows for travelling of these symbols across the plenum of practices. For instance, in a snowball-like manner, social practices that revolve around these symbols can attract more and more participants if they sense that these symbols belong to a group that is gaining more and more support, or when they sense they belong to a winning party. In this way, new political ideas and or the reputation of charismatic leaders can attract the attention in surges of emotional energy that spreads rapidly across the plenum (see also Collins, 1981). Waves of enthusiasm, or 'belief-desire-emotion flows' (Schatzki, forthcoming) bring about swift changes in many connected social practices. However, the support for these ideas or the belief in reputations may also decline dramatically. In addition to these emotion flows, emotions also directly affect the purposiveness of practical intelligence: they change what is important and meaningful for people to do, hence bringing about changes in the distribution of participants over (bundles of) practices (see again Chapter 4). In our view, the incorporation of emotions to study rapid, large scale social changes provides a promising domain for practice based research, both empirically and theoretically.

Note

1   As far as we know, practice theories are not yet discussed as such – as a category, a school or a bandwagon (Corradi and Gherardi, 2010) – in the major textbooks on contemporary social theory.

References

Castells, M., 1996. *The Rise of the Network Society*. Volume I of The Information Age: Economy, Society and Culture. Malden, MA/Oxford: Blackwell.
Castells, M., 2009. *Communication Power*. Oxford: Oxford University Press.

Collins, R., 1981. 'On the Microfoundations of Macrosociology'. *American Journal of Sociology*, 86 (5), 984–1014.

Collins, R., 2004. *Interaction Ritual Chains*. Princeton: Princeton University Press.

Corradi G. and Gherardi, S. 2010. 'Through the Practice Lens: Where is the Bandwagon of Practice-Based Studies Heading?' *Management Learning*, 41 (3), 265–283.

Geels, F.W., McMeekin, A., Mylan, J. and Southerton, D., 2015. 'A Critical Appraisal of Sustainable Consumption and Production Research: The Reformist, Revolutionary and Reconfiguration Positions. *Global Environmental Change*, 34, 1–12.

Gibson, J.J., 1979/1986. *The Ecological Approach to Visual Perception*. Boston: Houghton Mifflin.

Grin J., Rotmans, J., Schot, J., with Loorbach, D. and Geels, F.W., 2010. *Transitions to Sustainable Development; New Directions in the Study of Long Term Transformative Change.* New York: Routledge.

Higginson, S,. McKenna, E., Hargreaves, T., Chilvers, J. and Thomson, M., 2015. 'Diagramming Social Practice Theory: An Interdisciplinary Experiment Exploring Practices as Networks'. *Indoor and Built Environment* 24 (7), 950–969.

Holtz, G., 2014. 'Generating Social Practices'. *Journal of Artificial Societies and Social Simulation* 17 (1), 1–17.

King, A., 2010. 'The Odd Couple: Margaret Archer, Anthony Giddens and British Social Theory'. *The British Journal of Sociology*, 61 (1), 253–260.

Kuijer, L., 2014. *Implications of Social Practice Theory for Sustainable Design*. PhD Dissertation at Delft University of Technology. Pijnacker: Impressed.

Lamers, M. and Pashkevich, A., 2015. 'Short-Circuiting Cruise Tourism Practices along the Russian Barents Sea Coast? The Case of Arkhangelsk'. *Current Issues in Tourism*, online first.

Latour, B., 2005. *Reassembling the Social – An Introduction to Actor-Network Theory.* Oxford: Oxford University Press.

Naus, J., Spaargaren, G., Van Vliet, B.J.M. and Van der Horst, H.M., 2014. 'Smart Grids, Information Flows and Emerging Domestic Energy Practices'. *Energy Policy*, 68, 436–446.

Nicolini, D., 2012. *Practice Theory, Work & Organization. An Introduction.* Oxford: Oxford University Press.

Powell, W. and DiMaggio, P., 1983. *The New Institutionalism in Organizational Analysis*. Chicago: University of Chicago Press.

Sassen, S., 2006. *Territory, Authority, Rights: from Medieval to Global Assemblages.* Princeton: Princeton University Press.

Sayer, A., 2013. 'Power, Sustainability and Well-Being: an Outsider's View. In: E. Shove and N. Spurling, eds. *Sustainable Practices: Social Theory and Climate Change.* London: Routledge, 292–317.

Schatzki, T., 2002. *The Site of the Social. A Philosophical Account of the Constitution of Social Life and Change.* Philadelphia: Penn State University Press.

Schatzki, T., 2010. *The Timespace of Human Activity. On Performance, Society, and History as Indeterminate Teleological Events.* Plymouth: Lexington Books.

Schatzki, T., forthcoming. 'Keeping Track of Large Phenomena'. *Geographische Zeitschrift*, Volume 2.

Schmidt, R., 2012. *Soziologie der Praktiken. Konzeptionelle Studien und empirische Analysen.* Berlin: Suhrkamp Verlag.

Shove, E. and Spurling, N., eds. 2013. *Sustainable Practices; Social Theory and Climate Change.* New York: Routledge.

Shove, E. and Walker, G., 2007. 'CAUTION! Transitions Ahead: Politics, Practice and Sustainable Transition Management'. *Environmental Planning A*, 39, 763–770.

Shove, E., Pantzar, M. and Watson, M., 2012. *The Dynamics of Social Practice; Everyday Life and How It Changes.* London: Sage.

Spaargaren, G., Oosterveer, P. and Loeber, A., eds. 2012. *Food Practices in Transition; Changing Food Consumption, Retail and Production in the Age of Reflexive Modernity.* New York: Routledge.

Spaargaren, G., Van Koppen, C.S.A. (Kris), Janssen, A.M., Hendriksen, A. and Kolfschoten, C.J., 2013. 'Consumer Responses to the Carbon Labelling of Food: A Real Life Experiment in a Canteen Practice'. *Sociologia Ruralis*, 53, 432–453.

Stones, R., 2005. *Structuration Theory.* New York: Palgrave Macmillan.

Urry, J., 2000. *Sociology Beyond Society.* London: Routledge.

Urry, J., 2003. *Global Complexity.* Cambridge: Polity Press.